To Teresa Jackson Mack, (T. Mack) in appreciation for your friendship and your commitment to the gospel of Jesus Christ.

Powell Sykes

P.S. Candy is mentioned on pages 2 and 164-165.

OUT OF ORDER:

The Self-Destruction of a Mainline Denomination

Charles Powell Sykes, Sr.

In 1927 American Presbyterians chose to stop listing and insisting upon "the essential tenets of the Reformed faith"; instead, they emphasized tolerance and essential action. Since then, historic, biblically based Christianity has been supplanted more and more by a different religion, dubbed Religious Liberalism by the author, within the largest Presbyterian denomination in the United States. This, coupled with decades of removing practical means of holding pastors accountable for any of their beliefs and much of their behavior, is leading to that denomination's demise in the early years of the 21st Century.

OUT OF ORDER: The Self-Destruction Of A Mainline Denomination

Copyright 2012 by Charles Powell Sykes, Sr.

ISBN: 978-1-300-37728-3

Published by Lulu.com

Printed in the United States of America by Lulu.com

Distributed by Lulu.com

OUT OF ORDER – The Self-Destruction of a Mainline Denomination

ACKNOWLEDGEMENTS

Dedications:

Dedicated to my wife, Mary Kathleen Sykes, whose love is the greatest portion of grace God prepared in this life just for me;

To my mother, Barbara Jean Powell Sykes, who showed and sang to me the truth that Jesus loves me;

To my father, Lowell Beach Sykes, Sr., who taught me to love the Bible and Reformed Theology while being an inspiration to so many people;

To my children, Jodie and Chip Griffin, Christie and Jim Miller, and Chad Sykes, as well as to my three grand-daughters (so far!), Rachel, Emily, and Catherine. I love you all!

And to Fred Ward, who always wanted things done decently and in order.

Special thanks to my Editor, Cecelia Davis, and to my proof-readers: Greg Alty, Valerie Reid Jackson, Steve Moss, Mike Stewart, Kathy Sykes, and Lowell Sykes. They improved this book so much, correcting many mistakes, and any deficiencies which remain are solely mine.

A special thank you to all the congregations I have served and known within the Presbyterian Church (USA); may the Lord continue to guide you in the years to come. My life has been enriched by you.

Table of Contents

Introduction:..6

Chapter One: The Historic Presbyterian Fundamentals......................10

Chapter Two: A Clash Of Fundamentals..22

Chapter Three: The Problem Of The Miraculous..............................26

Chapter Four: Is There Such A Thing As Sin, And So What If There Is?..32

Chapter Five: What About Sex?..38

Chapter Six: The Mission Of The Church..46

Chapter Seven: The Lack Of Accountability.......................................52

Chapter Eight: Oxymoron – Presbyterian Bishops..............................62

Chapter Nine: The Connectional Nature Of Presbyterianism..............70

Chapter Ten: The Failure Of Theological Education..........................76

Chapter Eleven: Substituting Pagentry For Instruction.......................86

Chapter Twelve: The Cumberland Conundrum.................................92

Chapter Thirteen: The Nature And Role Of A Confession Of Faith..98

Chapter Fourteen: Right Action Trumps Right Belief......................108

Chapter Fifteen: 1983 – Reunion At Any Cost, Even Integrity.........118

Chapter Sixteen: Jurimandering..132

Chapter Seventeen: Ecclesiastical Defiance Is Ecclesiastical Assault..140

Chapter Eighteen: Why Religious Liberalism Will Fail....................158

Chapter Nineteen: The Biblical Case For Separation……………............168

Chapter Twenty: Ecclesiastical McCarthyism – "You Are Schismatics!...178

Chapter Twenty-One: The Glory Of The Church Universal, Militant And Triumphant………………………………………..............……190

Chapter Twenty-Two: Traditional Vs Contemporary……………........200

Chapter Twenty-Three: Where Do We Go From Here?............. 206

Chapter Twenty-Four: Answering Objections……………….................218

Appendix: Confronting Seminary Trustees, 1998…………………..........228

INTRODUCTION

"How did this happen?" So asked the elder, tears in his eyes. He was a man in his 70s, and a lifelong Presbyterian. I was his pastor, raised in the church, and had served Presbyterian congregations for almost half my 48 years. It was April of 2011, and we both were trying to make sense of what was happening in our denomination, the Presbyterian Church (USA). Emotions ran deep as we stood on the steps of the church, struggling with the news that our presbytery had voted overwhelmingly the previous weekend to remove the standards of fidelity in marriage and chastity in singleness from our national constitution. Soon the entire denomination would approve the change, and the forces of inclusivity would finally get their way after years of losing votes, then bringing it up again. This time they apparently had convinced the moderates that the only way to have peace was to make this change. Now they had 55% of the simple majority vote, and nothing would stop them from their dream of the ordination of practicing homosexuals, not even the prospect of thousands of congregations bolting from a denomination which already had lost more than half of its membership in less than fifty years, from over four million to less than two million. Gay ordination was not the only issue. In a culture which accepts many types of heterosexual couplings outside of marriage as standard operating procedure for human behavior, this also meant that general sexual anarchy would be let loose in the denomination.

"It's complicated, and this is just the tip of the iceberg," I finally replied. "We don't have enough time this morning to talk about all the stuff that has led us here." I talked to him a bit about the loss of accountability in our denomination, as many "pastors" who serve no congregations are given voice and vote in governing bodies, but even this just scrapes the surface.

My wife has been urging me to write about this for years, to explain to folks in the pew exactly how this happened. I also believe I must address the follow-up question, "How do we move forward?" Note I don't ask, "How do we get back to the way it was?" The way it was is a way it can never be again, especially in a post-denominational culture. Today people either don't care much about name-brands when it comes to their churches, or they care very much not to be associated with a brand over which they have no say and little control, and which seems to ignore the plain words of the Bible that people can read for themselves; see the rise of the non-denominational congregations in America and the world! We can't go back to the way it was, and it would be a waste of time and effort to try. Instead, trusting in Jesus' promise never to leave or forsake us, now we only can step forward in faith and discover the new thing He is doing in the world through His body, the Church.

As for me, I face the agonizing choice of leaving the denomination which nurtured and educated me. Truth be told, it abandoned me some time ago, along with its birthright of the Reformed faith, Calvinism. But I will never leave the Church, God's people in all times and places. I will seek and find people committed to the Lordship of Jesus Christ; together we will follow Him and share the good news of the gospel: Jesus died for our sins, He rose again, and He's coming back! Repent and believe the gospel!

In 1994 I was a commissioner to the General Assembly for the Presbyterian Church, in Wichita, Kansas. While having a meal sitting next to an international delegate from the Reformed Church of Yugoslavia (a country that even by then no longer existed), I asked if there were any churches in that area of the world which claimed to have been founded by the apostle Paul. I thought there might be since Paul mentions having preached the gospel from Jerusalem to "Illyricum", the ancient name of Yugoslavia, in Romans 15:19. Though Luke does not talk about this in the book of Acts, he certainly leaves room for it in the scant details of the third missionary journey.

"Yes," came the reply, and then the question, "Are you a seminary professor?" "No," I said, "I'm just a little preacher who reads his Bible." I have no special degrees, just the basic Master of Divinity required of all Presbyterian ministers. My expertise, if you want to call it that, comes from working in the trenches of spiritual warfare, pastoring three small congregations over the span of 24 years, since I was 25. I teach the Bible a lot. I pray a lot, though probably not as much or as consistently as I should. I read a lot of history and theology. I love Jesus, not some projection of my own desires upon a long-dead historical figure, but the risen and living Son of God incarnate, borne witness by scripture. I also love God's people, the Church, in spite of all of our foibles and failings. I believe there is a place in this brave new world for groupings of churches beyond the local congregation. At the same time, it is in the local congregation where the most important work of ministry is accomplished. I believe that there is no higher calling to which a Christian can aspire than serving a congregation as a pastor or an elder; many other "positions" available to Church leaders beyond the local congregation are a waste of time at best, and always a potential stumbling block.

This is how it happened. This is why I am leaving my denomination. And this is the way forward, I believe, into the new thing that God is doing in our time.

CHAPTER ONE: THE HISTORIC PRESBYTERIAN FUNDAMENTALS

Everyone is a fundamentalist. That statement may come as a surprise to some readers, especially since the word has shifted in meaning over the past century or so. But it is true. What I am saying is that everyone has a core set of beliefs, rarely questioned and without which that person ceases to be the individual he or she understands himself or herself to be.

One of the earliest uses of the word outside religious circles was connected with the Scopes Monkey Trial in 1925. The fictionalized account of that event from the play Inherit The Wind, popularized by its film adaptation in 1960, features the Clarence Darrow character running logical rings around the obstinate character approximating William Jennings Bryan. (In fact, Bryan, a mainstay of late 19th and early 20th century presidential politics, was a Presbyterian Elder.) Though Augustine himself, writing in the 4th century, acknowledged that the Hebrew word for day used in Genesis 1 and much of the Old Testament, "yom", did not have to mean a 24 hour period of time (the "Yom Adonai", the Day of the LORD, has no ending according to scripture), to the average viewer, what could be more plain than the blindness of this Bible thumper? Why would anyone want to be like that?

For me, growing up in Lynchburg, Virginia, home of Jerry Falwell and the Moral Majority, "fundamentalist" meant a narrow, xenophobic religious worldview that was suspicious of any new findings in scientific or historical research, as well as popular cultural trends. As a teen rock and roller in the 1970s, several well-meaning but ignorant fundamentalist Christians openly questioned my salvation for playing "the devil's music". What had begun as a religious movement struggling with the challenge of Darwinism to Biblical infallibility had by that time evolved into a big tent political movement attaching economic and cultural conservatism to the message of Jesus Christ.

Not surprisingly, by the end of the 1970s, the label "fundamentalist" had become a term of derision in the popular culture. Ironically, in my memory of the contemporary news coverage, no one associated the word with the events of

November 4th, 1979, when student radicals under the guidance of the Ayatollah Khomeini over-ran the U.S. Embassy in Tehran, Iran, taking dozens of Americans hostage. Though that 444 day long crisis finally was resolved peacefully, it was a foreshadowing of the events of September 11th, 2001, the largest and deadliest attack on the United States in our history. Suddenly a new version of the term was added to the American lexicon, "Islamic Fundamentalism". In addition to the narrow worldview shared by their Christian counterparts, Islamic Fundamentalists could be led to homicidal action given the right factors.

Is it any wonder then that educated, proper Presbyterians have sprinted and lept away from the concept of fundamentalism through the years? These same proper and educated Presbyterians do not know their own history. "Fundamentalism" as a term began with us, not as a willful ignoring of science and history, or a condemnation of the new, but as a compromise intending to allow church officers the opportunity to take their ordination vows with integrity. The pertinent questions were one and two: "1) Do you believe the Scriptures of the Old and New Testaments to be the Word of God, the only infallible rule of faith and practice? 2) Do you sincerely receive and adopt the Confession of Faith and the Catechisms of this Church as containing the system of doctrine taught in the Holy Scriptures, and do you further promise that if at any time you find yourself out of accord with any of the fundamentals of this system of doctrine, you will on your own initiative make known to your Presbytery the change which has taken place in your views since the assumption of this ordination vow?" (The Book of Church Order, 1950) The Shorter Catechism is quite clear; the work of creation took place "in the space of six days, and all very good." While the biblical definition of a day is somewhat ambiguous in scripture, the writers of the Westminster Standards in 1647 were quite sure that these were 24 hour periods of time. Must a pastor, elder, or deacon adopt the worldview of 1647 to answer his ordination questions with integrity?

Presbyterian fundamentalists, which included professors at Princeton Theological Seminary and elsewhere, concluded that the answer was no. With regard to the days of creation, the actual words of scripture gave more freedom than the writers of

Westminster realized. Scripture always trumps later, fallible confessions, which are amendable in the Presbyterian Church. Instead, those fundamentalists focused on "the system of doctrine taught in Holy Scriptures", particularly surrounding the person and work of Jesus Christ, "the Author and Finisher of the faith" (Hebrews 12:2). With this view in mind, they developed what they believed to be five essential beliefs for Christians, "the fundamentals".

The first fundamental is the authority of scripture. Charles Hodge, writing in the 1870s, expressed it like this: "Holy men spake as they were moved by the Holy Ghost. Moreover, as inspiration did not involve the suspension or suppression of the human faculties, so neither did it interfere with the free exercise of the distinctive mental characteristics of the individual. If a Hebrew was inspired, he spake Hebrew; if a Greek, he spake Greek; if an educated man, he spoke as a man of culture; if uneducated, he spoke as such a man is wont to speak. If his mind was logical, he reasoned as Paul did; if emotional and contemplative, he wrote as John wrote...There is no reason to believe that the operation of the Spirit in inspiration revealed itself any more in the consciousness of the sacred writers, than his operations in sanctification reveal themselves in the consciousness of the Christian...Nevertheless, and none the less, they spoke as they were moved by the Holy Ghost, and their words were his words. " (Systematic Theology, Volume 1, VI. 2 D, p. 157)

However, this view of "plenary inspiration" is not a blind rejection of new scientific knowledge. In the words of the Westminster Shorter Catechism, the scriptures principally teach "what man is to believe concerning God, and what duty God requires of man." The Bible, in this view, is not trying to be a science textbook. For example, Leviticus 11:6 expressly forbids the eating of rabbit because rabbits "chew the cud", a statement which is demonstrably untrue biologically. Instead, the Bible is infallible in all matters of faith and practice, again, what humans should believe about God, and what duty God requires as our response to this belief. God's nature, and His will for our response to His revelation of Himself, is unknowable apart from the Bible.

From here the fundamentals shift from how we know what we know about God and His will for our lives to the Person and work of Jesus Christ. This is by design. Later "neo-orthodox" Presbyterians made much of Jesus Christ as the Word of God Incarnate, which He was and is. But they did this over and against the Bible as the Word of God Written. Their spiritual descendants often call for following Jesus or the Holy Spirit away from what the Bible says; in fact, not only is such a division unnecessary, foolish, and wrong, it is self-defeating. Apart from the Jesus Christ found in Scripture, there is no real Jesus. Instead, those who reject biblical authority in all matters of faith and practice must reimagine Jesus in their own images, and He winds up looking a lot like them! That Jesus of imagination and preference does not challenge, He does not correct or convict; instead, He simply blesses that which the worshipper already wants and likes. The Jesus borne witness by the Bible is the real, historical Jesus: sometimes inscrutable, often mysterious, and always worthy of our complete devotion and praise because of His work and love for us. He is unknowable apart from the sure witness of the Bible; it is here we learn of His work for us and our salvation.

The second fundamental is "the Virgin Birth". At one level, this is a misnomer, because the doctrine actually revolves more around the conception of Jesus, "the virgin conception". However, since Matthew makes it very clear in his gospel that Joseph did not have sexual contact with Mary until after Jesus' birth, the doctrine certainly can stand under this heading. The miracle of Jesus' conception might, at first glance, seem an odd place to stake an essential belief of the Christian faith. Why this and not, say, Jesus' walking on the water, or the feeding of the five thousand? It's a fair question; I myself did not understand its importance in my younger days. It really comes down to Jesus' identity. Jesus was not merely a prophet, or a rabbi, or a good moral teacher. The Bible is quite clear that Jesus was God in the flesh. He believed Himself to be God; he forgave the sins of those who had not personally wronged Him, and He allowed Himself to be worshipped. How is it possible that God could become a man? The ancient Greeks had stories of their gods taking the form of humans, usually to commit some mischief.

Jesus' mission was much more benevolent and brave, and to accomplish it He needed to be both completely God and completely human. He was not merely human. This is revealed through the conception of Jesus in the womb of a virgin named Mary, without the aid of a human father. According to the witness of scripture, the eternal Second Person of the Trinity, God the Son, was conceived as the infant Jesus in the womb of Mary through the power of the Holy Spirit. His divine nature is delivered by the Spirit. His human nature came from Mary. While the biblical explanation leaves open questions of the percentages of Jesus' human and divine nature, the ecumenical Council of Chalcedon in 451 AD, which is accepted by Greek Orthodox, Roman Catholic, and Protestant churches, clarified that He was completely human and completely divine, in two distinct natures "without confusion, without change, without division, without separation".

The importance of this second fundamental becomes clear as we consider the third one, The Atonement. Basic to Christian belief, as explained repeatedly in the New Testament, is that Jesus' death on the cross was not an accident, it was not merely the unjust murder of an innocent man, but it was a sacrifice of atonement which truly paid for human sin. The concept of "substitutionary atonement" as the only way to bring peace between a holy God and sinful people does not begin in the New Testament. It is essential to the faith of Old Testament believers as well, as evidenced in the sacrificial system laid out in the book of Leviticus and elsewhere. Every ancient Israelite was required, at least once a year, to travel to the tabernacle, and later the temple in Jerusalem, and offer an animal as an atoning sacrifice. Before the animal was slaughtered by the priests, the man would lay his hand on the head of the animal, representing the transfer of his sins, or those of his family, on to the animal. Then it would be killed, and the person was free to go. The symbolism of this transaction taught two important lessons later embraced by Christianity: 1) the wages of sin is death, and 2) an innocent victim can die in the place of the guilty.

Of course, an animal cannot really pay for human sins. Though it may not be guilty of committing any sin (the physical perfection of the sacrificial animal is stressed in the Levitical code), it is not enough like a human to be a true substitute. In order for human sins to be eliminated truly, the only acceptable sacrifice would have to be a perfect human being, without sin. And yet human beings are sinful by nature, in open rebellion against God throughout our lives; no normal human is good enough to die for the rest of us. The universal condemnation of human sacrifice in the Old Testament, a practice widely observed in the cultures around them, was not simply about the evil of murder, but the blasphemy of thinking anyone who was less than perfect was worthy to die as a sacrifice. What was needed for atonement truly to work as presented in the Old Testament was a perfect human who did not need to die for his own sins, and yet was willing to die for the sins of others. And where can we find one of those?

The universal witness of the New Testament is that Jesus Christ was that sacrifice when He died on the cross. He was perfect, without sin, according to Hebrews 4:15. How is that possible, especially when the Bible is equally clear that all people are sinful? It only works if Jesus is completely God and completely human. This way He is enough like us to have his death count for us, a true substitute, but He is enough not like us, being completely God, that He could live a perfect life and not have to die for His own sins. Without the virgin conception, there is no atonement for sin, and Christianity as presented in the Bible collapses.

The fourth fundamental addresses the question, "How do we know Jesus' death really paid for our sins?" After all, thousands of people were crucified by the Roman Empire in the centuries surrounding the life of Jesus; what makes this one death so special? The bodily Resurrection of Jesus from the dead is the fourth fundamental. In Matthew's gospel the Jewish leaders demand a sign from Jesus, and He replies, "An evil and adulterous generation craves for a sign, and yet no sign shall be given to it but the sign of Jonah the prophet; for just as Jonah was three days and three nights in the belly of the sea monster, so shall the Son of Man be three days and three nights in the heart of the earth." (Matthew 12:38+39) The resurrection of Jesus from the dead is the sign that His death on the cross really paid for our sins. This is not a "spiritual" resurrection, or the "idea" of a resurrection; the New Testament writers are quite clear that Jesus, who died on the cross, returned to life in a spiritual body. This body was connected in some way with His physical body, and yet had amazing characteristics beyond those of a physical body. After the resurrection, Jesus could appear and disappear at will. He walked through walls. He sometimes was not recognized by disciples who ordinarily would have known Him immediately. At the same time, He could be touched, and He ate fish in the sight of the disciples. He was not a ghost, or some sort of intangible spirit.

As in the case of the atonement, the concept of resurrection has its origins in the Old Testament, so much, in fact, that most Jews in the first century were expecting a general resurrection of the dead to accompany the coming of the Day of the LORD. That day was a day of judgment, when all the dead would be raised to be paid in full for what they have done in life, good or evil. In the final verse of his book, Daniel is told by God to go his way and enter the rest of death, after which he will "rise again for your allotted portion at the end of the age." (Daniel 12:13) Pharisees especially believed in a coming resurrection of the dead, unlike their political rivals, the Sadducees. Sadducees only accepted the Torah, the first five books of the Old Testament, as authoritative, while Pharisees accepted all thirty-nine books. (The official designation of the larger list happened at the Council of Jamnia in 90 AD, twenty years after the destruction of Jerusalem by the Romans; the Sadducees were effectively wiped out by that military action, while the Pharisees, scattered throughout Judea and Galilee, survived and were present for the Council.) Jesus agreed with the Pharisees. When Sadducees questioned him about this matter, He answered them from the text they themselves acknowledged, the story of the burning bush in Exodus 3. In verse 6 God does not say, "I WAS the God of Abraham, Isaac, and Jacob," but "I AM the God of Abraham, Isaac, and Jacob." While not specifically mentioning a resurrection, Jesus took this to indicate that there was life after death, because "He is not the God of the dead, but of the living…" (Mark 12:27) Later on, in the book of Acts, Paul is able to bring a meeting of the Sanhedrin, the Jewish ruling council, to a screeching halt by shouting out, "I am on trial for the hope and the resurrection of the dead!" (Acts 23:6) The Pharisees will listen to this; the Sadducees will not. My point is this: the hope of the resurrection was shared by the believers of the Old and New Testament Church, people who knew as well as we do that dead people stay dead. Modern people have no new objections to raise against this fundamental of biblical faith; one either believes it, or does not, based upon the authority of scripture, upon the eye-witness accounts of those who saw the risen Jesus, the first one raised, but not the last. All who believe in Him will have a resurrection like His! (Romans 6:5)

The fifth and final fundamental of the Christian faith as presented by early 20th century Presbyterians is the return of Christ. This may come as surprise to those who know of Presbyterian opposition to Dispensationalism through much of the same century; in fact, the General Assembly of the southern branch of the Presbyterian Church in the United States proclaimed Dispensationalism a heresy in the 1950s. However, Reformed objections to end times speculation were never about whether or not Jesus would return, but the idea that hidden information as to when exactly this would be happening could be deduced from comparing biblical texts with contemporary history. Such speculation smacks of ancient Gnosticism, that first century heresy which often claimed to have secret knowledge only available to its adherents. At the same time, scripture says very clearly that no one knows the hour or the day of Jesus' return. Rather than fixate on discovering the unknowable date of that future event, Presbyterians have emphasized the importance of living for the glory of God; the best way to honor the returning Lord is not through idle speculation, but through being found doing one's duty should we be alive at the time, or completing up a life of thankful service to Him and His people should we not.

The return of Christ as a fundamental of Presbyterianism has a very different emphasis from that of Dispensationalism. It is not at all about guessing as to when the return will happen, but about acknowledging the nature of scripture, the nature of Jesus Christ, the nature of the redemption purchased by Him on the cross, and the helplessness of human nature in finally dealing with sin in a fallen world. In fact, some lists of the five fundamentals replace the specific return of Jesus with an emphasis more generally on the miracles of His earthly ministry. (The northern Presbyterian denomination listed Jesus' miracles as the fifth "necessary and essential" doctrine from 1910 until 1927, at which time the General Assembly declared that an Assembly could not designate certain doctrines as essential and necessary.) But either choice reaffirms the scripture, the Person of Jesus, and redemption, as well as our desperate need for divine aid in confronting sin.

The Bible is the Word of God written. Just as the Old Testament had prophesied over and over that the Messiah would come, and then He did, so the New Testament promises that Jesus will return. How was such Old Testament accuracy possible, such as Isaiah 53's description of Jesus' atoning sacrifice and burial, or Psalm 22's graphic description of Jesus' crucifixion nearly one thousand years before it happened, and centuries before crucifixions were common? It is only possible if scripture is divine in origin, inspired by the Holy Spirit. Jesus' return is spoken of with certainty in the New Testament, beginning with Paul's very first contribution, 1 Thessalonians, written around 50 AD on the second missionary journey. It is not some late doctrine tacked on to the apostles' teachings by overzealous scribes. The witness of the gospels themselves is that Jesus promised repeatedly that He would return for His disciples, and they tie the event to Judgment Day, the Yom Adonai, the Day of the LORD promised in books like Amos. God promised to send the Messiah in the Old Testament, and He did it in real history, though some had begun to doubt. Jesus has promised us in the New Testament that He will return again to establish Himself as the eternal Lord of all creation. If the Bible was right about the first time, so it will be proved right about the next time, when Jesus returns.

The return of Christ also affirms His own divine nature. How can a man who lived 2000 years ago return, like Arthur from Avalon, once and future king? And it may be many centuries or millennia yet. It is only possible if Jesus is God. To deny the future return of Christ, the so-called Second Coming, is to say that 1) the Bible is wrong, and 2) Jesus did not know what He was talking about, and had a high opinion of Himself unworthy of a religion's founder. Western Christians may not realize the theological implications of such blasphemy, or perhaps they do and just don't care. Reformed fundamentalists cannot believe any other way.

The nature of redemption also is revealed in the promise of Jesus' return. When I was a teenager I worked for two summers at a non-denominational camp in the mountains of Virginia. One night as I was walking to the building where I slept, a group of girls about the age of eight scurried by, sobbing and sniffing. "What was that about?" I asked their counselor. Apparently the evening Bible lesson had been upon death and heaven, and the counselor, an older teenage girl, informed the little girls that their dead pets would not be in heaven because animals don't have souls.

If heaven simply awaited the souls of the believers freed from the sinful cage of flesh by death (a gnostic heresy at odds with the plain teaching of both Testaments), the older girl's answer would have been correct. But the reoccurring witness of the New Testament is that redemption is much more encompassing. As Paul writes to the Romans, "…creation itself also will be set free from its slavery to corruption into the freedom of the glory of the children of God", and John echoes in the Revelation, "And I saw a new heaven and a new earth, for the first heaven and the first earth passed away, and there was no longer any sea." All the good of creation will be redeemed by the blood of Christ, not just the souls of Christians. The reference to no sea in Revelation is not a writing off of dolphins, orcas, and other magnificent ocean creatures. "The Sea" is a common metaphor for chaos in the ancient world, one used to great effect by the biblical authors. In the beginning God's Spirit is hovering over the face of the deep, the "waters" of chaos, and He brings order. Sin looses chaos upon creation once again, touching every corner of all that God had once proclaimed good. Christ's return means that He will not abandon His beloved yet now flawed creation to the ravages of sin forever. Instead, He will buy it back, along with the souls and bodies of believers. Jesus is the first one to be resurrected in a spiritual body. He will not be the last; the resurrection, which is good news for Him, becomes good news for us when we consider our present and future. It is also good news for things without souls. I don't know if my dog Peanut will be in heaven.

But I'm sure there will be dogs there. God likes dogs. He made them too.

Finally, hope in the promise of Jesus' return is an admission that the ultimate dealing with sin is beyond the power of human beings. Religious Liberalism (see Chapter 2), much like Marxism, believes that ignorance is the problem within human beings; once properly educated, or re-educated, human beings will be perfected and a golden age of peace and understanding will follow. This is unbiblical. Just as salvation was only possible when purchased by the blood of Jesus, God reaching down to save us, so the ravages of sin will only be stopped permanently by God reaching down one last time, when every knee shall bow and every tongue confess that Jesus Christ is Lord, to the glory of God the Father.

CHAPTER TWO: A CLASH OF FUNDAMENTALS

Do note that none of the fundamentals embraced by Presbyterians in the 1920s addresses questions of the origins of species, life, or the order of creation! I mention this because one of the heroes of the modern progressive movement for religion is Harry Emmerson Fosdick, whose 1922 sermon, "Shall The Fundamentalists Win?" is often cited as a brave statement of intellectual freedom from the height of this controversy. In fact, the sermon is intellectually dishonest, pulling the old bait and switch con on its listeners and readers. Fosdick, who was a Baptist pastor serving the First Presbyterian Church in New York City, began by stating that the Baptist and Presbyterian denominations are most affected by the modernist/fundamentalist controversy, and quickly suggested that the fundamentalists in both camps were opposed to new scientific knowledge. While that may have been true for the Baptists, it certainly was not with regard to the Presbyterians. He then went on to mention the doctrines of the atonement, the virgin birth, the inspiration of scripture, and the second coming of Christ, teachings never challenged by Darwin and completely beyond the powers of science to confirm or deny at this late date. (I suppose a thorough gynecological exam of Mary in the stable might have confirmed a virgin birth scientifically, though not the more important conception it indicates!)

I began the previous chapter by saying that all people are fundamentalists; everyone has a core set of beliefs which inform his or her actions, and without which the person does not know who or what he or she is, or what ought to be done. On rare occasions some fundamentals will be replaced by others, but the change is difficult; either the fundamental is eroded away by experiences which call it into question so much that behavior changes without much thought, or it is dropped suddenly during a crisis of faith, a moment of conversion. J. Greshem Machen, one of the heroes of Reformed fundamentals and a professor at Princeton in the 1920s, wrote a wonderful book in 1923 entitled <u>Christianity And Liberalism</u>. Today he might have called it Christianity and Progressivism, though I prefer to call that movement Religious Liberalism to distinguish it from its secular twin. Machen's point was that these two were incompatible, two different religions, the latter not being Christianity at all. This may be seen when Religious Liberalism's fundamentals are considered.

While Religious Liberalism began with a rejection of the authority of Scripture, followed quickly by the Virgin Birth, Substitutionary Atonement, and Christ's return, now it rejects all five fundamentals as essential for Christian belief, including the Resurrection. Fosdick suggested two fundamentals of his own: tolerance and doing the right thing instead of believing the right thing. In my own dealings with Religious Liberals in my denomination in the past 25 years, Tolerance has been replaced by Inclusivity, while deciding what is right to do is based upon cultural trends, not biblical revelation. Nothing else seems to matter. Not doctrine. Not ethics. Not reason. Not history. Not the plain meaning of words. All these take a backseat to the removing of any barrier to church membership, ordination, or any type of participation in the life of the Christian community, even leadership, followed by political action. All religions are basically the same, they say, and any Christian doctrine which highlights differences is to be condemned or ignored, NOT included, in the name of inclusivity.

Please do not misunderstand me. Of course non-believers are welcome in Church, to taste and see that the Lord is good. But to allow them to be members before making a profession of faith, let alone electing them to positions of leadership, is absurd and unbiblical. It would be like Jesus running after the rich young ruler, who rejected Jesus and went away sad when he realized that money was his idol, and Jesus then saying, "O, come anyway, and bring all your stuff! Just follow Me when you feel good about it!" Beyond this, within the Church and its leadership there is a type of inclusion, a diversity, which not only is desirable, but is to be sought. Years ago, when I was serving in rural North Carolina, I went to see a middle-aged woman who had visited the congregation. At some point in the visit she asked me if I would marry an inter-racial couple, meaning where one was black and the other white. I told her that I would want to discuss with them the challenges of an inter-racial marriage, and I would probably advise them not to live in rural North Carolina.

But if they both loved each other and they both loved Jesus, yes, I would marry them. This was not the answer she had hoped to hear. "Well," she replied, "birds of a feather flock together!" And I said, "Yes, but some animals eat their young." Just because something exists in nature, this does not mean it is morally right. (Not that birds are subject to the laws of morality!)

The more I have thought about this exchange, the more I have come to realize that the Church should be the most bizarre flock ever seen. Human beings naturally are drawn to people like ourselves; we do tend to flock with those of our "feather". But the Church is not of human origins; God calls all kinds of people to be the disciples of Jesus Christ. In the Church there should be hawks and doves, peacocks and penguins, mockingbirds and chickens, and yes, even a few turkeys like me! The unifying factor is not our backgrounds, race, education, or economic class, but our common commitment to the Lordship of Jesus Christ as He is presented in scripture (not as we would imagine Him to be) and our commitment to building each other up in that same faith in Jesus. This is only possible through the empowerment of the Holy Spirit.

My own denomination has lost sight of much of this understanding. Inclusivity as a fundamental has led to its slogan, "Unity in Diversity", the most inane linkage of words I believe I ever have heard or read. Basically it is saying, "We are so diverse that we are unified!" This is artificial, random, unworkable, and completely human in origin; it certainly finds no scriptural support. It stands in stark contrast to historical Christianity, which finds its unity, not in diversity of every imaginable type, but in a common commitment to the Lordship of Jesus Christ. Ironically, Religious Liberalism inherently must know that there is no unity in diversity apart from the limits brought by the fundamentals, because in practical application it seeks to impose a non-theological unity from above, through political constructs and maneuvers, intimidation and black-balling, and the embracing of the political agendas of secular liberalism.

Of course, the majority of modern Americans calling themselves Christians are neither Religious Liberals nor informed, Reformed fundamentalists. The majority "fundamental" in the United States has been handed to us, unthinking, by our secular culture, and has come to be called Post-Modernism. At its beginning, Post-Modernism was a reaction to the limitations and despair of Modernism. Modernism, a mechanical and materialistic world-view, posited all its hopes in scientific discovery and human achievement; reason and the physical world were its absolutes. At one level it is akin to Marxism, though the individual is elevated above the community in this agnostic approach to life, a reversal of Marx. But materialism does not satisfy; like all idols, it disappoints. It should come as no surprise, then, that the children of the Modernists have adopted a new, almost mystical world-view that rejected the absolutes of scientific achievement, while once again championing the individual. But Post-Modernism soon afterward also rejected the moral absolutes of Christianity, and in its place stands (shuffles? slouches?) a situational ethics where truth is relative, and inapplicable from one individual to the next. What is true for you might not be true for me. By this I do not mean preferences in attire or sports teams, but moral absolutes, especially in the area of sexual behavior. For example, living together with an active sexual relationship without being married might be wrong for couple A, but it might be OK for couple B. And who is to judge? Thus we live in an age of sexual anarchy.

When a minority Religious Liberalism meets a majority Post-Modernism, Inclusivity joining Whatever, the minority Biblical worldview loses. The fundamentals stand, and will stand, as long as there is a Bible which can be read and understood by the people in the pews. But biblical illiteracy is the norm in the Church today. The majority does not realize what is being sacrificed in the name of being tolerant. That is how we got here in 2011. But the problem runs much deeper than just the clash of fundamentals.

CHAPTER THREE: THE PROBLEM OF THE MIRACULOUS

When Francis Schaeffer wrote about the rise of secular humanism, he often spoke of its belief that the universe is a closed system, the idea that, however the world began, no type of divine being was involved in day to day history by miraculously "reaching in" from outside. Discomfort with the miraculous is not limited to the secular sphere; one could argue that the later writers of the Old Testament were less interested in an imminent God than they were with wisdom, seeking to understand of the make-up of the moral fabric of creation. Not unlike the deists of the Enlightenment, the wisdom literature of Proverbs and Ecclesiastes looks at the world as created by God and governed by a moral law; the Creator, like the proverbial watch maker, has put the pieces together, wound it up, and let it go. He is not involved in the day to day running of the universe because He does not need to be. Therefore, ultimately, if you are good you are rewarded, and if you are bad you are punished, not by God directly, but by the morality built into the fabric of creation. Early Judaism had a sense of God's intervention in life on a daily, moment by moment basis; its later form, and this seems to be the path on which the modern Judaism remains, sees God more as a casual observer. Live morally, according to the rules God has already put into place, and it will go well for you.

When Christianity arrived, it jumped back to the earlier version of Judaism, with more emphasis on God's miraculous intervention. What could be more of an intervention or more miraculous than God the Son becoming a human being, invading history as one of us? Some have argued that the apostles probably would have been more comfortable, given the state of 1st century Judaism, simply to have emphasized Jesus' teachings and the normal events surrounding His life, death, and the inescapable resurrection. After all, the glory of God's deliverance from the Babylonian captivity and the subsequent rebuilding of the temple and Jerusalem, is not that it was accomplished by plagues and the parting of seas, but that it was accomplished by the tedium of political expedience and bureaucratic red tape! The apostles spoke of His miracles, even though it might have made it harder for some to believe, because they had no other choice – He performed them. From this, Christianity developed the understanding of God acting through "the work of creation", things like physical law set up in the beginning, as well as through His "works of providence", by which He directs the actions of all creatures through miraculous intervention. The two need not be mutually exclusive. Jonathan Edwards wrote that, since God is so intimately involved in our lives that He prevents our atoms from flying apart at every second (Colossians 1:17), each moment of existence is as miraculous as the moment of creation. And, as G.K. Chesterton liked to say, "The sun does not rise by natural law. The sun rises because God says, 'Get up and do it again!'"

If this is so, all the observations of science would never be able to confirm or deny it. Science, in its purest form, can only report what it observes in a controlled environment; likewise, it cannot disprove miracles simply because they don't always happen. All science can say is what usually happens. How can anyone know whether water boils at 212 degrees F because of natural law or because an immanent God makes it happen in every pot on every fire and stove at any given moment? If He indeed holds the protons, neutrons, and electrons of our atoms together for everything in the physical universe at every moment, surely boiling the water a few million pots of coffee every day should not be too difficult!

Even so, human culture struggles with the concept of the miraculous. In part it is because we want to control our own destinies, not to be subject to the will of a deity. And in part it is because we do not wish to look like foolish children in the eyes of our peers, revisiting that moment in our lives when we figured out that our parents really were the ones putting presents under the tree though we had been arguing a different explanation with the neighborhood kids. Rather than struggle with the mystery of the miraculous and appear superstitious, modern men and women have preferred a more pragmatic religion, one which simply teaches us how to win friends and influence people, how to live a fulfilling life that lasts as long as possible.

This modern approach to religion actually seems to work with every faith except Christianity. Most religions are based upon the teachings of their founders, such as Mohammed, Buddha, L.

Ron Hubbard, even Moses with the Ten Commandments. If that person never had lived but someone else had taught exactly the same things, such as a Fred Smith receiving the tablets on Mount Sinai, the religion would survive unscathed. Christianity does not work like this. Christianity is not based so much on what Jesus taught as it is upon what He did. Jesus' ethical teachings are not that far removed from the Judaism in which He was raised. Even the much lauded Sermon on the Mount is a building upon the Ten Commandments, moving them from the realm of action to those of speech and thought. Of course, "You shall not take the name of the Lord your God in vain" is a commandment focused on speech, and "You shall not covet" can only be understood within the thought process, so any other Jewish teacher might have come up with this.

What is unique about Jesus' teaching is that He repeatedly claimed to be God. Think about that for a moment. What kind of people usually claim to be God, or expect the kind of devotion only a god might deserve? My short list includes Adolph Hitler, Joseph Stalin, Charles Manson, Jim Jones, and David Koresh. These individuals will never be mistaken for "great moral teachers". Yet this exactly is the type of nonsense trotted out by Religious Liberalism in attempting to remove the miraculous from the person and work of Jesus.

Jesus believed Himself to be God; all biblical accounts of His ministry are quite clear about this, and there are no other first or second-hand accounts to which others might appeal. The best Religious Liberalism has to offer in answer is to say, well, Jesus never really taught that; it was later generations of disciples which put those words into His mouth. Hogwash! Paul's letters are the earliest Christian documents, and he is quite sure that Jesus was God. How would he have gotten that notion? He, being a Pharisee, would not simply have made it up. It would have been blasphemous had Jesus Himself not claimed it and then been vindicated by the resurrection. There even is textual evidence that the claim did not begin with Paul. The Christological hymn quoted by Paul in Philippians 2 did not originate with the apostle; the Church was singing that Jesus, "who by nature being God, did not count equality with God as something to be grasped, but emptied Himself, taking the form of a servant and was obedient to death, even death on a cross," within the two decades between the resurrection and Paul's letters. That kind of radical teaching would only be present so early if Jesus Himself had taught it. As C.S. Lewis wrote, Jesus either was a liar, a lunatic, or God incarnate. He has not left open for us the option of being merely a great moral teacher. The non-biblical Jesus of Religious Liberals is merely the projection of their own desires.

Christianity is not based so much upon what Jesus taught as what He did. Even His teaching that He was God can only be accepted if He rose again. The resurrection is the miracle upon which Christianity stands or falls. If it did not happen, then the purpose of Christianity has been stripped away, and we all would be better off spending our Sunday mornings playing golf, watching TV, visiting family, or being kind to others. In fact, we might be better off just living for ourselves, grabbing all the gusto, eating and drinking for tomorrow we die, and hopefully dying young so at least we leave a good looking corpse. Is it any wonder that Religious Liberalism is a withering, dying religion? Cut off from its miraculous origin and historical, biblical moorings, Christianity devolves into a depressing works righteousness religion where one can never do enough to get right with a capricious Creator. It is without hope for this life or the next. It appeals neither to Christians who embrace the miracle of the resurrection nor to secularists without religious interests. Its one constituency is people raised in the Church who have fallen for the lie of Jesus as the merely moral and mortal teacher, people who soon tire of that façade and leave the Church entirely. They have received just enough of Christianity to inoculate them to the real thing, the miraculous thing, and fill their lives with other things which also fail to satisfy. Research done regarding the destinations of Presbyterians who have left their churches shows that the majority leave the Church entirely. Some Religious Liberals have crowed proudly that at least they are not syphoned off by more conservative churches; biblical Christianity does not seem to draw them. I take no solace in the idea that my denomination helps more people to hell than it does to fundamentalism, even the non-Presbyterian type.

The modern preference for non-miraculous religion is not based on science; science cannot comment on the existence of a deity, or how it might interact with a creation, like an artist with a canvass. The source of the preference is simply that modern people prefer a religion which is more manageable and less mysterious. To borrow from Lewis, they prefer a tame God. Unfortunately for Religious Liberalism, that kind of religion is not found in the pages of the Bible. Neither does it satisfy. After all, it is not true.

CHAPTER FOUR: IS THERE SUCH A THING AS SIN, AND SO WHAT IF THERE IS?

What is sin? When I was in seminary my preaching professor commented that we young pastors needed not to assume that our congregations defined words in the same way we did, coming fresh out of school. "Ninety percent of the time, when you say sin, they will think sex!" And though she did not say this, much of the time today members will not think that violations of biblical sexual mores are sinful for modern people, though they might still condemn adultery, especially if the violated is really nice and the violator is a pig. But human sexuality is just one area touched by sin. In fact, sin touches every area of our lives. The Westminster Shorter Catechism, one of the core historical documents of Presbyterianism in America, defines it like this: "Sin is any want of conformity unto, or transgression of, the Law of God." The Ten Commandments are the Law of God; once again, Westminster says it is here that the moral law is "summarily comprehended". Do note that sin is not merely breaking the commandments, it also is lack of conformity unto them, it is not doing them perfectly.

I would ask the reader something I repeatedly ask the members of my church, especially the teenagers: can you name the Ten Commandments? Years ago I said to the teens, "I know you think that what you have learned is stuff that everybody knows, but I want you to try an experiment this week. While you are at school, ask your friends to name the Ten Commandments." I'm sure they got some interesting answers; I can report that no one they asked could name even a few, let alone all ten. But one of the highlights of my ministry came the following week when one of the girls said to me, "I figured that if I was going to be asking people that, I had better know them myself. So I read them several times before I went to bed, and then I practiced saying them a few more times in the dark before I went to sleep." Would that all the Church would do the same!

After considering the words of the commandments, take another look at the tenth one, "You shall not covet." All the other commandments might be reduced to wooden, literal applications, no idols, being in worship every holy day, always waking up in the correct bed, etc. Likewise, if someone were to violate these narrow interpretations, anyone else present ought to be able to figure it out. Hey, that person is breaking a commandment! But someone can stand and covet in plain sight of an auditorium of spectators, and no one will ever know. This commandment, the tenth one, moves obedience from mere behavior to include our thoughts; if this is true, then maybe the other commandments also have applications to our thoughts, and our words. In fact, Jesus taught this way in the Sermon on the Mount; hating a brother is the same as killing him, and lusting after someone is as bad as committing adultery. The Pharisees of the first century were convinced they had kept the commandments throughout their lives. Paul tells the Philippians that his legalistic observation of the Law as a Pharisee had been perfect. The rich young ruler asked Jesus what he must to do inherit eternal life, and the Lord responded, "Keep the commandments." The man answered, "But I have done this since I was a child." Jesus' response is often misinterpreted. "One thing you lack – go and sell all you have and give the money to the poor, then come follow Me," is not a blanket command for all Christians to embrace a life of poverty. How could Prisca and Aquila have had a house which was being used as a meeting place for a Roman congregation if that were so, or how could Lydia have housed the missionaries in Philippi? How could Paul have said in 1 Corinthians 13 that if he gave all he had to the poor it would profit him nothing? Jesus simply was responding to the young man's declaration that he had always kept the commandments, showing him that he had not even kept the first one since his money was his god. He was showing the man that he could not do anything to inherit eternal life because he had broken the Law of God in thought, word, and deed all his life, and that God required perfection with regard to the Commandments. He was showing the man that he needed a Savior. We all do.

The seriousness of sin in scripture cannot be overstated. It begins with Adam, and continues down to each one of us by ordinary generation. Each one of us bears its scars from birth, and we contribute our own violations very quickly afterward. It is being self-centered instead of God-centered. It is not only missing the mark of God's standard, like a novice archer whose wild shots never come near the target, it is not getting a bullseye every time. And it is the exact opposite of God's perfect nature.

Sometimes when I teach the youth about this, I ask them to imagine a shaker filled with pure salt. Then I ask, "If I put one grain of sugar into that same container, is it still pure salt?" It might look like it, but no, the kids always reply, it would no longer be pure salt. This image helps me understand the nature of sin as it is presented in scripture. It is the exact opposite of God's perfection, and to allow it into His presence indefinitely, uncorrected, would be to ask the Lord to deny His own nature. This reality is illustrated very powerfully in the Old Testament ritual connected with the Ark of the Covenant. That artifact represented the very presence of God, His footstool or throne. It was kept away from everyone ordinarily, sequestered in the Holy of Holies in the center of the tabernacle, and later the temple. A thick veil separated it even from the priests and Levites who worked in the place of worship. One priest once a year was able to go in and offer a sacrifice for the people. When he did he wore bells on his robe and had a rope tied around the his foot; this way, if the bells stopped ringing for very long, those outside would know that something was wrong and would be able to pull the injured or dead priest from the throne room of the Lord. There was no other option. You can't go barging into the presence of a holy God, covered as you are in sin, even on a mission of mercy. That's how serious God's holiness is, and how devastating our sin is in severing the relationship. And our desire for that relationship, to worship and adore Him, is so strong, so basic, that if we do not worship him, we will worship something or someone else. That something or someone always lets us down, always disappoints, in addition to adding to our account of sin via idolatry (Commandment 2).

And though the Bible does not spell this out specifically, I have come to see hell as God's sin disposal site. Just as human beings and nuclear waste cannot coexist, so God and sin cannot exist side by side. It's not that sin is dangerous to God like nuclear waste is to us, but instead, just as we can't live side by side with things that kill us, God cannot and will not reside with things which deny Who and What He is. Karl Barth emphasized the root meaning of the Hebrew word for "holiness", which is "apart". The utensils in the temple were "holy to the LORD", that is, set apart for His use. So also the people were called to be holy, set apart for God's use. God Himself is holy, completely apart from His creation like an artist is separate from his or her canvass. This in itself is an important image; like a person on the shore throwing a life ring to a drowning friend, God is not caught up in the problem of sin which plagues all His creation, and thus is free to save us. But unless He moves to save us, we are helplessly tied to the miseries sin brings to this life, and eternal separation from Him in the life to come.

The good news of the gospel is that God has moved to save us out of His love through sending His Son. When Jesus died on the cross, THE essential sacrifice was made; all the previous ones, even those made in front of the Ark, were merely foreshadowings of what happened on Golgotha in the spring of 33 AD, the day before Passover. The fact that this sacrifice of Jesus worked was proclaimed even before the Resurrection, on Good Friday, when the veil in the temple, before the Holy of Holies, was ripped from top to bottom. It was as if God Himself had stooped down from heaven and tore it apart, saying, now, finally, the way has been made clear for sinful humans to be accepted into the presence of a holy God! It's what we've always wanted, even when we don't recognize that longing for what it is. How can we say no to Him? Why would we want to?

Religious Liberalism does not have this understanding of sin. Some versions of it, the ones with universalist, "all religions are the same" tendencies, see sin as ignorance, and salvation as education. Those with a more Marxist bent see sin as the rich and powerful exploiting the poor and weak; in this scenario, the poor are without sin because they have no power by which to implement any evil. Both versions deny the plain teaching of scripture. It is important to note that the biblical definitions of sin and warnings against it are first directed to the individual, not the group. Though it is not obvious to English readers, the Queen's English having no distinct versions of the second person singular pronouns and the verb to be which accompanies them ("you are" is the same either way!), the Commandments are written to individuals. You, the individual, shall have no other gods before Me. And so it goes. Yes, we have our collective sins. But never forget that you are guilty all by yourself, as am I. Jesus did not come just to save a whole bunch of people. He came to save you. How will you respond?

CHAPTER FIVE: WHAT ABOUT SEX?

I always have liked what C.S. Lewis said about the ridiculous nature of the sex drive in human beings in his wonderful book, Mere Christianity. He begins with the scenario of a foreign country where there was plenty to eat, no starvation, and yet where one could fill a room with people to see a show where a cover over a plate was slowly lifted until it could be seen, just before the lights went out, that beneath it was a bit of mutton or a pork chop. Wouldn't we say that something was wrong with the desire for food in that country, especially if there was no famine in the land? Or simply consider the biological purpose of eating compared with appetite. A person might eat more than he should, maybe even enough for two, but most fill up at a reasonable level, not much beyond that. By contrast, sexual desire as it exists, especially in men, is absurdly exaggerated beyond biological necessity. Lewis imagines a young man who acts on his sexual impulse each time he has it, and observes that if each of these unions produced a child, the biological purpose of sexual intercourse, he would easily populate a small village within a few years.

When we turn to the Bible itself, it is clear that of all the desires which human beings have, shelter, food, security, only one is singled out with its own commandment: you shall not commit adultery. It is as if God knows that with our fall into sin the sexual drive has become so warped that it needs special attention and curbing. Ironically, there are many other pleasant sensations available to human beings which do not seem to rule us so harshly. My wife's college sociology teacher put it this way: the most over-rated sensation in life is sex; the most under-rated is a good bowel movement!

Since the sexual revolution of the 1950s most Americans assume that sexual activity is not only a right, but a necessity. It is no exaggeration to say that, in the minds of many, if you are an adult and not having sex with somebody, anybody, there is something wrong with you. Your head surely is going to explode if you don't get lucky. Beyond this, the accepted age for sexual activity among peers has dropped far below 18 now, so that young teens, emotionally unprepared for the commitment sexual intimacy promises and rightly expects, blunder through the door of sexual experimentation into self-loathing, betrayal, and mistrust.

Sexual imagery abounds in this culture, from advertisement to entertainment to the most vile of pornographic debasement. When I was a teen in the 1970s softcore porn was only available at the local news stand; I never glimpsed hardcore in those days. Today all of it is available on the home computer via the internet; any preschooler might stumble across it while searching for a favorite cartoon character. Is it any wonder that so many are confused?

Add to this the destruction of the American family. Again, when I was a boy in the 1960s I knew of one couple that had divorced; their children were friends of mine. Today more than half of American marriages end in divorce, the vast minority due to the biblical allowances for adultery (Matthew 5:32) and abandonment (1 Corinthians 7:15). The family is the basic building block of society. It is there we learn to trust, we learn to respect authority, we learn self-confidence. It also is in the family that we learn our earliest lessons about God. I once heard a preacher say the hymn really ought to be changed to say, "Jesus loves me, this I know, for my mother told me so." The Bible surely teaches it, but as children we believe because we see the faith of our parents. But what happens in a society where a majority of children are not raised in loving, stable homes? Granted, in a fallen world, some marriages will fail. But what happens in a society where most marriages fail, and the ideal of a mother and a father married till death parts them is not stressed or celebrated, but simply is one of a plethora of coupling arrangements all touted as equally good, or bad, or disposable? Where do those young ones learn self-worth, or trust, or respect for authority? Where do they develop an understanding of a God who loves them and will not abandon them? And what happens when they cannot discern reality from appearance in our mass media, eager to sell whatever illusion will make the fastest buck? I think we are seeing this today as sexual anarchy slashes and burns its way through our teens and twenty-somethings.

Of course, in a society where sex outside of marriage is accepted as normal, desirable, and necessary, acceptance of homosexual behavior is completely understandable. Coupled with the fundamentals of tolerance and "whateverism", most people feel that what one chooses to do in his or her bedroom 1) is nobody else's business and 2) cannot be called wrong. Additionally, while no "gay" gene ever has been discovered, people assume that homosexuality is a genetic condition, therefore natural for those who have it, and never to be condemned. (Even if such a gene exists, it would not automatically make the behavior right, just as contemporary theories of gene-driven adultery do not make adultery right. Sometimes being moral means fighting against what feels natural!) But in a society which assumes that sexual activity is basic to being human, it is the height of cruelty to preach sexual abstinence for anyone, including the homosexual.

The Christian answers that cruelty is not found in expecting abstinence for the unmarried, but rather in encouraging anyone to participate in behavior the Bible calls sinful. Sinful behavior has negative consequences, whether or not our society wants to acknowledge it. American culture does not truly believe that such a thing as sin exists; therefore calling a behavior sinful is bigoted, narrow-minded, and mean-spirited. But suppose just for a moment that sin is real and does have consequences. Wouldn't the real cruelty be not to warn those attracted to it? Were our parents cruel for not allowing us to play in the middle of busy streets when we were children?

According to the Bible, the most basic desire in human beings is to have a relationship with our Creator, to worship Him. When that relationship is severed, we seek intimacy elsewhere. And with apologies to Freud, intimacy is what human beings most desire, not sex. Unfortunately, 21st century America uses this formula – sex equals intimacy, intimacy equals sex. While it is true that sexuality is a part of the intimacy between a husband and a wife, there are many close, satisfying relationships throughout life which do not involve sex; in fact, sex would ruin them.

While the origins of homosexual behavior are still disputed (heredity vs environment), one of the most intriguing non-genetic theories I have discovered was suggested by representatives from Exodus International, which is a ministry formed in the 1970s to support and assist people out of the gay lifestyle. When asked, they asserted that often homosexuals are raised in families where the opposite sex parent is overbearing, while the same sex parent is absent or distant. Because of this, the child grows up longing to connect with the parent of the same sex. Such a desire is understandable. But then puberty kicks in, and the desire becomes sexualized. The people from Exodus International claimed that, at the heart of homosexual behavior, is simply a desire to be close to someone of the same sex. To bolster their assertions, they offered this observation: in all their research, no gay person ever went to a gay bar the first time for sex. Instead, they simply were lonely, longing to connect with someone, looking for companionship.

    I believe these observations also can be applied to heterosexual relationships. While sexual attraction is part of the mix, the connection, the intimacy is the promise for which everyone is looking. If it were not so, why bother with any selection process beyond "He/she looks good to me," and "Do the parts fit?". (As far as I know, at least between men and women, they always do.) What is that mysterious factor which says in our hearts, "I do not connect with this person," but "I know this is the one."? It is about intimacy. Beyond marriage, why is this person my best friend, while I don't seem to bond with this other person, though we have so much in common? There are types of intimacy which do not involve sex; often they are just as important in our lives as the relationship we have with a spouse, though different. And to add sex to the mix would ruin them.

    From the Christian point of view, one which runs counter to the culture, our fulfillment does not come from sexual encounters at all, but from our relationship with God through Jesus Christ. The Westminster Shorter Catechism explains this in question and answer one: "What is the chief end of man? Man's chief end is to glorify God and to enjoy Him forever." As a married man I can say, sex is nice, but it is not everything, and it neither defines me nor completes me. My relationship with Jesus does both. Beyond this, Jesus never had sex a single time in His life, yet He was fully and perfectly human in a way every other human being never will be. Sex did not define Him. It should not define

Christians. When sex defines us, it has become an idol, and disaster looms.

And so, the Christian answer to the question, "What about sex?" begins with this – "Do not let that desire run your life." Beyond this, the biblical standard for sexual activity is this: chastity in singleness and fidelity in marriage. Does this mean every Christian will live up to these standards perfectly? No, of course not. But the standard remains there, and is unchanged by culture or fashion. It means that every Christian will try to live by that standard, fighting against the natural, fallen nature which desires otherwise. Not only is this pleasing to a loving heavenly Father, it also is in our own best interest.

In the mid-1990s Time magazine ran a cover article entitled "Our Cheating Hearts". It explored the idea that marital infidelity had genetics at its source. Our genes "desire" the best and most opportunities to be passed on, so men cheat to have more children than one woman could possibly bear (see C.S. Lewis' small village illustration!), while women desire the best provider for their genetic material, conveniently deposited in their offspring, and cheat more often with richer men. In just a few pages love, marriage, and child-rearing were reduced to the mechanical lurching of genes. I call that "genetic fatalism". But in the final paragraph even the writer could stand it no more. After fretting that people might use this new understanding of adultery as an excuse to stray, he concluded with this statement: "Perhaps the first step to being moral is to realize how thoroughly we aren't." And that, sisters and brothers, will preach!

The ancient Greeks believed in fate, that a person's life was completely mapped out from the day he was born to the day he died. Nothing he did would change what the Fates had decided for him, no matter what he did to change himself, no matter what lengths were taken to stop some horrible event prophesied from happening. The story of Oedipus illustrates this so well. The oracle at Delphi told his parents, the king and queen of Thebes, that he would kill his father and marry his mother. The king attempted to kill the baby by exposing him, but a kind shepherd found and saved him. Eventually he was adopted by the king and queen of Corinth, who raised him as their own. Oedipus visited the oracle himself as a young man, and was told of his destiny to murder his father and marry his mother. Thinking they were in Corinth, in order to save them he fled to Thebes, where, through a series of adventures, he fulfilled his irrevocable destiny with his unrecognized birth parents. No matter what he did, his fate was determined.

In the first century, one of the great gifts of Christianity was that it freed believers from cruel and inescapable fate. It didn't matter where you were born, or who your parents were, or your social standing – the only thing that mattered was and is that you, as a follower of Christ, are adopted and adored by the God of the universe, and in His service you will find your deepest joy. This is a message the 21st century needs desperately to hear. The secular world believes that we are locked in a genetic fatalism, and if we do not act on whatever our genes might be compelling us to do, then we will be miserable: nothing can prevent this, because nothing is greater than our genes, not even Jesus Christ. But this is a lie, and Christians need to denounce it as such, all the while living in the power of Jesus and daily surrendering our wills, actions, thoughts, and words to Him. This will not lead to misery, but fulfillment. Misery comes when we surrender to fleshly desires, treating human beings created in the image of God merely as means to our own selfish ends, and leaving a trail of broken promises and people in our wakes.

Chastity in singleness and fidelity in marriage are realistic and achievable goals for Christians. To live otherwise is neither just nor kind, to others or to ourselves. To live otherwise is to destroy the very human intimacy we innately desire. The intimacy of marriage is not limited to sex; the best marriages are based on friendship and mutual respect, mutual edification.

I also believe that fidelity in marriage and chastity in singleness is a workable solution for individuals attracted to people of the same sex. By this I do not mean gay marriage; the Christian definition of marriage is a union between one man and one woman, a visual representation of the love shared between Christ and the Church. Many of the gay people I know have been married to someone of the opposite sex at one time or another; sometimes this is explained as fulfillment of a desire to have children, with the opposite sex partner then abandoned once the birth or births have occurred. Sometimes it is dismissed as mere "bisexualism", and too bad for the opposite sex partner now cast aside. At the same time, I know people who have come out of the gay lifestyle who have married someone of the opposite sex and lived faithfully and happily in the intimacy promised.

Perhaps the solution for those drawn to members of the same gender is not simply to have sex with any willing partner or partners, but instead to build friendships with people of the same gender without attempting to sexualize those relationships. Here the type of intimacy which everyone desires with other people can be realized without compromise. Certainly the individual would need to beware of being in situations where he or she is tempted to act on sexual urges and so avoid them, just as heterosexuals married and single must do. He or she might be wise to develop that close friendships with people who do not struggle with same-sex attraction; it would help if these friends belonged to the same congregation too. Marriage to someone of the opposite sex would remain an option in such a case; many married couples have close friends beside their spouses. In wedding ceremonies I usually remind couples that their needs are going to be beyond what this other, finite person can meet. Christian marriages are not based on how one feels at a given moment, but upon the commitment to keep the promises made months or years or decades ago. True love does not promise how it is going to feel, but what it is going to do and not do. This understanding does not lead to loveless marriages, as caricatured in American media, but to a comfort and a trust upon which a life can be built. And, contrary to another American caricature, there are people who live a celibate single life and find it quite fulfilling. Our peace and purpose comes from Jesus Christ, not our reproductive organs.

Augustine wrote that God made our hearts restless till they find their rest in Him. The ultimate expression of intimacy which satisfies the soul will not be found in any single person in your life, nor within a group of family or friends. The intimacy we most long for is a connection with our Creator.

CHAPTER SIX: THE MISSION OF THE CHURCH

The New Testament Church had a very narrow focus on its mission. Within congregations believers gathered regularly to encourage one another in the faith, to worship the risen Lord Jesus, to hear the Word of God proclaimed by preachers with the gift of prophecy, and to receive instruction in the meaning of scripture (both Old Testament books and the parts of the New Testament which existed, Paul's letters being the first things collected and shared). Beyond this, social ministries were focused on caring for poor church members, such as distributing food to widows (Acts 6), and the collection of funds from Gentile churches to send to the culturally predominantly Jewish Christian mother church in Jerusalem. Ministry to non-believers was primarily that of sharing the good news about Jesus, the Son of God, who had died on a cross in Palestine as a human sacrifice to pay for human sins, and then rose again as the evidence of the success of His death in our places. From non-New Testament sources we also learn of the efforts of Christians to locate and rescue the newborn babies legally left to die of exposure on trash heaps. Individuals were commanded to live at peace with everyone so far as it depended upon them, and to do good to all people, especially with those in the Church, but everyone else as well. There does not seem to have been a standardized program for addressing social ills.

One might argue that since early Christians were a small, powerless group on the fringe of first century Roman society, we should not be surprised that no larger social program is adopted by the New Testament writers. When we look to the Old Testament, the concern for social justice is more pronounced. The Lord speaks through Amos, "Take away from Me the noise of your songs; I will not even listen to the sound of your harps. But let justice roll down like waters and righteousness like an ever flowing stream." (Amos 5:23+24) The Old Testament Church was a society which needed this kind of structuring, where all law, if it was good law, was based on God's Law. Kings and religious leaders were in places of power and authority, and God wanted them to know that merely going through the outward motions of religious services was not enough to satisfy His expectations of loving Him and one's neighbor as oneself.

Once Christianity became the only religion legal in the Roman Empire, it became necessary for Christians to consider how to apply principles of the gospel to ruling. Augustine's Just War Theory was developed in the decades which followed, where certain rules applied to Christian warriors regardless of the rules observed by their enemies. However, through the centuries the power of the Church often became merely an extension of state power and, to the extent it existed, the corruption of government. The checking of power by Calvinists in Scotland by holding pastors and lay leaders accountable, and the subsequent refusal of the United States' founders to establish a state church as a guard against ecclesiastical tyranny, have proven to be reforming forces within the Church from the time of the Reformation until today.

But the struggle to engage our communities without allowing our communities to co-opt the Church for their own ends remains. The 1850s were a watershed decade for American Presbyterians in grappling with the demands of Christ and the culture. While the theological climate of the day was dominated by the Old School/New School debates connected with the Second Great Awakening, with most southern churches firmly Old School while the New School gained ground in the north, the political climate was defined by the question of slavery. White abolitionists tended to argue apart from the words of the Bible, preferring instead to talk about the "spirit of freedom" as the overall theme of the New Testament. White defenders of slavery, such as Dr. Robert Lewis Dabney of Union Theological Seminary in Virginia, argued from the words of scripture itself, pointing to specifics like slaves owned by Abraham, or Paul's sending Onesimus back to Philemon without demanding the runaway slave's emancipation. Interestingly, the black abolitionists of the day were much more likely to argue from the words of scripture than their white counterparts, correctly noting the differences between biblical slavery and the modern, race-based version; unfortunately, few whites read black abolitionists' work at this time. Prior to the Civil War, the pro-slavery, pro-text camp was winning the argument. Then the war came and, as Church historian Mark A. Noll has noted, "the matter was settled by those great theologians, Ulysses S. Grant and William T. Sherman."

Perhaps because abolitionists were not winning the theological debates of the 1850s, when the crisis of secession loomed in 1860, northern Presbyterians rallied to the side of the federal government, and demanded that all Presbyterian churches nationwide pledge their fealty to Washington. Slavery may have caused the war, but the division of the Presbyterian Church into USA and CSA branches in 1861 was caused almost exclusively by northern demands that southern Presbyterians choose federal government over state government, an argument only decided conclusively by the war itself.

Into this maelstrom stepped an unlikely champion from Princeton Theological Seminary, Dr. Charles Hodge. Hodge later would become famous for his three volume Systematic Theology, which today remains one of Princeton Seminary's most popular reprint publications. But in 1861 he was concerned for his Christian brothers and sisters in the south, including Robert Dabney. Hodge argued for a doctrine of "the spirituality of the Church", the idea that the Church should focus on spiritual matters, such as the preaching of the gospel, the building up of the faith of believers, and teaching basic doctrine, matters beyond the expertise or scope of other societal institutions, and that the Church should refrain from entangling itself in temporal matters, such as federal vs state rights. Following the war, most southern Presbyterians adhered to this understanding of the Church, staying out of the political debates of their times.

The strength of the doctrine of the Spirituality of the Church is its refusal to allow itself to be co-opted by current political debates. Its weakness came to light in the 1950s and 1960s, during the height of the Civil Rights Movement, as many churches used the doctrine as an excuse to remain silent in the face of the oppression of African-Americans, especially in the South. In reaction, many young pastors who came of age in those decades rejected the Spirituality of the Church and embraced the Social Gospel, a politically active Christianity. Though they would probably blanch at the comparison, their liberal brand of political activism, informed by the Civil Rights Movement, has much in common with the conservative religious brand of political activism made popular by Jerry Falwell and the Moral Majority in the 1970s. With an emphasis on political action instead of theological fundamentals, each can be hijacked by the secular political movements with whom they share common concern. Therefore, while Religious Liberalism has become a captive of pro-union, pro-choice, and pro-gay normalization movements nationwide and beyond, conservative Christianity can easily be over-shadowed by pro-free market, pro-military, and pro-nationalism secular movements which also have nothing to do with the spread of the good news of Jesus Christ. I believe it is time to revisit the glorious doctrine of the Spirituality of the Church.

Religious Liberals within my denomination, the Presbyterian Church (USA), have spent much time and effort in recent years condemning modern Israel for its handling of the Palestinians who live within its borders. This has hurt our witness to American Jews; one of my best friends, who happens to be Jewish, usually forwards to me news articles about the latest pronouncement from Presbyterians against Israel. He notices, he cares, and our actions infuriate him. Two facts must be stated: 1) It's a complicated situation, and to pretend otherwise is dishonest; 2) Most of us are not living there, and don't know exactly what is going on.

A few years ago I was attending a meeting of Synod Council, a body whose responsibilities do not include the monitoring of overseas human rights violations; if they did, certainly Cuba and Syria should get as much attention as Israel. Nevertheless, we were treated to a lengthy presentation on Israeli oppression of Palestinians, with much time devoted to condemning the building of the security wall between Israeli and Palestinian communities in the West Bank. "This makes farming very difficult for Palestinian families, some of whom must travel for miles to get through the gate to get to the section of their land on the other side of the wall," we were told. But the situation is much more complicated than we were told, sitting in the air-conditioned comfort of the conference room in Richmond that day.

After the speaker was done, I raised my hand and asked, "Tom, isn't it true that everywhere that wall has gone up, suicide bombings of Israeli citizens by Palestinians has stopped completely?" Yes, came the answer. I continued, "You know, no less an expert on war than Ulysses S. Grant said that the Mexican War was the most unjust war forced by a stronger nation upon its weaker neighbor. And we got about half of Mexico out of that deal, California, New Mexico, Arizona. Now, suppose a group of Mexican nationalists appeared today, demanding that those states be returned to Mexico. Suppose they started blowing themselves up in malls and on busses, murdering innocent people, until their demands were made. What would be the American response to such actions? I don't know. But I do know this: whatever the Americans decided to do, Sweden wouldn't have a lot to say about it, because it's not their problem." The presenter had no response.

Certainly individual Christians need to be aware of current events and to form political opinions on which we act. There are many groups throughout our open society dedicated to political and social change. But only the Church has been charged by God with the task of proclaiming the perfect, atoning sacrifice of our now risen and soon returning Lord Jesus. Nobody and nothing else can do that. Of course schools can teach the historic facts about Christianity, as well as other religions. Of course congregations can choose to join in ministries of compassion in their communities and beyond, working with those with whom they disagree about fundamental things while supporting common causes. (In our community we work with many different churches and religious groups to support a soup kitchen and over-night shelter.) Of course churches can equip their members with information to deal with worldviews which agree or clash with their own. But the proclamation of the gospel from the Church must remain clear throughout it all.

CHAPTER SEVEN: THE LACK OF ACCOUNTABILITY

Many people know that Presbyterians are Calvinists, which is to say that our theology is based on the work of John Calvin, the 16th Century reformer who lived in Geneva, Switzerland, and others who continued his train of thought. All together this branch of theology is referred to as Reformed. But we do not identify ourselves by our theology. We are not the Reformed Church, or the Calvinistic Church, we are the Presbyterian Church. In taking that name we have chosen to identify ourselves by our polity, our system of government.

Churches around the world are governed in one of three ways. Many are <u>hierarchical</u>; they are governed from the top down to the local congregation. The best example of this is the Roman Catholic Church, where the pope is at the top, and he and the bishops underneath him inform the local congregations of their decisions, which are to be obeyed. The second type of polity is <u>congregational</u>; most Baptist churches are congregational, where most decisions are brought before the local church for a vote, and no one has authority over the church beyond the local congregation. <u>Presbyterianism</u> is the third option; we combine the best of these other two forms, with real authority given to people outside the local congregation, but never to individuals, like bishops. Locally, our form is more like a republic than a democracy. The congregation elects elders who they trust to make most of the decisions for the church, making the deliberative and voting body much smaller than the local congregation, but also hopefully more informed than the average member as well.

Many people are unaware of the fact that the American system of government, with separation of powers and checks and balances, is based upon the Presbyterian system of government. After all, the Presbyterians were here first! Basic to this view is the understanding that human beings are flawed, frail, and tend toward idolatry, even idolatry of self. Therefore, no one individual is given final say in any matter of importance in the life of the Church.

In the place of the bishops who rule the Roman Catholic, Episcopalian, and Methodist churches, Presbyterians have ruling councils. No individual has authority over a council, even over councils closer to the local congregation, or even if that individual is working at the national level. In fact, it is no exaggeration to say that there is no hierarchy in the Presbyterian Church, only pastors and elders. At each level, the local session, regional presbytery, multi-state synod, and national General Assembly, historically referred to as "courts of the Church", local pastors and local elders are the only members, the only ones with voice and vote.

Sometimes when I hear people explaining why they do not attend church, they will say, "There's too much politics in churches and not enough spirituality!" Now, if they mean too much church focus on local or national politics, I might be inclined to agree. (See Chapter 6) But what they usually mean is struggling within the membership between different groups. If this is the case, a Presbyterian should reply, "Politics is spirituality." How we work together, and love each other, through disagreements is a great witness to the world of the power of Jesus Christ. It also is how sanctification happens, as we knock off each other's rough edges. Paul put it like this: "For there must also be factions among you in order that those who are approved (by God) may have become evident among you." (1 Corinthians 11:19) In other words, as the group gathers and discusses a problem, God will reveal His will in the understanding of the majority, so long as the majority position is in harmony with scripture. Historically speaking, Presbyterians have not believed the majority is always right; the words of the Bible do have veto power! But a minority ought humbly to consider what the majority is saying, especially if there is a biblical warrant, and be willing to submit their understanding to that of the majority.

One of the best examples of this in scripture is found in Acts 15, the Jerusalem Council. Here the Church was considering what to do about all these Gentiles who had been flocking to faith in the Jewish Messiah, Jesus. This was an unexpected turn of events for most Christians of the day, all raised as Jews. Some Christians, who had been Pharisees in Judaism, were very sure that Gentiles who became Christians also needed to be "circumcised according to the custom of Moses." They needed to become Jews. Countering this argument was Peter, who reminded the listeners that he had been sent by God to the Roman centurion named Cornelius and his family (Acts chapter 10), and that after Peter had preached to them, the Holy Spirit fell upon them. They began speaking in tongues, just like the apostles and other disciples experienced the Holy Spirit's baptism on Pentecost in Acts 2. If God accepted Cornelius as he was, in the same way that He accepted the original 120 disciples at Pentecost, surely adding Judaism to Christianity was not necessary. Later on Paul would argue to the Galatians that adding Judaism to Christianity for Gentiles not only is unnecessary, it is a damnable heresy because it nullifies the work Jesus did on the cross; it is saying Jesus did not do enough, and that our work enhances our salvation. But at the Jerusalem Council he and Barnabas simply added their support to what Peter was saying, telling about Gentiles who had been coming to Christ during the first missionary journey of Acts 13 and 14.

At this point in the meeting, James, the biological half-brother of Jesus, who had come to lead the church in Jerusalem, stood up and reminded the group that they should not be surprised that these things were happening. Old Testament scripture had foretold this. "With this the words of the Prophets agree," he said. So knowing God's will is not just a matter of one's personal experience, and it is not just a matter of majority rule. It is also a matter of finding precedent in scripture, or some type of harmony with what already is written there. Though the minority might not completely agree with the majority position, or even the majority biblical interpretation, only if the majority ignores the plain words of the Bible should the minority feel free simply to rebel against the majority. This is what happened at the Jerusalem Council. The former Pharisees who treasured their Jewish heritage were the minority, and yet also were willing to submit their understanding to that of the majority. The majority had personal experiences to support their claims, plus the greater number convinced, plus the words of scripture itself. This is the spirituality of politics within a congregation or denomination.

Because of this understanding, Presbyterians have developed a theology regarding meetings. Prior to the meeting those who attend cannot be instructed by those they are representing on how to vote. Presbyterian representatives to higher governing bodies, even just to presbyteries, are not delegates, who may be instructed by their constituencies on how to vote. They are commissioners. They are commissioned to act on behalf of those they represent. They certainly are to prepare before going to the meeting, but they still are called to arrive with an open mind, listening for the leading of the Holy Spirit. At the meeting their minds might be changed, and they should be open to the possibility. This also is why voting by proxy is not allowed in any Presbyterian church meeting. You can't phone it in or mail it in. You must be there to hear what is said, to listen for the Spirit's leading through experience (both yours and that of others), the majority opinion, and the words of scripture itself. Of course, that's one more reason to know your Bible as well as possible!

Sometimes, perhaps because they have been spending too much time with bishops in the hierarchies of other Christian churches, leaders in the higher governing bodies forget the role and value of councils over individuals. Years ago, after a scandal had rocked the denomination and a local session in Wilmington, NC, voted to cut funding to the larger denomination as an act of protest and good stewardship, a presbytery official took it upon himself to write a letter to that session, criticizing them for their decision to withhold money. My father, who also is a pastor, made this comment: "The Session should send a letter back to that person which says, 'And who are you, an individual, to speak thusly to a court of the Church?'" What scripture says certainly is more important than decisions of courts of the Church; one of the foundational understandings of Calvinism, formed during the Protestant Reformation while doing away with non-biblical Roman Catholic traditions, is that Councils do err, they are not infallible. At the same time, the opinion of the individual, certainly when it is apart from scripture, and even when it concerns interpretation of scripture, is to be held in lower regard than that of a duly elected ruling body.

One of the glories of the Presbyterian system which should be observed here is that at each level the lay leadership, the elders, MUST outnumber the professional leadership, the pastors. Historically the elders were called "ruling elders", while the pastors were called "teaching elders"; unlike most other Christian denominations, the offices of pastor and elder are seen as the same office with different functions. Think about that for a moment. How would the American Medical Association be different if more than half of the voting members could not be doctors? Or how would the Bar Association be different if half of its voting members could not be lawyers? While Presbyterians have placed high value upon an educated clergy, they also recognize that education is no substitute for the calling of God. While one's vocation might not be into full-time ministry, a plumber or a mechanic or a nurse (or any other calling) may well be called by God into lay leadership within the Church. This is also shown by who has authority to ordain pastors; while seminaries provide the education needed, that's all they do. Only presbyteries made up of pastors and elders can ordain and install pastors.

Up until the 1960s the process of calling into the pastorate was three-fold. 1) An individual felt the call of God to become a pastor. 2) A presbytery had to concur with that call. 3) A congregation had to call the pastor to serve it. If you did not have all three, you could not become a pastor. The story was told of a young man plowing in a cornfield; looking up into the sky, he saw the clouds forming the letters "P" and "C". "This surely must mean, 'Preach Christ!'" he exclaimed. Filled with enthusiasm, he went to the next meeting of his presbytery and presented himself to be considered as a candidate for the ministry. But upon examination, the presbytery decided that the letters in the clouds must have meant, "Plow Corn!" True calling from God into ordained office is not known simply by the individual.

In the 1960s the Presbyterian Church decided, after years of studying scripture, to ordain women as elders, deacons, and pastors. In doing this, it went against centuries of tradition and the vast majority of Christians worldwide. However, I believe it was right to make this change. While there are passages of scripture which seem to forbid women in positions of authority over men in the Church, closer examination of the actual texts reveal a first century Church which had many women in leadership positions. Phoebe was a deaconess. (Romans 16:1)

Pricilla, whose name almost always comes before that of her husband, Aquila, probably indicating that she was of more noble birth, taught alongside him in correcting what was lacking in the preaching of Apollos. (Acts 18:24-26) Syntyche and Euodia of the Philippian church shared in the struggle with Paul and Clement. (Philippians 4:2+3) For me, the key text is Acts 21:7-9, where Paul is travelling to Jerusalem and stays in the home of Philip the Evangelist, one of the original seven deacons. Luke tells us that Philip by this time had four virgin daughters who were prophetesses. The gift of prophecy is interpreted differently by different groups of Christians, as either the telling of the future or preaching. Whichever is correct, these women were not being silent in their churches, and Paul seemed to have no problem with this since he stayed with Philip and his family in Caesarea for several days. Because of this I believe, along with the majority of Presbyterians in my denomination, that Paul's commands for women to be silent in church were meant for specific problems in specific churches, not for all time.

While the denomination allowed for the ordination of women in the late 1960s, it could not force churches to call women as their pastors. The practical result of this was that many women graduating from seminary in the early 70s could not find jobs as pastors. What was to be done? The solution chosen was to remove the third tier of the call process; a person would feel the call, and a presbytery would confirm it through the ordination process, but no longer would someone have to receive a call from a congregation to become a pastor.

The unintended consequences of this well-meaning change have been catastrophic for the Presbyterian Church (USA). Today there are many individuals called "pastor" who are not pastoring churches and who are accountable to no one. Some are college or seminary professors. This in itself is troubling. Dr. John Leith of Union Theological Seminary in Virginia used to say that ideas which wouldn't last ten minutes in a congregation can be kicked around in seminaries for decades. Others are "specialized clergy", counselors and chaplains and campus ministers and such. Some are "members-at-large", pastors who for whatever reason are not installed in congregations. Still others are retired clergy. And then others are presbytery staff members, executives, associate executives, and the like. The one thing each person in these groups has in common is that none is serving a congregation, none is accountable to a session or a congregation, before whom most pastors preach and teach each week. As such, they tend to be more influenced by cultural values, and less by biblical values.

Even so, each of these has the same voice and vote on the floor of presbytery that pastors serving congregations have. Often they have more flexibility in their schedules, and thus are more likely to serve on presbytery committees and in higher governing bodies. I represented my presbytery for seven years at the Synod level, 2001-2007. Of course, as required, the Synod Council of about thirty always had as many elders as pastors for every meeting. But the reality was quite different from the ideal. Once, after a particularly troublesome vote, I observed to the leadership, "You know, I'm the only pastor here who has to go home and explain this to a congregation." This was not unusual; at the most there might be one other serving pastor, accountable to elders and members. The other "pastors" were chaplains, professional counselors, or retired. I cannot speak to how things are done at the national level, having only served there once as a commissioner to General Assembly in 1994, and never having even visited the national offices in Louisville, Kentucky. After all, our representative to the General Assembly Council in the first years of the 21st century was a retired pastor.

Another innovation in Presbyterian government from the 1960s has gone a long way to remove the possibility of holding pastors accountable, the rotation of ruling elders. Prior to that decade ruling elders were elected for life; for a man to be elected to that position while in his twenties or thirties was extremely rare, and only those of exceptionally sterling character were considered to fill vacancies in the local church ruling council, the Session, upon the death of another man who had held the office for decades. Once women had the possibility of being elected to the office, the only way to insure that they would be considered for the office of elder sooner rather than later was to limit how long an individual could serve before stepping down. Today, though elders still are elected for life, their terms are broken up into three year increments, ordinarily followed by at least one year off. The advantage of this, obviously, is that elders are given a break, and new people with new ideas are allowed to try their hand at running the church. The disadvantage is that elders are less likely to know what is going on, sometimes in their own churches, but certainly at the higher governing body levels.

The problem is not limited to mere knowledge of previous votes and decisions made by the governing bodies. Sometimes it devolves to misunderstanding parliamentary procedure. A controversial vote sent to presbyteries by the General Assembly of 2000 involved denying permission to pastors and churches the right to hold gay union services as a means of ministering to homosexual couples. The previous year the "supreme court" of the denomination, the General Assembly Permanent Judicial Commission, had ruled that since there was no specific prohibition against gay union services in the Church's constitution, they were legal. "Amendment O" was an attempt to add that specific prohibition, in response to the PJC's decision. It said, in part, "Church property shall not be used for, and church officers shall not take part in, conducting any ceremony or event that pronounces blessing or gives approval of the church or invokes the blessing of God upon any relationship that is inconsistent with God's intention." But confusion reigned when elders unfamiliar with Robert's Rules of Order tried to weigh in on the matter, because a "yes" vote meant "no" to gay union services. I personally sat through an impassioned speech from an elder urging the presbytery to vote no, though I knew him well and understood he was opposed to gay union services. All the pastors understood that he was confused, for while he rose to oppose the amendment, his arguments supported it. "That's a yes comment," noted the stated clerk. "No," this dear man insisted, "I am opposed to this, I mean no." And then he voted no. How many others did not understand what they were voting on simply because their parliamentary procedure skills had atrophied while they enjoyed their year or more off the session? But every pastor, even those not serving a congregation, understood clearly what was at stake. We live and breathe this stuff so much it is like second nature to us.

Beyond this, the rotation of elders also guarantees that first-time commissioners to presbytery, as well as many others, will not be steeped in Reformed theology, or even theological language and concepts, like their ancestors were. A few years ago a college chaplain was being examined on the floor of my presbytery; in response to a question from the floor, she answered that she believed that adherents to other religions can be saved apart from the work of Jesus Christ. She cited John 14:2, "In My Father's house there are many dwelling places; if it were not so, I would have told you, for I go to prepare a place for you." Of course, her interpretation was absolutely incorrect; she was reading into the text what she wanted it to say, not taking from it what it actually means. Jesus' teaching here is not about many ways of salvation, it is that there will be room for all who repent and believe in Him. Not surprisingly, this chaplain, who would go on to serve without being held accountable by any elders or church members, received a significant number of no votes. There were not enough to stop her from taking her position at the college, or to prevent her later from having voice and vote on the floor of the presbytery, but the no votes resounded in the room enough to let everyone know that there were problems with her beliefs.

The next person being examined, a young pastor, had no problems in his written statement of faith or from his orthodox answers on the floor. Even so, when the votes were voiced, a lone individual called out, "No!" At that moment an elder leaned forward and said to me, "Why did that person vote no?" I said, "He probably was annoyed that the previous person had gotten so many no votes, and was voicing his dis-satisfaction with those of us who did it." The elder then responded, "Well, why did she get no votes?" I replied, "She's a universalist. She believes that there are ways to be saved apart from Jesus Christ." And the elder answered, "I didn't hear her say that." How much more clear could the chaplain have been? The pastors all understood it. This elder, and perhaps many others, did not. Rotation of elders is not the only reason for the problem (see Chapter 10), but it has served to exacerbate the problem. The dearth of an informed laity has meant that the professional clergy have taken more and more power for themselves. Nowhere is this more clear than in the non-constitutional office of the Presbytery Executive.

CHAPTER EIGHT: OXYMORON – PRESBYTERIAN BISHOPS

COCU, Churches Of Christ Uniting, was an orchestrated attempt from the 1960s through the 1980s by Religious Liberals in several branches of the mainstream denominations to bring about their organic merger, mirroring the union of the United Church of Canada. Biblically, the proof text cited by COCU advocates was John 17:11, the request of Jesus in the High Priestly Prayer that His disciples would be one. The National Council of Churches and the World Council of Churches are surviving expressions of this ecumenism run amok from those days; at the heart of each is not a unity based on fundamentals of faith, but structure and mission. Theological differences were to be de-emphasized and ignored for the sake of a surface unity. In practice, however, mission follows theology, and so it is no surprise that many denominations and churches have refused and continue to refuse to support the false unity offered by an ecumenical movement where missions emphasized are in basic disagreement with their theology.

However, it was not theology which killed COCU in the Presbyterian Church (USA); it was polity, our system of government. The issue was that of bishops. Presbyterians do not have them; our sisters and brothers in those other denominations do. To have organic union with Methodists and Episcopalians, Presbyterian elders were informed that they would have to be re-ordained by bishops. All future ordinations also would need a bishop in attendance. And the Presbyterian pastors and elders would have nothing to do with that; our ordinations were fine, thank you very much.

A few years later, having given up the dream of organic union with our sister denominations, an amendment to the Presbyterian Church's constitution was suggested which allowed pastors to use the title "bishop". The argument was presented that this would make it easier for Presbyterian leaders to have parity of title with actual Methodist and Episcopal bishops, with whom they might deal in ecumenical relations. Since Presbyterians always have argued that the title bishop in the New Testament applied to all presbyters, it seemed like a rose by any other name, and received the majority vote nationwide. But not in my presbytery.

In one of those rare moments when my argument from the floor actually swayed commissioners, I stood and said, "Mr. Moderator, I see here that pastors will be allowed to be called bishops, but there is no provision that elders will also be allowed this right. I cannot vote for this. Presbyterians have always believed that the office of pastor and elder is the same, with different function." (In truth, I overstated my case; this understanding comes from the southern stream, going back to Thornwell in the 1800s. It was not the understanding in the north, as championed by Hodge. But since we were in North Carolina, I guessed that such distinctions were unnecessary.) The amendment went down in flames here as elders realized what was at stake. Nationally, however, it passed, and so now, while you may refer to me as Bishop Sykes, my elders do not have that right. No Elder does.

I cite these two examples as practical expressions of Presbyterian resistance to the office of bishop as exercised within the polities of our sister denominations. No one individual should have that kind of authority. Instead, the authority is given to councils, groups of elders and pastors; their deliberation and votes, in so far as they are in harmony with the plain testimony of scripture, are seen as the work of the Holy Spirit. It is a means of spreading out the self-centered nature of sin, and seeking the will of God.

However, the position of the Presbytery Executive, which is nowhere to be found in the constitution of the Presbyterian Church (USA), completely undermines this understanding. What is a Presbytery Executive? His job title explains that his function is to execute the will of the presbytery body; a retired pastor friend who once was an Exec said the position developed after World War 2 because pastors wanted to hire someone else to do presbytery work while they focused on their congregations. Usually the position is held by a pastor, and is considered a career advancement beyond shepherding a congregation; certainly the pay grade is far beyond that of a pastor in a church. And though executives have zero official authority over the pastors and churches they serve, often they act as the guardians at the gate and the keepers of the keys, seizing and being granted powers which mirror that of bishops in other traditions.

When I was approaching graduation from seminary in 1988, and interviewing with churches, my polity professor advised all of us to contact the Executives of the presbyteries to which those churches belonged. Had I known then what I know now, I would have asked, "Why?" But the message was clear. These individuals could prevent us getting into those churches, regardless of what the Committee on Ministry or the Examinations Committee said. And that is un-Presbyterian. But I dutifully called the two Executives of the two churches which seemed to be the best fit. The Exec for the presbytery of the church to which I did go was familiar with that congregation; soon after I arrived he stopped being Executive and went back into the pulpit. The other Executive said he knew someone who had served that church years earlier. Beyond that he knew nothing. But he stayed in that position until he retired, several years later.

As my former Presbytery Executive friend said, the position did not exist prior to World War 2. Up until that time the only presbytery "position" was that of Stated Clerk, the individual responsible for recording and preserving the minutes of presbytery meetings. There also was no need for a central presbytery office, or other staff personnel. An office and a filing cabinet at one of the larger churches was all that was needed. The presbytery's "missions" were carried out by the local congregations: missions of compassion, foreign missions, education, and even church planting. In the second and third decades of the 20th Century First Presbyterian Church in Burlington, NC, was a church planting machine, founding Second, Shiloh, Piedmont, and East Burlington Presbyterian churches in different quadrants of the city, in little more than a dozen years. This case was not exceptional for the time. Ironically, in the modern Presbyterian Church (USA), presbyteries, not congregations, found churches, and in 2010 a mere twelve congregations were begun nationwide.

The main job of the presbytery in those days was to encourage the member pastors serving within their jurisdiction, and to vet new pastors entering the presbyteries; the latter process was completed by the ordination and/or installation of those new pastors standing in their churches. Several committees were tasked with various aspects of these duties. Even so, examination of new pastors coming into the presbytery was not limited to the committee; examinations on the floor of presbytery by pastors and elders of new pastors might last an hour or more. Today most "oversight" is done in the committees. As presbyteries have gotten larger and larger, the time available for meaningful theological discourse has been swallowed up by ceremony, committee reports, and administrative items. This begs the question: if bigger does not mean better presbyteries, overseeing the spiritual health of pastors and empowering the ministries of congregations, why have them? Part of the answer (see Chapter 16) is that only large presbyteries can afford an executive. And most presbyteries today are not content to have just one!

"But Presbytery Executives are pastors to pastors," comes the reply. Not in my experience. In 24 years of ministry the Lord has provided me with many friends and pastors in the ministry, several from other Christian traditions, but I have pretty much been on my own as far as the Executive goes. There have been some kind ones. There have been some not-so-kind ones. But whether the neglect has been benign or malicious, I have been off their radar. One might say, "Well, have you been involved in presbytery so they could get to know you?" More than I care to admit. I have chaired that committee most dreaded by most pastors, Sessional Records, in both my presbyteries. (I volunteered to serve each time.) I have been a commissioner to General Assembly once. I have been a commissioner to Synod two or three times. And for seven years, 2001-2007, I was the sole representative of my presbytery on Synod Council. (While ordinarily this would have been illegal, a reorganization made it OK. Plus, nobody else in the entire presbytery wanted to drive the three to five hours one way it would take to get to the meetings in Richmond, Virginia; nobody else wanted the job! Since I had lived there for five years, in college and seminary, I did not mind the trips.) Through all this service in higher governing bodies, including being an ex officio member of presbytery council for the seven years I served on the synod council, the only time I saw my presbytery executive was when I initiated the contact, and if I went to him.

In 2011 the façade of exec as pastor to pastors was ripped away very clearly for me. It was in April that year that our presbytery voted overwhelmingly to remove sexual standards from requirements for pastors, elders, and deacons. In the past this had been a close vote, won or lost by five to fifteen votes. This time it passed in a landslide, 2/3 of the presbytery voting in favor of this unbiblical change, almost 90 more votes. The arguments in favor of the change were weak; the arguments in favor of not making this change were strong and Bible-based. One of the proponents of the change even lampooned "the Fundamentals" of the 1920s with nary a reaction from a presbytery too ignorant or too jaded to care. I have never felt more spiritually eviscerated than I did on that Saturday. When I reported it to my congregation the next day I broke down into tears, something I had never done before.

But as I limped out of the meeting on that Saturday, I saw my Executive and said to him, "I don't think I can do this anymore. I don't even know if I can be a pastor." He told me that he would be out of town the following week, but would return afterward. And I waited. And I heard nothing from him. I found this incredibly puzzling. If a member of the church I pastored told me something like this, the sun would not have set before I would be knocking on his door. At the July meeting, three months later, I walked up to my Executive and told him I was extremely disappointed that I had not heard anything from him since the last meeting. "About what?" came his reply. So I told him again. Three weeks later we finally met. Call him many things. Call him an Executive. Call him a Bishop if you must. But please don't call him a pastor to pastors. I know something about being a pastor, and that is not how it is done.

It's hard for people to care about something when they have no say in what happens there. Likewise, the building of personal relationships within every level of the Church is the glue which holds us together, as was accomplished when Gentile churches collected funds and sent them to the mother church in Jerusalem, made up almost exclusively of cultural Jews, in the first century; remove the personal contacts, and cohesion, as well as accountability, go out the window. Nowhere has this been more apparent to me than in the demise of Synods, the governing body between the General Assembly and the Presbytery, over the past few decades. And in the middle of the fray, yanking literal and figurative support away from the Synods, has been the Presbytery Executives.

I have a friend who was a Presbytery Executive before becoming the Executive of our Synod. Someone asked him what that change was like. He answered, half-jokingly, "Well, first I found out what it was like to be top dog. And now I have found out what it is like to be the hydrant." Top dogs like to secure their positions. Top dogs who answer to no one are especially ruthless in securing their positions. Say what you want about bishops in the Roman Catholic, Episcopalian, and Methodist traditions; at least they have someone to whom they must answer. Presbytery Executives, imported from these other traditions without the natural checks and balances of those hierarchical polities, have none. Power corrupts. And absolute power corrupts absolutely.

In the years prior to reunion of the northern and southern streams of the Presbyterian Church in the United States, which occurred in 1983, the middle governing body above the presbytery was the Synod, and the Synods were limited to the geographic American states. For example, Union Theological Seminary in Virginia received that name when it was founded in 1812 as a "union" project of the Synods of Virginia and North Carolina. Prior to reunion in 1983, every southern pastor in the state was a commissioner to his or her Synod, which met once a year, and every church in the state was able to send an elder commissioner to that meeting as well. It was a time of reunions, of building and rekindling relationships within the larger Church as old seminary classmates gathered for a bit of business, much more worship, and discovering common interests for ministry across presbytery lines.

One of the conditions of reunion, however, was that synods would no longer be "state-sized". They were "super-sized," the Synods of the Virginias, North Carolina, and Piedmont (encompassing the District of Columbia, Maryland, and Delaware), becoming the mega Synod of the Mid-Atlantic. And obviously, all the preachers and all the churches in that region would never fit into a single meeting; even if they met at RFK Stadium, the costs of travel, boarding, and meals would have been prohibitive. Instead, each presbytery was told to elect commissioners as representatives to Synod. No longer was everyone allowed to attend. And with fewer people involved, fewer people took ownership in Synod.

My first Synod meeting was in 1992. It was held at the Hilton Hotel in downtown Raleigh, and it was an opulent affair! It was like a mini-General Assembly, with fancy meeting rooms and large groups of commissioners from each of the 13 presbyteries. Even then we knew the Synod was cash-strapped. I joked to my roommate that if I were in charge, we would have been meeting at Motel 6. That comment proved to be prophetic.

In the years which followed, the Synod meetings were downsized. Even fewer people were allowed as commissioners. By the time I returned for my seven years of duty on Synod Council, the meetings were held in churches, with commissioners housed at colleges and conference centers already owned by or operated for the denomination. And yet again the commissioner delegations were made smaller. Finally the decision was made simply to make Synod Council be the Synod every other year for one meeting. Almost no one outside these few people has any idea what is going on in the synod. And no one cares. Their duties slowly have been stripped away. No longer do they approve trustees to the seminaries within their bounds. No longer do they initiate any ministry within the presbyteries or churches. No longer do they support Presbyterian college campus ministries. They simply dole out money to those who know enough to ask for it. But almost no one asks because almost no one knows or cares.

Who have been the beneficiaries of the demise of the synods? Certainly the power of the presbytery executives has been enhanced. Though I cannot speak to what took place prior to 2001-2007, both of the reorganization plans that I did see in those years, which had fewer people involved at the synod level and thus less people who might actually hold them accountable, were developed and promoted by the presbytery executives.

At one point in these discussions, as every presbytery executive initiative was embraced and passed without any objection, I had had enough. I fired off an email to the entire Synod Council urging the members not to make the group smaller and smaller. Make Synods smaller if you have to, go back to state-sized so more people can be involved while travelling shorter distances if that's what it takes, but do NOT let the presbytery executives dictate what the Synod will be. "Until they see their jobs as doing the will of the presbyteries, like janitors without toilet-cleaning duties, we will have this problem." At this point an irate presbytery executive sent a furious response to me and the entire Synod Council, "You have denigrated my ministry!" To this I calmly replied, "Being a pastor means receiving insults. Having a 12-year-old laugh in your face and call you weird, that's just a part of ministry." This Executive, trained as a pastor but now apparently above such things, had forgotten. Not all of them had. One Executive privately send me a response and said, "I cannot say this to the others, but I love what you have said. I too am a janitor."

I should say that in those days I also was in conversation with the Synod leadership about the need to make North Carolina presbyteries smaller. Nothing was done, so I wrote the Synod Executive to ask about where that initiative might be. He replied that he had asked the Presbytery Executives about this, and that none of them thought the presbyteries needed to be smaller. I'm sure they didn't.

CHAPTER NINE: THE CONNECTIONAL NATURE OF PRESBYTERIANISM

Sometimes when I complain about problems in my denomination someone will say, "Well, why do you put up with it? Why don't you and your church just become independent?" While I understand the sentiment, that person usually does not understand the high value Presbyterians place on being connected with other Presbyterians. We just don't go off on our own, and it's almost impossible to get most of us to go off with another group. I tell my members that an "Independent Presbyterian Church" is like a bull with an udder. It just doesn't happen, or if it does, it is a freak of nature!

At the heart of this understanding is the doctrine of election. Some of you may be familiar with the "TULIP" acronym of five-point Calvinism, developed in Holland in 1619 within The Canons of Dort. The focus of each point is the sovereignty of God over and above the efforts of human beings. T is for Total Depravity, the belief that sin permeates human existence, along with all of creation, and all of our best thoughts and works still are tainted by it. U is for Unmerited Election; God chooses Christians to be His children from before the foundations of the world simply because He does, and not because His foreknowledge lets Him see how good we will be if He were to choose us, or for any other reason beyond His sovereign choice. L is for Limited Atonement; Jesus' sacrifice on the cross was sufficient for all, but only is effectual to the elect. In other words, if you don't accept what He has done, it doesn't do you any good. I is for Irresistible Grace; God's calling to salvation, for the elect, must be answered with a yes. And P is for the Perseverance of the Saints, often summarized as "once saved, always saved." My purpose in listing these is not so much for debating them, as Christians have for centuries, but for highlighting the Reformed understanding of God as supreme, the prime mover in all things, and especially salvation.

If God has chosen you to be saved from before He created anything (Ephesians 1:4), then He also has chosen other Christians, including the ones with whom you worship on a weekly basis. Therefore, you are not in your particular congregation by accident. He led you there as He led the others, by various means, and He ordinarily wants you to stay there unless drastic circumstances occur, such as a move to another city, or a gross violation of theological or ethical standards taking place and not being corrected. Sometimes I have heard people complain about their churches, "I just didn't get anything out of worship today." My first reaction is to want to ask, "Well, what did you give?" According to Paul in 1 Corinthians 12, the purpose of gifts from the Holy Spirit is to build up other believers in their faith. Just as the preacher has a responsibility to use his, or hers, the members also have a responsibility to one another.

Well, what about members I personally don't like? I thank God for difficult members! The Lord has placed them in my life with three specific functions. 1) They might be right! And I might be wrong! They may have something I need to hear and consider that otherwise I would not. 2) They might be wrong and need my guidance. 3) Regardless of what other reason God has for placing them there, He is using them to knock off my rough edges.

When I was in eighth grade I had a science teacher named Mr. Wilson. He was notorious for his silly jokes and puns, such as, "This is the study of geology. But don't get stoned." "This is igneous rock, but don't take it for granite." One fascinating experiment we did in that class was to dump some gravel into a small mechanical drum which then spun around slowly like a cement mixer. Mr. Wilson left it running all night, and the next day, when we opened the drum, out came sand and beautiful, polished stones, like those you might find in a creek bed. The pieces of gravel had knocked the rough, jagged edges off each other, polished each other, and become things of beauty. The Church is like that. Congregations are supposed to be like that.

Denominations also are supposed to be like that, on a grander scale. Though the real work of sanctification, that process of becoming more like Jesus after accepting Him as Lord, happens best at the local level, in a congregation regularly meeting together, it should come as no surprise that there will be persons in our larger church bodies with whom we will disagree, and who rub us the wrong way. That's part of the sanctification process. We are not to abandon them simply because we don't like them.

Just like in our congregations, we believe God has placed them in our denominations, just as He did with us.

Our ordinations, in the Presbyterian Church, also are connected. When a person is ordained as a deacon, elder, or pastor, it is not only for the particular congregation which he or she is serving; it is for the entire denomination as well. After a pastor is ordained, according to our Book of Order, part 2 of our Constitution, the following statement is made: "You are now a minister of the Word and Sacrament in the Church of Jesus Christ and for this congregation. Whatever you do, in word or in deed, do everything in the name of the Lord Jesus, giving thanks to God the Father through him. Amen. (For a minister previously ordained say only: You are now a minister of the Word and Sacrament in and for this congregation. Whatever you do,…etc.)" (G-14.0510c) An identical statement, save for the title of the office, is made after the ordination of deacons and elders.

Do you see what this means? A church officer is not only ordained for that particular congregation, but for the entire denomination, that section of the Church of Jesus Christ over which the body has authority. For this reason, a person is ordained to these offices only once. I was ordained as a pastor in 1988. Unless I renounce my ordination, which only can be done by formally declaring to the presbytery, "I renounce my ordination," I always will be a pastor in this denomination, and never will be ordained again. If I change churches within the PC(USA), as I did in 1996, I will not be re-ordained, I will only be installed in the new call. (Note the parentheses of G-14.0510c.) The ordination is for life, for the entire denomination. And the ordaining body, the presbytery in the case of pastors and the session in the case of elders, ordains in the name of the entire denomination, including me.

But what happens when an ordination takes place of someone with whom I have serious theological or moral disagreement; what if the historic fundamentals are denied by that person? What if I am not the only person troubled; what if it is a majority, or even a sizable minority, of the denomination? At this point in the life of the PC(USA), my opinion, our opinion, does not matter. With the removal of ordination standards through

Amendment 10-A in 2011, the sole arbiter of who should or should not be ordained is the ordaining body itself; you should trust, they say, the wisdom of the sessions and presbyteries which know the situation, as they ordain this objectionable person in the collective name of the denomination, including me.

Trust is a funny thing. Anyone whose marriage of decades ends after a sudden series of indiscretions is discovered knows that trust takes years to build and little time to destroy. For centuries trust was built as pastors, elders, and deacons promised that they believed the faith once delivered to the saints in their ordination vows, and proved it by the living of that faith. (James 2:18) The rise of Modernism and Post-Modernism has changed all that; the former sees the ancient writers of scripture as naïve and culture-bound, while the latter believes that the meanings of words are only given by the one speaking, not the collective understanding of the denomination, the culture, or any group. For the Post-Modernist, a word means what it means when it means it; it means what I say means right now, nothing more, and nothing less. To illustrate this point, let us examine the current versions of the first three ordination vows to which all ordained persons in my denomination must agree before taking office.

"(1) Do you trust in Jesus Christ your Savior, acknowledge him Lord of all and Head of the Church, and through him believe in one God, Father, Son, and Holy Spirit?" The plain meaning of this vow should be clear – the person is declaring that he or she is a Christian and accepts the foundational and mysterious doctrine of the Trinity. Yet the contemporary Modernist might reason that the Trinitarian formula is merely historic Christian language, and so answer yes, secure in the knowledge that this is merely a human approximation of the mystery of God's being, not something actually revealed by God, and thus optional. The Post-Modernist ordinarily doesn't use reason when it comes to matters of doctrine, and thus may answer yes simply because it feels right at the moment. Or he might redefine " trust in Jesus Christ your Savior" as "Jesus saves me, but other religions are fine for saving their adherents." A few years ago there was a brouhaha in the denomination when someone wrote that *"for us Jesus is the Savior."* What did that mean? Officially denominational leadership, trying to stave off yet another ecclesiastical crisis (usually resulting in a drying up of funds sent to General Assembly offices in Louisville, Kentucky), clarified that this meant that, speaking from the biblical, Christian perspective, Jesus alone is the Savior and there is no salvation in any other religion. However, a few months later a Latino denominational official from Louisville told me privately that this meant Jesus is the Savior only for us, only for Christians, but other religions are fine for others. I told him this was exactly the opposite of what Louisville had just said; he got angry with me and told me that I was just like the missionaries who came to Latin America, and I thought I knew everything. I don't. But I do know what the Bible actually says about sin and the only One who can save us from it.

"(2) Do you accept the Scriptures of the Old and New Testaments to be, by the Holy Spirit, the unique and authoritative witness to Jesus Christ in the Church universal, and God's Word to you?" Please note how this question has been changed since 1950 in an effort to make room for the Modernists; sixty years ago it read: "Do you believe the Scriptures of the Old and New Testaments to be the Word of God, the only infallible rule of faith and practice?" (See Chapter 1) Scripture is not "the Word of God" anymore, but merely "the unique and authoritative witness to Jesus Christ in the Church universal, and God's Word to you". The Modernist, with his hope fixed on a rational, non-supernatural religion, is more comfortable with the Bible being a unique and authoritative witness to Jesus (since almost no mention of the life of Jesus exists outside the New Testament and the other writings of early Christians and Christian heretics), especially when that authority is granted by a nebulous Holy Spirit who inspires the reader more than the original writers. The orthodox Christian counters, "How can one test the spirits to see whether they are from God (1 John 4:1) without the plumb line of scripture itself?" But this vagueness has become the refuge of Modernists. Likewise, the Post-Modernist is quite comfortable with the Bible being "God's Word to you," since what is true to me might not be true to you. Of course, it is possible to read these vows with an orthodox, historic understanding; these are the vows I took when I was 25 years old. But I don't need all the possible hedge words; I truly believe the Bible is the Word of God, the only infallible rule of faith and practice.

"(3) Do you sincerely receive and adopt the essential tenets of the Reformed faith as expressed in the confessions of our church as authentic and reliable expositions of what Scripture leads us to believe and do, and will you be instructed and led by those confessions as you lead the people of God?" The insincerity of this question as it is asked today is beyond the pale. Since 1927, when bureaucrats who cared more about peace and a "big tent" denomination sought to shove the modernist/fundamentalist controversy under the rug, the Presbyterian Church has refused to list any essential beliefs. How can anyone sincerely receive and adopt anything without knowing what it is? The Modernist can answer yes without having to affirm any of the miracles of Jesus' life, death, or return. The Post-Modernist doesn't care for lists anyway, and also answers yes. The orthodox, sincere Christian, who does sincerely receive and adopt the fundamentals of faith, answers yes. No one's conscience is violated.

But what is the result of these broad questions which can be interpreted in so many ways? It is the same lack of trust which occurs when marital infidelity is discovered. It is the same fury that rises as one says, "I took the vow, and I meant it – you took the vow, and you are a liar!" Refusal to define terms and a willful blurring of meaning may lead to a short-term peace as each assumes the other means the same thing I mean. But in the long run, when the real intention of each party becomes clear, the peaceful illusion is stripped away and all that remains is the shock and rage of betrayed friends all around. Et tu, Brute?

CHAPTER TEN: THE FAILURE OF THEOLOGICAL EDUCATION

Those who know me well probably expect this chapter simply to be a rant against the seminaries of the denomination. Those institutions swapped the glory of the proclamation of the gospel in the Reformed Tradition decades ago to become gathering places for professional scholars longing to be accepted by their secular counterparts in other institutions of higher education. That's no small problem in the PC(USA) today, and I will speak to it, but that is not where I will begin. The debacle of theological education in my denomination, as well as throughout the Church, has its origins in the local congregations. When I have complained to seminary professors that they have not adequately prepared pastors to teach and preach the message once delivered to the saints, they have responded, "It is not my job to catechize seminarians." And to a certain extent, that is true.

Theological education begins at home, but not home in a vacuum; it is a home supported by a local congregation. How can parents teach what they have not learned, or what has not been reinforced as essential? Pastors have a responsibility here, true, but what about the responsibility of the elders who hear his or her sermons every week? I tell my congregation that they have a duty to listen to my sermons with two ears, one pointed toward what I am saying, listening to the conviction and leading of the Holy Spirit, and the other pointed at scripture itself. The words of the pastor in the sermon will not match the words of scripture, but they must always be in harmony with scripture. I tell the Youth Group, if I say God is telling me to rob a bank to help our budget shortfall, how do you know I am wrong? Because the eighth commandment is, "You shall not steal." Of course, if the members do not know the Bible, then how will they know if the words of the sermon are in harmony with it?

For this reason I urge the members to read their Bibles, and I teach multiple Bible studies every week, in addition to my Sunday worship duties. It's not only for their good – it is for mine! I need to know the Bible better than I do, and though I would not purposely mislead my congregation, I certainly have been known to be wrong about things! Years ago I was teaching the story of Moses killing the Egyptian who was beating a Hebrew, and how the murder was discovered. I asked why the class thought Moses fled Egypt at that point, and a member responded that it probably was because Pharaoh tried to kill Moses afterward. "Well, I guess that is possible, but he probably got out before Pharaoh could have found out about it," I replied. The class member, a godly and humble elder who had an open Bible sitting in his lap, replied, "Well, it says in Exodus 2:15 that Pharaoh did try to kill Moses, and that's when he fled." Oh. I forgot!

Theological education begins at home and in the local congregation. But what is being taught? Youth ministry today is a train wreck; either neglected, or so focused on relationships that little is taught, or so focused on service that a type of works righteousness is the message given. In part it seems to be because "Youth Pastor" is the job of friendly lay people, an energetic college student, or an associate pastor whose only ladder for career advancement forces an eventual end to working with the youth.

As a teenager coming of age in the 1970s, relationships were important in my youth group. In fact, I am still friends with our former Director of Christian Education and her husband, and deeply appreciate their attention to my spiritual development in those formative years. We had a muppet ministry in those days, and performed in various venues throughout my high school years. And the emphasis for which I am especially grateful, which I have brought to my own youth groups through the years, was on the now greatly neglected discipline of apologetics, defending the faith.

Some of you may recall that the section of Plato's Republic in which Socrates gives a defense of his actions is called The Apology. It is not the philosopher's expression of regret for what he has done, as the word has evolved in contemporary English, but it is an explanation of his actions, why he has done what he has done. Mainstream Protestantism has ceased to teach Apologetics, as well as Systematic Theology (I never had a class in either during my seminary days) because modern scholars have come to believe that there is no one system of theology being taught in scripture, and reason cannot be invoked to explain the things of the inscrutable Deity; after all, these are simply the musings of men, they say, not actually God's revelation of Himself, and faith will always be blind. But cut the legs out from under Scripture, and we have eviscerated Christianity; we might use the same words, as Religious Liberals do, but they will not be following the faith once delivered to the saints, and they will not be worshipping the risen Lord and Savior Jesus Christ. Apologetics and Systematic Theology still have an important role to play in the life of the thinking Christian, and they should be a part of our regular Christian education program in the local congregation and beyond.

The biblical command to practice apologetics is found in 1 Peter 3:15, "…sanctify Christ as Lord in your hearts, always being ready to make a defense to everyone who asks you to give an account for the hope that is in you, yet with gentleness and reverence." As a teenager two authors were held up as guides for us in apologetics, C.S. Lewis through his book Mere Christianity, and the much lesser known but much more focused Paul Little, whose book Know Why You Believe gave me a foundation for faith which has remained unshaken since I was about 15 years old. The main focus of Little's work was three-fold: 1) The trustworthiness of the Hebrew and Greek manuscripts from which our Bibles are translated, the fact that they have not been corrupted so terribly through the centuries that modern people are unable to discover what the original writers wrote; 2) Jesus really did claim to be God, this is not something attributed to Him by later, overly enthusiastic disciples; 3) Jesus really did rise again, since there is no other reasonable explanation for the empty tomb, the actions of Jesus' disciples and enemies, and the limited time between His resurrection and ascension, after which no one claimed to see Him in His spiritual body on earth. All Christians, but young Christians especially, must be taught the reasonable nature of our faith. How else can we explain the hope within us to those who ask? And how else will this faith survive the storms of life which threaten to strip it away?

Faith itself must be explained in our congregations. What is faith? A child once said, "Faith is believing something that you know can't be true." While this might work for Santa Claus or

The Great Pumpkin, nothing could be further from reality when it comes to the biblical understanding of faith. In the Bible, faith must have an object, you must put your faith IN something or someone. And faith, which cannot be seen, is shown by what the person does. This happens repeatedly in chapter 11 of the book of Hebrews, the so-called "Hebrews Hall of Fame". BY FAITH these Old Testament believers did what they did. As we believe, so we do. And as we don't believe, so we don't do! How different is this understanding from that of modern people, who often base faith either on what they feel at the moment, or confuse faith with mental assent to a series of propositions, like agreeing (believing?) that Christopher Columbus discovered the New World in 1492, something which has zero effect on their day to day lives.

My father, to teach what the Bible means by "faith" to my communicants' class, used an illustration I have never forgotten:

> In years gone by carnivals were held at Niagara Falls, and sometimes a daredevil would stretch a high wire from the American to the Canadian side. He would then walk across in a death-defying stunt that thrilled the on-lookers. But once, as the story is told, a man stood before the crowd and asked, "How many of you believe that I can walk across this high wire safely?" And the crowd cheered, oh yes, they believed! And the man did it! Then he said, "How many of you believe that I can walk across the wire with a wheelbarrow?" Once again the crowd went wild, they believed, and the man did it! Finally the man said, "How many of you believe I can walk across the high wire with a wheelbarrow, with a man sitting in it?" The crowd erupted in a frenzy, this show was better than they had bargained for! And the daredevil looked into the crowd, saw one man who was especially vocal in his belief that this could be done, and he said, "OK, how about you?" And the man said, "No!" Biblical faith, which is shown by what we do, means getting into Jesus' wheelbarrow, putting your life into His hands.

Now, I have thought about this from time to time, and I have to say that I would never get into a wheelbarrow pushed by some idiot with a death wish on a high wire over Niagara Falls, or even a few inches off the ground! Why not? Because I do not have that kind of faith in any human being. Ironically, all people have faith in something, they put their lives into the control of people or things greater than themselves, but the Bible is clear that faith in anyone or anything besides Jesus is idolatry, it is a faith that will let you down. You may not agree with me, or scripture, about this. If this is the case, all I would ask is that, when that other thing, whatever it is, drops you into the Niagara River, you would consider getting into Jesus' wheelbarrow instead. Biblical, saving faith in Jesus Christ cannot be based on feelings exclusively, and it cannot be based on reason exclusively, though each has its place. Biblical, saving faith in Jesus accepts what He has done for me that I could not do for myself when He died on the cross, and that same faith now seeks to live for Him as an act of thanksgiving to Him for His kindness. He alone is worthy of this kind of devotion.

I learned a lot that I needed to know about my faith as a teenager, but I was not exposed regularly to Reformed Theology through the Westminster Shorter Catechism, as generations of young Presbyterians had in earlier generations. I believe I was poorer for the omission. The Shorter Catechism is one of two which supplement the Westminster Confession of Faith, written at Westminster Abby in London in 1647, during Oliver Cromwell's Protectorate. The significance of the Westminster Standards, especially in North America, cannot be overstated. The Confession itself set the tone and nature of Presbyterianism in the United States, beginning with Chapter One, on Scripture and how it is to be interpreted. The Larger Catechism was an in-depth series of questions and answers designed to help pastors grapple with the Reformed theology of the Confession. The Shorter (not Smaller!) Catechism, originally designed to teach children, actually has become one of the most succinct and accessible encapsulations of Calvinistic theology ever put to paper. I sometimes refer to it as "A Seminary Education in 107 Easy Questions And Answers."

One of my favorite stories about a famous Presbyterian deacon is related by his widow, Anna Morrison Jackson, in her biography of Thomas "Stonewall" Jackson. The general had not been raised in church at all; he came to faith in Christ as an adult. Both of his wives, Ellie, who died in childbirth, and Anna, were the daughters of Presbyterian ministers; in fact, Anna's father was the founder of Davidson College outside Charlotte, North Carolina. The wives had memorized the Shorter Catechism as children, but Thomas had not. Those who know about the general's idiosyncrasies during the war know his commitment to remembering the Sabbath Day; not only would he not read a letter that arrived on Saturday night until Monday, he would not mail a letter late in the week on the off chance that someone might have to carry it on Sunday. Anna relates in her account that soon after she married her then Virginia Military Institute professor husband, Thomas asked her to help him memorize the Catechism on Sunday afternoons. This was a duty appropriate to the commandment. He would sit in a chair facing the wall, and she would patiently read the questions and help him with the answers. Thus it had been for most young Presbyterians for centuries, and thus it would remain for about one more.

In the 1960s Christian educators decided that rote memorization was a bad thing. Though the Apostles' Creed never came under such censure, the Shorter Catechism was quickly dropped from most Sunday School curriculums. Part of this, I suspect, was because of the war against the Westminster Confession of Faith which had culminated in the adoption of a Book of Confessions in 1967. (See Chapter 12) At any rate, the one time I remember having exposure to the Shorter Catechism was at Bible School in 1975, when I was twelve years old; an older teacher had us memorize the answers to the questions about the Ten Commandments, and I set the fourth commandment to a tune, a part of which I can still remember today.

Dr. John Leith, who taught me theology his final year before retiring, was the one professor at my seminary who took Westminster seriously. He had his students memorize the answers to about twenty of the one hundred seven questions, and I found myself quoting them the next year as I wrote the answers to my ordination exams. I passed easily. But Dr. Leith was the exception. Most other professors were less interested in exposing us to Westminster than they were in warning us of its troublesome doctrine of double predestination and its rationalistic (read: "non-Barthian") approach to theology. They did not argue with Westminster, they lampooned and then neglected it. Ironically, years later I suggested to the Chair of the Board of Trustees that the seminary would do well to emphasize the Westminster Standards more, and he replied that they already were emphasized in many classes. I thought that to be untrue, so, unlike that trustee, I directly asked the two theology professors if they emphasized Westminster. One replied that there were more confessions than just Westminster. In other words, no. And the other wrote me that, as I have already said, it was not her job to catechize theological students, but that it was her job to get them to "think theologically", whatever that means. (I don't recall that being a priority for John Leith.) She, never having been a pastor, might be surprised to learn that congregations do not ask to be taught to think theologically, they ask what they must do to be saved, and how then they should live in light of the precious gift of salvation purchased by Jesus' blood.

My father's co-pastor at Rivermont Presbyterian Church in Lynchburg, Virginia, in the 1990s, graduated from Columbia Seminary in Decatur, Georgia, in the 1970s. He told dad that, prior to taking his ordination exams, at the end of his seminary years, he decided that it might help him to read the Westminster Standards. When he did, he was shocked and dismayed. "This is what I should have been studying all along," he said. But it was not.

What is so great about the Westminster Shorter Catechism? Just as a mastery of the book of Ephesians is the doorway to understanding all of Paul's letters, the Shorter Catechism opens the other parts of the Confession of Faith to the readers, providing a theological framework by which scripture can be understood. In his wonderful little book from 1901, <u>The Creed Of Presbyterians</u>, Dr. Egbert Watson Smith wrote that the Confession and its two catechisms "are not three creeds. They are three statements, varying in form, fullness, and purpose, of one and the same creed. Each is complete in itself. Each contains all the essential truths of Scripture. Each is a complete epitome of the Calvinistic system. Whoever intelligently accepts the teachings of the Shorter Catechism is a true Calvinist. Should he extend his studies to the Larger Catechism and the Confession of Faith, he will find in them the same system of doctrine with which the briefer statements of the Shorter Catechism had already acquainted him." (page 13)

What is my purpose in life? Is this not the question for which every person must seek an answer? It is the first question of the Shorter Catechism, worded thusly: What is the chief end of man? The answer: Man's chief end is to glorify God, and to enjoy Him forever. And how do we know what glorifies God? The Bible alone tells us. What does the Bible mainly teach? Two things: what people are to believe about God, and what God wants us to do. All this in the first three questions and answers!

Questions 4 through 6 address the nature of God, while 7 through 11 discuss the fulfillment of God's purposes by the work of creation, natural law established in the beginning, and His works of providence, God's governing of all creatures and their actions every moment of every day. Questions 12 through 19 explain sin. Questions 20 through 28 explain how Jesus Christ was able to save His chosen people from sin. Questions 29 through 39 discuss how we are able to become a part of God's people, and the benefits Christians receive in this life and the life to come. Many believers, even those who are not Calvinists, appreciate the clarity with which basic Christian doctrine is set forth in the first 39 questions of the Shorter Catechism.

Questions 40-84 discuss the Ten Commandments, along with the sins forbidden and the duties required, and the fact that no one can do it perfectly, so all deserve God's condemnation. Questions 85-87 address faith in Jesus Christ and repentance; questions 88-98 address reading the Bible and hearing it preached, then sacraments and prayer. And the final ten questions explore the meanings of each petition in the Lord's Prayer. As I have said, this is a seminary education in 107 questions and answers. But modern seminaries neglect this and most of the classic statements of the Reformed faith in favor of focusing on pastoral care, personality types, conflict resolution, and theological innovation. Certainly there is nothing wrong with knowing about the first three, or knowing how to answer the last one. But the main job of the pastor and the Church is the proclamation of the biblical gospel. A theological framework is essential to that task.

Soon after I arrived at my current call, the appropriately named Westminster Presbyterian Church in Burlington, North Carolina, I contacted denominational headquarters in Louisville, Kentucky, and attempted to buy small, individual catechisms for distribution within the congregation. The woman with whom I spoke had no idea what I was talking about. "We have the new catechism for study," she suggested. That modern attempt to replace classic catechisms was offered to the Presbyterian Church (USA) in the mid-1990s; in the years since its introduction, no one has ever sent an overture to General Assembly in an attempt to get it included in the denominational book of confessional statements, though whether that is due to theological weakness within the document or theological apathy within the denomination is more than I can say. But it wasn't what I wanted. "I need the Shorter Catechism, the one already in the Book of Confessions." The woman replied, "How do you spell it?" I couldn't believe my ears. "How do you spell it?" "Yes," she replied, "is it a name, like Schorter?" "No, it's shorter, like not longer." "Well, we don't have that," she assured me. "The only other catechism we have is 'The Westminster Shorter Catechism with Scripture proofs'." "Yes!" I said. "That's it! That's what I want!" And I bought about one hundred copies.

I found that interchange enlightening. It meant two things. First, the people working the phones in our denominational offices were not lifelong Presbyterians. That's fine; they can hire who they want, so long as the people are competent. Secondly, and this was the troubling revelation to me, almost nobody in the denomination is ordering the Westminster Shorter Catechism with Scripture proofs from the Louisville offices. How else could she not know what I was talking about? And how will our children, who grow up to be our seminarians and then our ministers, know what Presbyterians have believed historically if no one, from the congregation to the seminary, teaches them? Agree with Westminster or not, this is the standard by which Presbyterians have understood the faith. How can you argue with something you have never known? Or how can you accept something you have never been told?

At my first church, the day that I arrived in the high school Sunday School classroom as a teacher, I mentioned the catechism to which I had been exposed as a boy, the Children's Catechism. Though it was written as a teaching aid by the General Assembly of the old southern Presbyterian denomination, it was never officially added to the Westminster Standards. That morning I quoted the first three questions and answers. Who made you? God. What else did God make? God made all things. Why did God make you and all things? For his own glory. At this point a ninth grader, who had been raised in the congregation and who prided herself on being the youth expert on all things church, said, "Well, that's pretty arrogant!" And I said, "No, it is not arrogant. If it were anyone besides God, it would be arrogant. But God's glory is the most important thing of all." Again, how can you accept something you have never been told?

CHAPTER ELEVEN: SUBTITUTING PAGENTRY FOR INSTRUCTION

The historic, Reformed understanding of a church calendar is very simple: it is a weekly one which begins with Sunday, the Lord's Day, the day He rose from death. It is not an annual cycle. And yet in the same years that the Presbyterian Church has been failing miserably to pass on the faith once delivered to the saints, it has embraced more and more the pageantry and liturgy of our "high church" sisters and brothers, especially as linked with the annual Church Calendar.

Admittedly, an annual Church calendar has origins in the annual festivals of the ancient Hebrew people. Passover was celebrated in the spring, "in the month of Abib"; seven weeks later was the Feast of Weeks. The Feast of Booths took place in the fall, seven days after completing the threshing of wheat and the pressing of wine. A Sabbatical year was commanded for every seventh year, when fields were to lie fallow and rest, an early version of crop rotation. And every fiftieth year was to be the Year of Jubilee, when all debts were to be forgiven, and all land was to be returned to the families which originally owned it in the days of Joshua. Churches which adopt an annual calendar are not to be condemned for following a biblical precedent. But it has not been the Presbyterian way, historically; we are not Catholic light.

The annual Church calendar also has origins in paganism, particularly when it comes to feast days. Christianity arose in the pagan Greco-Roman world, and when it became legal with the Edict of Milan in 313, and the only legal religion in the Empire by the 380s, the question of what to do with popular pagan holidays became important. The people were going to celebrate something, after all. The Church's solution was to co-opt the pagan holidays by holding competing celebrations with similar, yet sanitized, themes. Lupercalia was a Roman fertility festival held on February 15th. As part of the fun, young men ran naked through the streets carrying strips of goat flesh, striking women who lined the way. (Female goats go into heat every other day, and thus were considered extremely fertile!) If a woman was hit with the goat flesh, she was supposed to become more fertile, and given the orgies which often followed, many did become pregnant. In response, the Church instituted Valentine's Day on February 14th; rather than a celebration of erotic love, considered by the Greeks to be the most base of loves, it became a celebration of a type of self-sacrificing love akin to agape, which only flows from God.

Samhain was a Gaelic harvest festival held on October 31st. Many Celts believed that here, at the end of their year, the veil between the living and the dead was most permeable. They would present offerings of food to their ancestors, and place large turnips with frightening carved faces to ward off evil spirits. Divination was practiced that night, as well as séances, seeking audiences with and guidance from the dead. In response, the Church developed All Saints' Day on November 1st, a celebration of saints who did not already have their own days on the Church calendar. This competing feast took place without the biblically forbidden divination or séances.

Of course, the biggest pagan holiday co-opted by Christians within and beyond the Roman Empire was the winter solstice celebration. Close to Rome it was called Saturnalia. In the far north of Scandanavia, it was Yule, where huge logs were burned in December and January to provide fuel for the dying sun; it must have worked, because the sun always got stronger afterward! To answer these celebrations, the Church developed the Christ Mass, focused on the birth of Jesus as a baby in Bethlehem.

Jesus was not born on December 25th. Jesus was not born in December at all. Jesus was born in the spring. We know this because the shepherds were out in the fields at night with their sheep; why would anyone be out at night with livestock in the winter? In Palestine today shepherds have their sheep in the fields at night in the spring, when the lambs are being born. They have done this for millennia. Jesus was born in the spring.

But no one knows exactly when Jesus was born. The date of Easter every year is relatively simple to determine accurately because the date of the Jewish Passover was established at the time of the Exodus. Jesus was executed on the Friday before Passover, and rose on the first day of the week, the day after the Passover Sabbath. But since Easter always will be in the spring, an historically accurate celebration of Jesus' birth in the spring sort of defeats the purpose of the annual cycle of fasts and feasts. Therefore, when Christianity became the only legal religion in the Roman Empire and Church leadership desired to have a celebration to compete with and ultimately supplant Saturnalia, the seasonally inaccurate but conveniently vague date of Jesus' birth was useful, and December 25th was chosen.

My point is this: the annual liturgical Church calendar, for the most part, is a human construct which has far less to do with biblical instruction than ancient political struggles. Until the 1960s, Presbyterians never used it. Until the 1870s Presbyterians did not celebrate Christmas at all; they realized it was a political compromise from the first millennium, and often was celebrated, not as a religious holiday at all, but with the pagan revelry of a modern New Orleans Marti Gras. That was the reason Christmas was outlawed in parts of colonial New England.

But the modern Presbyterian Church, forgetting earlier objections, has wholeheartedly embraced many aspects of the liturgical denominations' annual observances, substituting style for substance. When it simply is a matter of liturgical colors, purple for Advent and Lent, white for Christmas and Easter, red for Pentecost, and green for "normal time", probably no harm is done, so long as one does not take it too seriously. I heard once of a non-denominational church pastor calling a liturgical church's pastor to ask which colors should be used at Christmas. "Should it be red or green?" (Of course, the color is purple, the color of mourning; Advent is to Christmas what Lent is to Easter. But no Presbyterian that I know fasts during December.) One of these days I hope to convince our worship committee to mix the red and green paraments for the entire month of December!

As a great example of denominational schizophrenia, our Book of Order, Part 2 of our Constitution, says specifically that Presbyterians observe the season of Lent; however, our Book of Confessions, Part 1 of our Constitution, which includes The Second Helvetic Confession of Faith, says this: "The fast of Lent is attested by antiquity, but not at all in the writings of the apostles. Therefore it ought not, and cannot, be imposed upon the faithful." (5.230) So, which one is correct? (For the answer, see the closing paragraphs of Chapter 13.)

It is not that Presbyterians are opposed to all art or pageantry; it is that we have been opposed to them when they become idolatrous, or even when they become a hindrance to understanding God's will for our lives. Simplicity in worship guarantees that the preaching will not be lost in a sea of smells, bells, sounds, and colors. But that approach to worship has not been the emphasis in recent decades.

Jack Rogers was Moderator of the General Assembly in 2001 and 2002. He began as an evangelical in the 1980s, but crossed over to the side of Religious Liberalism in the 1990s, much to my dismay. (Sitting through his sermon at my presbytery in 2002, in which he compared Presbyterian fundamentalists to the terrorists who less than a year earlier had flown airplanes into the World Trade Center and the Pentagon and murdered thousands, was almost more than I could bear.) However, I still appreciate his explanation of the Calvinistic approach to the Reformation as contrasted with the approach of Lutheran and other more liturgical denominations, illustrating the difference with a man cleaning out his sock drawer. When a Lutheran cleans his sock drawer, he gently lifts it from his dresser, places it on the bed, and then systematically takes out only those things he knows he will not need. When a Calvinist cleans his sock drawer, he rips it from the dresser and flings all the contents on the bed. Then he only puts back in the drawer the things he knows he will need. This was the difference between Calvinists and Lutherans when it came to reforming Roman Catholic dogma and worship. The Lutherans kept whatever was not against scripture. The Calvinists kept only what was specifically commanded by scripture, with the New Testament Church, not the Roman Catholic Church, as the normative standard.

In those days, the Liturgical Calendar was disposed of by Calvinists, and along with it, the three year cycle lectionary. For those unfamiliar with the lectionary, it is an unchanging list of 156 weeks-worth of scripture readings from which the pastor is expected to produce his or her sermons. Each Sunday in the cycle has a selection from a general Old Testament lesson, a Psalm, an epistle, and a gospel; Matthew, Mark, and Luke are featured in the so-called A, B, and C years, while John is reserved for the Sundays leading up to Easter. The lectionary is based on the annual liturgical calendar, and so, quite randomly, the gospel reading will be related to the church calendar, not the previous week's text. For example, on Transfiguration Sunday, regardless of the previous week's text, the gospel selection will be the story of Jesus being transfigured into his luminous glory on the mountain, talking with Moses and Elijah, and terrifying Peter, James, and John. The following week's lesson will be unrelated to the transfiguration.

The reasoning behind the lectionary, as it was explained to me in seminary, is to prevent a pastor simply from preaching the same dozen favorite texts over and over. This way, I was told, the entire gospel will be preached. And I was urged to follow the lectionary, at least for the first three years. I tried. And I didn't last a month! My first sermon was from Mark, chapter 4, the parable of seed that grows seemingly by itself and the mustard seed which grows into a large plant. Next was the stilling of the sea, also in Mark 4. But then we were to skip the story of the healing of the Gerasene Demoniac in the first 20 verses of chapter 5, and start with verse 21, as Jesus went to heal the little girl and the woman with a hemorrhage touched the hem of his garment along the way. The lectionary had gotten us to the eastern shore of the Sea of Galilee, and then plopped us back on the western shore for no reason. I pitched the lectionary that day, and preached about the Gerasene Demoniac, a powerful story of the gospel.

Imagine reading a book by skipping around in it, starting with chapter three, then over to chapter ten, a bit of five, then half of chapter one. How could you ever hope to understand what was going on? The way to understand most books is to read them from start to finish. That's what I started doing in the first month of my ministry; I started preaching through books. It was not how I was trained in seminary. But it was better. In doing this I also stumbled across an almost forgotten term of the Protestant Reformation, Lectio Continua, a Latin phrase which literally translates "continuous reading." The Reformers also were concerned that the full message of scripture be preached, but they accomplished this, and successfully taught those in their charge, by preaching through entire books of the Bible, not hopping around an arbitrary annual Church calendar. I was standing alongside Calvin and Bullinger without even realizing it, though it should not be a great surprise since our priorities are the same. Modern Presbyterians would do well to reform our worship according to the Bible, with the primitive New Testament Church being the norm, as it was for our ancestors. But when teaching and understanding the Bible are no longer important, what remains but empty pageantry or political activism?

CHAPTER TWELVE: THE CUMBERLAND CONUNDRUM

In completing Chapter 11, as I mentioned Lectio Continua, I was reminded of a discussion I had with one of my seminary classmates about a decade after our graduation. He was shocked to learn I had abandoned the lectionary, and even more shocked that I was preaching through entire books of the Bible. "Every pericope?" he asked. (That is pronounced "per-i'-co-pee". It's a Greek word that means "section".) I had to think about it for a minute, what is a pericope? I had almost forgotten because I purposely set out to eliminate seminary-spawned jargon from my vocabulary once I graduated. I did not want to use words which would cloud my teaching for those who did not have my education. I stopped talking about pericopes and the "sitz im leben" (a German phrase meaning "situation in life") and such, and just explained the text so anyone could understand. But once I remembered, I said yes, I preach through every pericope. After I preached the pericope about the calming of the sea, the next week I preached the pericope about the healing of the Gerasene Demoniac, and then continued on.

When telling this story to another friend, he told me that he learned about this when he got back his ordination exams. Those exams are graded by ordained people in the denomination, both pastors and elders. In his answers my friend had referred to the pericopes. When he got back one test a reader who was an elder had written the comment, "What's all this talk about periscopes?" Even as I am typing these words my spell check keeps trying to change "pericope" to "periscope"!

Anyone who knows me or who reads this book must understand that I have great respect for Ruling Elders, the lay leadership in congregations. They are essential to the health of the Church. But they have not had the specialized training that pastors, Teaching Elders, have had. In matters of theology they are much more likely to defer to the pastors; this would have been less likely in the days when Presbyterian laity were steeped in Reformed theology through the Westminster Standards. (See Chapters 10 and 13) As it is, modern Ruling Elders often are timid when it comes to theological debate with Teaching Elders, the professional clergy. Nature abhors a vacuum; what the elders cede to the pastors, the pastors will take.

It happens regularly on the floor of presbyteries, where elders, who are not professional speakers, sometimes become befuddled at a microphone. And sometimes they are brow-beaten by the pastors. One of the most egregious examples I ever have seen of this occurred when a new pastor was being examined by the entire presbytery. After all these years I do not remember exactly what was odd about the pastor's statement of faith, but it was something about God raining down blessings on earth which went beyond Jesus' words about God causing the rain to fall on the good and the bad. An elder rose to question this pastor, who apparently resented the question. He replied, "Well, this has to do with the doctrine of Creation Ex Nihilo."

There was only one purpose for the pastor to use this Latin phrase – to intimidate the elder into silence. And it worked for the moment. Then I jumped to a microphone and said, "For those of you who do not know, Creation Ex Nihilo just means 'creation out of nothing'. And it is true that a god raining blessings down on the earth is a biblical image, but it comes from Baal worship, so we might not want to use that in the Church." The preacher being examined didn't deny that what I said was true.

All of this is preface to the point of this chapter, the Cumberland Conundrum. Some of my readers may be familiar with the small denomination called The Cumberland Presbyterian Church. The Cumberlands formed in Kentucky around 1810 following division in the larger Presbyterian body regarding the current revival which was sweeping that part of the country. Two presbyteries, Springfield and Cumberland, were dominated by pro-revival factions, and believed the revival to be an extraordinary situation which required exceptions to the requirements of pastors formally educated in the eastern seminaries, and subscription to the Westminster Confession of Faith. (Revivals in and of themselves are problematic to a wooden reading of Westminster, which states "By the decree of God, for the manifestation of His glory, some men and angels are predestinated unto everlasting life, and others are fore-ordained to everlasting death. These men and angels, thus predestined and fore-ordained, are particularly and unchangeably designed; and their number is so certain and definite that it cannot be either increased or diminished." (Chapter III, paragraphs 3. and 4.) Would not revivals thus be an expression of doubt in God's sovereignty, that such extreme measures must be taken? I don't believe this, but many Old School Presbyterians did!) The pro-revival presbyteries believed there was no time to wait for educated clergy, especially when they had enthusiastic men, some of them elders, right there, ready to preach and lead. But Kentucky Synod, the next higher governing body, did not agree, and would not grant the exceptions. Frustrated, Springfield Presbytery withdrew from the denomination in 1803; in 1804 Kentucky Synod dissolved Cumberland Presbytery. In 1810 some pastors from the now defunct Cumberland Presbytery reformed it independently, and the new denomination was born. Though begun with religious fervor, the Cumberland Presbyterians have remained a small group through two centuries of existence. In 2007 they had about 800 congregations with an active membership of less than 50,000. By contrast, the descendants of the Presbyterians they had left, the ones who insisted on an educated clergy beyond home-grown enthusiasts, still had over 11,000 congregations in their largest denomination, with more than 2 million members.

My reason for giving this example is to highlight the historical emphasis in mainstream Presbyterianism on an educated clergy. Like the centralization of sacrifices for worship in the Old Testament, centralization of education for pastors at seminaries like Princeton, Union Theological Seminary in Virginia, and Columbia, guaranteed that pastors would have the theological tools at their disposal to open scripture for their congregations and preach the whole Word of God, free from heresy. However, as time passed and theology began to be eclipsed by psychology, Pastoral Care became required, Church History was reduced from a year to a semester, and classes on specific books of the New Testament (Romans, Philippians, Galatians, etc.) became electives. Theology classes became less about preparing pastors to explain Reformed theology to congregations and more about presenting a smorgasbord of modern theological substitutes for orthodoxy (Liberation Theology, Feminism, Process Theology, etc.) to the students. Theological certainty was ridiculed, and replaced with questions and "thinking theologically." Is it any wonder that our denomination's seminary attendance plummeted in the 1990s?

During that decade my own alma mater continued to send mailings out to alumnae, crowing the record-setting sizes of their new students each year. A friend confided in me, "They're playing a numbers game. They are mixing their Doctor of Ministry students in with their Master of Divinity students." Those are very different degrees. Doctor of Ministry degrees are not as difficult to get as the scholastic Ph. D. seminary professors usually hold. At the risk of ticking off a lot of folks, including dear friends and family, the D. Min. almost is a vanity degree, the kind gotten by preachers who want to be called "Dr. Smith". Large churches often encourage their pastors to get D. Min. degrees; it sounds better to say, "Our Senior Pastor is Dr. Smith," instead of merely Pastor Smith, or the grammatically incorrect Reverend Smith. Presbyteries sometimes have funds set aside to help their pastors get D. Min. degrees. Though the requirements have gotten stricter since the 1980s, those who graduated from my seminary the year before I did benefited greatly from a D. Min. program which only required an additional one year internship, with a requisite written thesis, in the middle of their quest for the Master of Divinity degree, to graduate as Dr. Jones, not Pastor Jones. Truthfully, it's not a vanity degree. There is work required; you can't order it off the internet! But it is not equivalent to the same kind of work done to become an academic or medical doctor.

Still, one type of person pursues a Doctor of Ministry degree – one who already has a Master of Divinity. Historically, those who seek Master of Divinity degrees do so for one purpose, which is to become pastors of churches. However, today some scholars who have no intention of becoming pastors will seek the M. Div. because it looks good on their academic resume. About half of current Masters of Divinity students have no intention of going into the ministry.

Because of these factors, the question to ask overzealous seminary promoters for a more accurate read of their service to the Church is this: How many on-campus first year M. Div students do you have? When I asked this of my seminary in

1998, the number shrank from over 100 students to 30. Of these, statistically speaking, half would not be entering the ministry. That cuts the number to 15. Of those, many of whom would be second-career folks, about half would be unwilling to go to small, rural churches where they would receive the presbytery minimum salary. Let's say 8. Eight new pastors per year, from an institution that once provided pastors for most of Virginia and North Carolina, states densely populated by Presbyterians. At the same time, my own presbytery, with over 150 churches and about 32,000 members, had zero students attending that seminary to earn a Master of Divinity degree.

What to do then, for churches seeking pastors when so few are available? In my first call, my solution was to become "Temporary Supply" to a church of about ten members, eleven miles from my main church. I preached there most Sundays at 9:00 AM, and then rocketed up the road to be ready to teach Sunday School back home at 10:00. That position had to be re-approved by my main church's session and the presbytery every year. It always was, unanimously, without debate, for seven years. I said on many occasions that this was a good solution to the dearth of pastors, that called pastors be willing to get up a little earlier, drive a little further, and preach the same sermon they would be repeating a little later on that morning. But very few pastors took up that challenge.

In my current call there has been no need for me to supply empty pulpits. There are many retired pastors in the area willing to preach at least a few Sundays per month; some who have volunteered to do so simply get no reply from the presbytery. But many of our small churches now are being served by an innovation of the past 20 years, the Certified Lay Pastor. The main church of my first call is served by a CLP today, a good man who loves the Lord, who I know well and admire, and whose daughter I thought someday might be my daughter-in-law when our children were in pre-school together! The smaller church I served as Temporary Supply for seven years was dissolved by its presbytery, and the property given to an Hispanic ministry which failed; afterward the building was bulldozed and paved over for extra parking by the Baptist church next door, to whom the presbytery finally had sold the property. That's a different way of solving the empty pulpit problem!

What is a Certified Lay Pastor? Originally they were called Certified Lay Preachers; they are ordained Presbyterian elders who belong to churches other than to one at which they preach. In 2012 in my PC(USA) presbytery, they received special training in a program which lasted about nine months, six of which they spent interning with an ordained Pastor. They also took five or six classes on-line from Dubuque Seminary in Iowa. In the beginning, they were certified to preach, but now, apparently, they do the entire pastoral gig. After all, most of the churches they serve have pretty much given up the search for an installed, seminary trained pastor.

Here is the practical reality: within the PC(USA), the Clergy has won another round in the struggle with Lay people for accountability. CLPs are wonderful folks. I admire them. They would not do what they do without a strong commitment to Jesus Christ and His Church. But they will not stand in the way of Clergy at any level of church governance beyond the local congregation. To the CLPs, the Pastors are the ones who are seminary trained. They know best. I have seen elders on Synod Council vote overwhelmingly one way at one meeting when the Moderator, who was a Pastor, indicated this is the best way, and then vote overwhelmingly the opposite way one month later when the same Moderator wanted the opposite, without one question being raised.

And here is the historical irony: the Cumberlands have won their argument.

CHAPTER THIRTEEN: THE NATURE AND ROLE OF A CONFESSION OF FAITH

What is the purpose of a confession of faith? For me, the best historical image of a confession is found in the life of the great Reformer, Martin Luther, standing before Emperor Charles V at the Diet of Worms in 1521. Asked to renounce his criticisms of the Medieval Roman Catholic Church, begun when he nailed his 95 Theses to the door of the Castle Church in Wittenberg four years earlier, the former monk replied, "Here I stand, I can do no other, so help me God!" The purpose of a confession of faith, then, is to articulate one's faith to the surrounding world. In the case of a denomination, historically the purpose of a confession of faith was to articulate essential beliefs and practices of this group to the surrounding world.

But beliefs change through the centuries; what is to be done with old confessions which no longer articulate the view of the majority? Some would simply dispose of them and write new confessions. But in the United States, Presbyterians, understanding that the words of the Bible are the words of God, not the words of our confession, adopted a system by which the Westminster Standards could be amended. Today, to amend our confessional statements, a two thirds majority of the General Assembly must vote to make the changes, then a two thirds majority of presbyteries must vote to make the changes, and then a second General Assembly must once again vote by a two thirds majority to make the changes. In years past it had to be a three quarters majority each time! By contrast, the system for changing Presbyterian policies and procedures, historically contained in the Book of Church Order, was a much easier process: a simple majority at General Assembly, followed by a simple majority of presbyteries. Because of the difference, changes to what now is called the Book of Order happen almost as often as the General Assembly meets. Only occasionally have attempts been made to change our theological documents in my years as a pastor, and rarely do they succeed. But never in my years as a pastor, and not since 1983, has there been an attempt to change the words of the Westminster Standards. Why not? It is because they no longer matter. Few people understand the purpose of a confession, and fewer still actually read or care what the confessions say.

As I have already written, Religious Liberals and denominational bureaucrats chafed at the restrictions of the Westminster Standards for years. Changes were made as they were needed, the last one being in the 1950s, when a very good and biblical rethinking of marriage, divorce, and remarriage replaced an earlier version of that chapter in the Standards for both the northern and southern streams of American Presbyterians. 1967 was the year which ended confessionalism in the northern Presbyterian churches. There, in the height of the struggles for civil rights for all Americans, a new confession was presented which emphasized the need for reconciliation among races, the Confession of 1967. It is a short document, taking up only ten of the 391 pages in the current Book of Confessions; by contrast, The Westminster Standards are 127 pages. As such, there was no way the Confession of 1967 could stand alone as a replacement for Westminster. This is acknowledged in the preface to "C-67", as the fifth paragraph states: "This Confession is not a 'system of doctrine', nor does it include all the traditional topics of theology. For example, the Trinity and the Person of Christ are not defined, but are recognized and reaffirmed as forming the basis and determining the structure of the Christian faith." Instead, the confession is divided into three sections, "God's Word of Reconciliation", "The Ministry of Reconciliation", and "The Fulfillment of Reconciliation." Since it was never intended to be a stand-alone confessional statement, but a "tack on", the northern denomination was able to avoid the sentimental war which likely would have erupted had the Westminster Standards simply been set aside. More than 90% of the presbyteries voted in favor of adopting C-67 and an entire "Book of Confessions". (By contrast, when the southern denomination's Religious Liberals attempted to replace the Westminster Standards with a completely new confession in the 1970s, it went down in flames while traditionalists shouted, "They're trying to do away with Westminster!")

Almost fifty years later, there appears to be little about which to complain within the Confession of 1967. Based upon 2 Corinthians 5:16-21, where, through Christ, God was reconciling the world unto Himself, and now has committed to us the ministry of reconciliation, it certainly was a proper word for a decade rent asunder by racial unrest. Its only inherent weakness is the Karl Barth influenced lines, "The Scriptures, given under the guidance of the Holy Spirit, are nevertheless the words of men, conditioned by the language, thought-forms, and literary fashions of the places and times at which they were written. They reflect views of life, history, and cosmos which were then current. The church, therefore, has an obligation to approach the Scriptures with literary and historical understanding." (Book of Confessions 9.29) While these sentences might be interpreted in an orthodox way (of course it helps to know something about the Roman Empire while reading the New Testament), they also open the possibility that some might use Jesus Christ as the Word of God Incarnate against Scripture as the Word of God Written. In fact, since its adoption, some have commented on the struggle which has developed between those who hold a "Westminster view" of the inspiration of scripture versus those who hold a "C-67" view, though I find a harmony between the two with which I can live. Many do not bother trying to hold the two together at all, and most have no idea what either statement says. An axiom of 21st century Presbyterianism is this: The Book of Confessions is an unread and unmissed "core" document.

When I went to General Assembly in 1994, my roommate was a pastor from Bellevue, Washington, an older gentleman who had been at the northern Assembly which had ratified the Book of Confessions in 1967. He told me about a man in the old northern denomination who was something of a gadfly, always complaining about new things being done within it, and sometimes staging elaborate stunts to make his points. At the 1967 Assembly, this man staged a mock wake for the denomination, complete with a coffin. He invited attendees to come and look into the coffin of Presbyterianism, and those who did found their own faces staring back at them; the man had placed a mirror at the head of the dummy which lay in state!

Truthfully, I do not know what this man's specific complaint was. In all likelihood, he was opposed to something within C-67. If this is the case, he was much like the Old Testament prophets who, according to 1 Peter, did not understand what exactly they were prophesying as they indicated by the Spirit the coming of Jesus. The problem was not the Confession of 1967; the problem was the adoption of a Book of Confessions in the place of a single confession.

What is in the Book of Confessions? Most pastors can tell you since we have to study this stuff in seminary, but most elders (closer to 99% instead of 51%, especially if they can't run and look it up!) cannot. Originally it was ten documents: The Nicene Creed, The Apostle's Creed, The Scots Confession, The Heidelberg Catechism, The Second Helvetic Confession, The Westminster Confession, The Larger Catechism, The Shorter Catechism, The Barmen Declaration, and the Confession of 1967. Since my ordination in 1988 another section has been added, "A Brief Statement of Faith". And, in 2009, an attempt was made to add a new confession from South Africa, The Belhar Confession, adopted in that country in 1986, before the abolition of apartheid.

Can you see the problem here? Maybe they could not in 1967 when this new approach to confessionalism, the only way Westminster could be marginalized, was adopted. And maybe it was not seen once again at reunion in 1983, when the southern church adopted the northern denomination's Book of Confessions in exchange for the northern churches adopting the southern Book of Church Order. Perhaps with all the energy and focus which went into forcing that reunion (see Chapter 15), it was not noticed in the intervening 16 years. But from the beginning of my ministry in 1988, it has been clear to me, and I have complained about it to anyone who would listen. A Book of Confessions is no confession at all. It becomes a library, a collection of time-locked historical artifacts, the significance of which is determined by the reader. One might ask of it, "What did we believe in 1547?", and consult The Scots Confession, or "What did we believe in 1560?", and consult The Second Helvetic. What did Reformed Christians in 1930s Nazi Germany believe? You can find that in the Barmen Declaration. But what do we believe now? As the fights of the past three decades have clearly shown, that is found in the Book of Order, not the Book of Confessions; in other words, in the modern, mainstream Presbyterian Church, polity, how we govern ourselves, is more important than theology, what we believe. In spite of the denomination-wide rallying cry of "Theology Matters" following the heretical 1993 Re-Imagining Conference, in practice, theology does not matter.

The Book of Confessions is filled with statements that no modern Presbyterian believes. The Scots Confession condemns the Roman Catholic Church for allowing women to serve communion. "(T)heir ministers are not true ministers of Christ Jesus (indeed they even allow women, whom the Holy Ghost will not permit to preach in the congregation to baptize)..." The answer to Question 80 of The Heidelberg Catechism includes the following evaluation of the Roman Catholic Mass: "...the Mass teaches that the living and the dead do not have forgiveness of sins through the sufferings of Christ unless Christ is again offered for them daily by the priest (and that Christ is bodily under the form of bread and wine and is therefore to be worshipped in them). Therefore the Mass is fundamentally a complete denial of the once for all sacrifice and passion of Jesus Christ (and as such is an idolatry to be condemned)." The harshest confession is the Second Helvetic, written by John Calvin's associate and John Knox's teacher, Heinrich Bullinger. Often he included condemnations of sects, heretical and otherwise, in his confession. As examples, "we therefore abhor the impious doctrine of Arius and the Arians against the Son of God, and especially the blasphemies of the Spaniard, Michael Servetus, and all his followers, which Satan through them has, as it were, dragged up out of hell and has most audaciously and impiously spread abroad in the world...we detest the dogma of the Nestorians...we thoroughly execrate the madness of Euthyches...we by no means approve of or accept the strained, confused, and obscure subtleties of Schwenkfeldt and of similar sophists with their self-contradictory arguments...we also condemn those who thought that the devil and all the ungodly would at some time be saved, and that there would be an end to punishments;" all these condemnations are found in just one chapter of the Second Helvetic, Chapter XI, Of Jesus Christ, True God and Man, the Only Savior of the World. A true, working confession would have none of these statements; instead, a supermajority of the presbyteries would delete obsolete arguments and no longer held points of view, and insert new insights we have gained through closer study of the Bible and the guidance of the Holy Spirit. This is exactly the way American Presbyterians understood the Westminster Confession prior to the adoption of a Book of Confessions in 1967. Read the modern chapter "Of the Civil Magistrate" (Chapter XXV, PCUS) and then the footnote which gives the paragraph from 1647; the earlier version has much to say about the civil government using its power to suppress heresy, for example. American Presbyterians don't believe that, so we changed it! After all, a working confession is not a pristine document, hung on a museum wall. The Bible is written in ink; a confession is written in pencil! The Bible is the Word of God Written, infallible in matters of faith and action; a confession is the words of people, always susceptible to error and in need of revision. At the same time, a confession is needed as a witness to the world and to ourselves as to what we believe is essential, and what we will do because of our beliefs.

However, this is not the understanding of a majority of Presbyterians today. This became clear to me in February of 2011 as my presbytery debated whether or not to approve the Belhar Confession. Some in the denomination opposed its addition because they believed its emphasis on opposition to "injustice" and "unity" might be interpreted as removal of standards for action and belief for Religious Liberals, and a new club to be wielded against "schismatics" by bureaucrats (see Chapter 20); some supported its addition because, in the words of one elder, "it's against racism, and we all ought to be against that." I was opposed, as I explained to the presbytery, because we should be deleting from this behemoth Book of Confessions filled with conflicting statements, not adding to it! But my argument fell on deaf ears, and the presbytery overwhelmingly voted in favor of the addition; nationwide, though, Belhar failed to receive the necessary two thirds supermajority needed for inclusion in the Book of Confessions. Ironically, the 2012 General Assembly decided to send it back to the presbyteries again, following the Religious Liberal pattern of wearing down resistance by vote after vote after vote until their way is accomplished.

But in 2011, because I spoke against Belhar first in my presbytery, I got to hear first-hand how far the denomination had fallen from the traditional understanding of a confession, as pastors who should have known better attempted to refute my "less is more" position. "I like a library of theological thought," said one. Another spoke of the joy of showing teenagers how we had changed through the centuries. One sought to reassure me, since the Larger Catechism had been deleted by the northern denomination in 1967, only to be re-instated at reunion in 1983, that statements added now could be deleted later. Nobody addressed the issue I had raised, that by having a Book of Confessions, we had no coherent statement to the world as to what we believe and what we will do, and no means of learning for ourselves what we did or didn't believe in 2011. They preferred the museum piece, hung on a wall, unchangeable. Of course, up there it cannot bother anyone.

In 2000 I attended a presbytery sponsored event entitled "Embracing God's Diversity". It was a train-wreck: offensive, at least to those of us of orthodox persuasion, who got to endure being called bigots by one unapologetic speaker; disappointing, since we had been assured that all theological points of view within the presbytery would be represented by the speakers (ours never was); and superficial, basically staged to justify acceptance of the homosexual life-style for as many as could be persuaded. One of the key moments of that event occurred for me on the first day, when a group of us were gathered together and asked to write a completion to this statement, "I believe…". Some used it as a moment to be silly, "I believe in dragons." Others used it as a moment to be confrontational, "I believe homosexuality is no big deal." I decided to be theological, and I wrote this: "I believe that 'The Word of God, which is contained in the scriptures of the Old and New Testaments, is the only rule God has given by which we may glorify and enjoy Him.'" No one there, not even those who considered themselves to be orthodox, evangelical Christians, recognized this as the answer to the second question of the Shorter Catechism. More troubling, I was the only one who believed this statement to be true. Granted, most of the evangelical leaders in our presbytery had steered clear of this conference which I had naively believed also would be an opportunity for us to share our positions in a neutral environment, as we had been promised. But our influence is small. Theology does not matter in our presbytery or our denomination; God help us all when it ceases to matter in our congregations!

Even among denominational friends my cry for a single confession is that of a lone voice in the wilderness. In 2006 I was part of a small group of evangelicals which formed something called "Constitutional Presbyterians". We even held a denominationally advertised and rather well-attended gathering at First Presbyterian Church in Greenville, South Carolina! Originally Constitutional Presbyterians was "A New PCUS", the initials of the old southern Presbyterian Church in the United States. We dropped that when it was learned that some potential allies believed that to be an offensive name; after all, the PCUS began in Augusta, Georgia, in 1861 as the Presbyterian Church in the Confederate States of America! But while Constitutional Presbyterians wound up simply being another short-lived evangelical special interest group, which, like third parties in American politics, was a honeybee which stung and then died as our concerns were addressed by larger groups, in the beginning we were talking about a new denomination, just as the Fellowship of Presbyterians was talking in 2011. To that end, a group of us gathered at Montreat College in March of 2006 to discuss what a new denomination would need to look like. I brought out my insistence that only one confession be used, and since we are in the United States, the only logical single confession to be used is Westminster, used in America before the United States existed. Two of our number were seminary professors, and immediately they said no. Westminster depends too much on natural theology, they said; Karl Barth has shown us that God is so much more than what we can grasp, and unless He reveals Himself, we will understand nothing about Him or His will for our lives. It was a fair argument; after all, only reason can give us double-predestination, since the words of scripture do not. But which is the better option? The continuation of a Book of Confessions that includes a Barthian correction but still results to no clear statement of faith, and then the elevation of polity by default? Or would it be better to have a single, flawed confession which we can and will correct as needed? If you don't like the double-predestination section of Westminster, amend it with the gentler and still very orthodox section on predestination from The

Second Helvetic! Yes, two-thirds of the presbyteries would need to vote in favor of such a change, but that is a discussion which would greatly benefit the Church, and in the end, our witness to the world would be much clearer.

Meanwhile, the denomination as it currently exists lurches along rudderless, swinging and attempting to hit at some political issue in which it can impute some righteous indignation, thus justifying its existence. In practical use, our modern Book of Confessions generally serves pastors as a theological buffet, from which they can pick their favorite lines and ignore the rest, while the laypeople go hungry. Confessionalism was created for more than this. It is about essentials. Here we stand, we can do no other, so help us, God!

Ironically, on Friday, July 6, 2012, several months after the completion of this chapter in my manuscript, the General Assembly of the Presbyterian Church (USA) voted overwhelmingly (70%) that the Book of Order, our polity, takes precedence over the Book of Confessions, our theology. At issue was an overture to the Assembly to redefine marriage within the Book of Order as something other than between one man and one woman; the traditional definition is given three times within the Book of Confessions: in the Second Helvetic Confession, the Westminster Confession, and The Confession of 1967. A commissioner asked the Moderator to rule the overture out of order because it conflicted with Robert's Rules of Order, upon which Presbyterian parliamentarianism is based. Robert's Rules states in section 10, p. 111, lines 4-6, that any motion which conflicts with a body's constitution is out of order. The commissioner reminded the Moderator that The Book of Confessions is Part I of the Constitution, while the Book of Order is Part II.

The Stated Clerk called on a member of the Advisory Committee on the Constitution, whose answer confirms everything I have said as a criticism of the polity over theology approach to "confessionalism" as practiced within the PC(USA). Discussing Part I, the Advisory Committee member said, "This collection of statements spans a vast selection of theological perspectives, and there is no small amount of difference and conflict within the Constitution itself…but more specifically, it is important to understand that because it is a large sweep of history, and a fairly broad representation of theology, it ought not to be treated as though it were a rule book. It is, in fact, a document from which we draw our basic theological views."

The Advisory Committee member continued, now describing Part II, The Book of Order. *"It contains the standards by which we operate.* (emphasis mine) We have been asked occasionally if it is necessary to amend the Book of Confessions in order to amend a similar provision in the Book of Order. The answer is no. The Confessions are deliberately broad, and allow us to draw different ecclesiological conclusions on the basis of our theology. It would be the Advisory Committee on the Constitution's opinion that a statement in the Book of Confessions might not pose a conflict with a proposal to amend the Constitution (Part II, the Book of Order, clarification mine)."

The Stated Clerk recommended that the Moderator accept the recommendation of the Advisory Committee on the Constitution. He did, and ruled that the overture to amend the definition of marriage to "between two people" instead of "between one man and one woman" within Part II of the constitution was in order, even though Part I defines marriage exclusively and repeatedly as between one man and one woman. The Moderator was challenged. A debate ensued. A vote was taken. The Book of Order won by 70% over the Book of Confessions. The Bible was never considered.

In the Presbyterian Church (USA), polity trumps theology.

CHAPTER FOURTEEN: RIGHT ACTION TRUMPS RIGHT BELIEF

As I wrote in chapter two, Harry Emmerson Fosdick's 1922 sermon, "Shall The Fundamentalists Win?", suggested replacing traditional fundamentals with two new ones: "Tolerance" and "Doing the right thing instead of worrying about believing the right thing". *Correct belief* is known as "orthodoxy", a word with which most of us are familiar. *Correct action* is summed up in a more obscure word, "orthopraxy", doing the right thing. At the conclusion of the modernist/fundamentalist controversy of the 1920s, the northern Presbyterian denomination removed the requirement of subscription to theological fundamentals, and from 1927 on, though Presbyterian officers continue to swear that they sincerely receive and adopt the "essential tenets of the Reformed Faith" when we are ordained and installed, no list of essential tenets has existed. Denominational bureaucrats, who longed for peace within the denomination at any price, as well as looking attractive to as many non-Presbyterians as possible, developed this slogan: Theology Divides, Mission Unites. It is the triumph of Fosdick the Baptist, tolerance and orthopraxy: a tolerance based upon vagueness and a common language, and an orthopraxy determined either by denominational leadership or the larger, increasingly more secular, culture. Why worry about whether or not someone actually believes the Bible is God's Word, or believes that Jesus truly rose from death? Instead, give your money to this hospital that we are building, or to this orphanage, or to this Presbyterian college or seminary.

While this pragmatic approach may sound appealing in the short term, and many of these missions are worthy of support, it ignores the basic principle that action follows belief, not the other way around. The generic letter to the Ephesians models this understanding clearly. The first three chapters discuss what we are to believe. The last three chapters discuss how we should live in light of what we believe. In the same manner, Paul's letter to the Romans, written to a church he had yet to visit, and thus without the personal notes addressing specific crises in the congregation which fill most of his letters, has eleven chapters of theology, followed by three chapters of ethics. This you are to believe. Therefore, because of these things you believe, you are to do these things. Belief precedes action.

As we believe, so we do. Abraham believed God, and his faith was shown in what he did in offering Isaac as a sacrifice. Had he not believed, and Hebrews says that he believed that if Isaac was killed, God would bring him back to life, had he not believed, he would not have been willing to take Isaac up the mountain. As we believe, so we do. I believe that tithing, giving back to God 10% of my gross income, is a practice which shows my love for Jesus, and that it is a guard against the idolatry of loving money. If I can give part of it away, I can't be taking it too seriously. Therefore, my wife and I have tithed ever since we got married, when I was in college. As we believe, so we do.

By the same token, as we don't believe, so we don't do. Years ago a couple came to me, very concerned about their teenage son. He had gotten into trouble with the law, and as they tried to understand what was happening to make him act out, he confessed that he did not believe in God. They were very concerned, and called me to come talk with him. I said I would, and then observed that they themselves did not attend our church, their family's home church. "If you want to help his unbelief, you need to show him that you believe, that you want to make your relationship with God a priority."

I met the boy, and he and I hit it off at once. We liked the same kind of music, we both played guitar, and he began coming to the church. He attended regularly for about six months. Sometimes he brought his younger brother with him. He helped with a musical production the church was putting on during that time. Through it all, his parents rarely darkened the door of the church. And then he sort of drifted away, still friendly with me, but with other priorities. As we believe, so we do. His parents showed him what they didn't believe by what they didn't do. Action always follows belief.

Orthopraxy as a substitute for orthodoxy is the proverbial cart before the ox. The best we can hope for is nothing happening, but usually something does happen, and it is bad. While the short-term result of declaring that theology divides and mission unites may have stopped the fighting within the northern, and then the southern streams of Presbyterianism, allowing unprecedented growth up until the 1960s, long-term it has aided the weakening and collapse of the combined body.

Orthopraxy led to a denomination that simply lurched from addressing one social concern to another, allowing the culture to determine the Church's action instead of allowing the Holy Spirit to control through the study of scripture. It began with the purpose of foreign missions in the 1930s; are missionaries there to win converts to Christ, or should they simply improve the lives of people in other countries through medical aid and general education, without attempting to encourage conversion? One Presbyterian foreign missionary who insisted on merely addressing temporal needs was Pearl Buck, best known for her novel, <u>The Good Earth</u>. Her challenger in those days was a man who also was her friend, Dr. J. Greshem Machen, by then of Westminster Seminary in Philadelphia. His concern that mission be primarily about the proclamation of the gospel, about winning souls to Christ, was so deep that he and other Presbyterians formed an independent board of foreign missionaries as an alternative to the compromised denominational board of foreign missions. The bureaucrats in New York at the headquarters of the northern Presbyterian Church, were willing to support Buck's position, but not these upstart Presbyterians concerned about saving souls. The General Assembly of 1935 demanded that all Presbyterian officers on the Independent Board for Presbyterian Foreign Missions resign, and some did. Machen refused. He was summarily defrocked. Buck was never reprimanded.

The Orthodox Presbyterian denomination left the northern Presbyterian Church in 1936, and Machen died suddenly the following year. The fallout from the shift away from orthodoxy and to orthopraxy, short-term, was over. But long-term the effects have been devastating to Presbyterianism in the United States. By the 1960s the two major denominations in the north and south had reached their numerical peak and begun their decline, a trend that continues to this day. Two church court rulings from 1975 and 1981, respectively, illustrate the practical problems of orthopraxy without orthodoxy. They were the Kenyon case and the Kaseman case.

Walter Wynn Kenyon was the son and grandson of Presbyterian ministers. In 1974 he was a pastoral candidate under the care of Pittsburgh Presbytery, and during his examination by that body he declared that, as a matter of conscience based upon his reading of scripture, he could not participate in the ordination of women as pastors, elders, or deacons, though he was willing to work with them once they were ordained. The presbytery approved his ordination, but it then was set aside by the General Assembly Permanent Judicial Commission (GAPJC), the Presbyterian equivalent of the Supreme Court. They overturned his ordination and showed him to the door. "Neither a synod nor the General Assembly has any power to allow a presbytery to grant an exception to an explicit constitutional provision," they wrote in their decision. "A candidate who chooses not to subscribe to the polity of this church may be a more useful servant of our Lord in some other fellowship whose polity is in harmony with the candidate's conscience."

Mansfield M. Kaseman was a pastor in the United Church of Christ denomination before being called to pastor The United Church of Rockville, Maryland, a union church between the two denominations; National Capital Union Presbytery, as it was then called, was the governing body with oversight responsibilities from the Presbyterian side. According to Time magazine, Mr. Kaseman denied that Jesus was God ("Jesus is not God, God is God," he said), was not sure that the resurrection happened, and was unclear as to what he believed regarding the Trinity. Nonetheless, he was overwhelmingly approved by the presbytery as a pastor. Evangelicals were appalled, and appealed his approval to the General Assembly Permanent Judicial Commission, not once, but twice. The final decision of the GAPJC is telling, speaking less about what Kaseman believed, and more about what they believed:

> "The arguments presented by both parties in this case force us to recognize that there are several valid ways of interpreting the creedal symbols and the confessions of our faith. Theological pluralism is a reality which is both desirable and present in our midst. Whether one begins his/her quest for truth with faith and experience as the path that leads to knowledge (creedal or otherwise), or whether one begins the quest with knowledge (creeds)

that leads to faith, is not an important issue. There is room in the church for both approaches to reality and for the honest differences of opinion that will result. Tolerance is called for – tolerance, sympathy, understanding, and mutual respect and love in Christ. Mere differences in methodology of Bible study, in theological investigation and in opinions need not divide or polarize the church. Jesus Christ and the realities of the Christian faith are far too big and broad and gracious to be confined within the limits of human thoughts and creeds. We must be instructed and guided by the creeds in our quest, but we must not stop with that. Led by our living Lord we must go on to find and test and confirm the creeds in our own ways – in our own experience, if we as a church and as individuals are finally to know the truth that will set us free forever. This is the approach which Mr. Kaseman has chosen to follow. National Capital-Union Presbytery has attested to its validity. The commission believes that it is valid and in accord with the basic tenets of our Reformed tradition."

Harry Emmerson Fosdick would be proud. Well, in fact, though his 1922 cry for tolerance is lifted up here, the man himself probably would be appalled by the unforeseen consequences; I have known many otherwise orthodox older liberals who now deeply regret their lack of theological concern in the 1950s and later. But look at how far we had fallen by 1981! Though couched in flowery and soothing language, there is no sense of God revealing Himself in scripture, or in the teachings of Jesus of Nazareth regarding Himself. There is no concern about false teaching, warned against in every book of the New Testament, because teaching does not matter anymore. There is no right teaching. There only is right practice, which is tolerance of anything (except, apparently, those who question the ordination of women) and unity above all things.

Reunion between the northern and southern branches of the Presbyterian Church in the United States of America occurred in 1983, and concerns over theological drift into Religious Liberalism were quieted as the institutional reorganization of two bodies into one took precedence. Then in November of 1993 a conference entitled "Re-Imagining God" took place in Minneapolis, MN, which at first seemed to be a huge swing to the left; instead, denomination-wide horror at the blatant paganism and pluralism on display resulted in a reversal of the theological direction declared in the Kaseman ruling. The 1994 General Assembly in Wichita, KS, actually declared that parts of the conference not only went beyond the Reformed tradition, but also beyond "what the Reformed tradition understands as being Christian." The commissioners, of which I was one, voted overwhelmingly, 98%, to adopt this language in addressing the conference. Much of the credit for this response must go to The Presbyterian Layman, a much maligned independent newspaper published in North Carolina, whose circulation far out-paced anything the denomination had to sweep the truth under the rug. This time the decision was not being made quietly by denominational elites. This time people in the pews were reading first-hand accounts of milk and honey rituals to replace communion; of declarations that no doctrine of atonement is necessary since Jesus' life should be emphasized, not his death; of the traditional atonement being dismissed as "folks hanging on crosses and blood dripping and weird stuff," and condemned as justification for child abuse because, since God the Father did this to His Son, therefore abusive parents can say to their cowering children, "You should just take it like Jesus did!" All these things were said at the conference, to which the PC(USA) was the largest financial contributor. Cassette tapes of the conference were available for purchase; there was no denying the content or context. And there was no denying that monies within the denomination dried up quickly. The Bi-Centennial Fund, begun in 1988 with the intention of raising six million dollars for the denomination, and which donated about $50,000 to the Re-Imagining God Conference, quietly shut down a year or so later because the giving to it had stopped. The 1994 General Assembly reacted quickly and well by placing parts of the conference's teachings outside orthodoxy; it also declared, "Theology matters."

But 1994 turned out to mark the last discussion of theology at the national level. The following year the General Assembly

Permanent Judicial Commission declared that the 1978 Authoritative Interpretation regarding the incompatibility of homosexual practice with Christian teaching regarding ordination of church officers must be set aside since nothing in the Book of Order, the polity portion of the denomination's constitution, specifically forbade it. In 1996 a majority of presbyteries voted to put that language in the Book of Order, declaring the scriptural norms of fidelity in marriage and chastity in singleness to be requirements for ordination. Religious Liberals were furious; not only did they hate the practical result of this wording, they also chafed at the fact that homosexual behavior was not specifically named so homophobia could not be charged easily. And when they attempted to replace the 1996 language with more permissive words in 1998, they lost by an even larger margin.

But in 2011 they finally got their way. Ironically, it was not the permission to ordain practicing homosexuals they truly wanted which they got, but simply permission to de-standardize ordination standards. This has been referred to as the "states' rights" solution, the one originally granted when women's ordination initially was allowed in the 1960s. They sold it to the majority of the denomination with the promise that if the local church did not want to ordain gay elders or deacons, or hire gay pastors, they would not be forced to do so. "Nothing will change for you if you don't want to change," they assured elders on the floors of presbyteries. "This will just bring an end to all the fighting; don't we have better things to do, like missions?" They convinced a denomination which obviously had forgotten about Walter Wynn Kenyon. What is allowed today may very well be required tomorrow.

In November 2011, following the removal of fidelity and chastity standards, The Covenant Network of Presbyterians, a group formed in 1997 for the sole purpose of allowing the ordination of practicing homosexuals, published a paper entitled "Guidelines for Examination of Church Officers." Though the author claimed not to speak for all members of the group (who can speak for all the members of any sizable group?), the paper was made available on the Network's webpage. Certainly he was not simply speaking for himself. And his reasoning was flawless given the history of the denomination, as well as troublingly familiar. "...lower councils can neither ignore, nor add to, these churchwide standards. Thus, the GAPJC has admonished that 'no lower governing body can constitutionally define, diminish, augment, or modify standards for ordination and installation of church officers...Likewise, local efforts to add requirements that are stricter than those which have been adopted by the whole church are unconstitutional." Thus, presbyteries or sessions who now want to add fidelity in marriage and chastity in singleness to requirements for pastors, elders, or deacons, restating the biblical standards removed in 2011, should prepare themselves for challenge in the church judicial system. (In fact, in October of 2012 the GAPJC declared "unconstitutional and, therefore, void" the fidelity in marriage and chastity in singleness requirements for pastors added by Los Ranchos Presbytery on September 15, 2011. And so it begins.)

It gets worse when the paper moves from governing bodies to individuals. One of the promises repeated over and over by those advocating the removal of fidelity in marriage and chastity in singleness for church officers in 2011 was that there would be no "Kenyonization", which is to say, no one would be forced to ordain a practicing homosexual if this violated his conscience, as Kenyon was forced out for his refusal to ordain women. Therefore it is chilling to read the following words penned mere months after the change went into effect:

> (A) person who wishes to engage in ordered ministry must be prepared to carry out the functions of the office. General Assembly has affirmed that an examining body 'cannot excuse a candidate's inability to perform the constitutional functions unique to his or her office (such as administration of the sacraments).' Consistent with this, a series of judicial cases has made clear that a presbytery may not ordain or install someone who declares that he will not participate in the ordination of women. Indeed, it is *fundamental* (ironic emphasis mine) to our polity that the responsibility of assessing the fitness of officers-elect is vested in the *councils* (sessions and presbyteries), not individuals. Accordingly, the pastor who officiates at an ordination thereby performs a *ministerial* act that is required by the Constitution (not a

discretionary one), and the act of officiating indicates neither approval nor disapproval of the congregation's choice of leaders and the council's approval of them. This point pertains primarily to pastors, who must officiate at child baptisms, ordination and installation of church leaders, and the like. While candidates who cannot agree to perform such functions in conformity with Presbyterian polity may be fine Christians, they may not be ordained or installed in the PC(USA).

So much for the promise of no Kenyonization. If I declare my unwillingness to participate in the ordination service for an actively gay pastor, even as a matter of conscience because of the way I understand scripture, at best, my career in the denomination is over, because I will never be allowed to be installed as pastor in another church. At worst, the Covenant Network and its friends, who see this as a justice issue, will work to remove me from the church I currently serve, sooner rather than later. And, for the record, I declare here that I am unwilling to participate in such a service of ordination. It would be a violation of my conscience, which is supposed to be "free from the doctrines and commandments of men which are in anything contrary to (God's) Word..." (Westminster Confession of Faith, Chapter XXII, 2.) (See Chapter 20)

Here's one more reason for me, and all Evangelicals, to leave; eventually they will be coming to kick us out anyway. Better to go now before the exit rules get changed on us again! Religious Liberals do not care about orthodoxy, right belief; any belief will do. They only care about orthopraxy, right action, and refusal to ordain practicing homosexuals is always wrong to them.

I shared this position paper with the executives of my presbytery. They assured me that nothing like this would ever happen here. But all it takes is one disgruntled member of the Covenant Network in our presbytery (one of whose names is included as a contact person on the document) to file a complaint against me. "But that would get nowhere in our presbytery PJC," they answered. If you say so, but then it would be appealed to the Synod PJC. "Well, the Synod won't be around for much longer," came the reply. OK, then it would go directly to the

General Assembly PJC. And who knows what they will decide? They will not care what promises were made to get the votes for rescinding fidelity and chastity standards. They do not care about orthodoxy, obviously. They do care very much about orthopraxy.

CHAPTER FIFTEEN: 1983 – REUNION AT ANY COST, EVEN INTEGRITY

In 1983 the two major Presbyterian denominations in the United States reunited after over a century of estrangement. That break occurred at the beginning of the Civil War, and most of the southern branch still resided within the geographic area of the old Confederacy. Talk of reunion began as early as 1870, but most southerners were opposed to it then. In 1914 they managed to add a provision to the southern constitution which made reunion nearly impossible; the process would be like that for amending the Westminster Confession of Faith, needing the approval of a General Assembly, the approval of three quarters of the presbyteries, and finally the approval of a subsequent General Assembly. This guaranteed that only near unanimity of desire for reunion in the south would allow it.

The rise of the ecumenical movement in the early 20th century and the formation of the World Council of Churches in 1948 inspired many Presbyterian individuals, both north and south, to work toward reuniting the fractured Presbyterian Church. As I type this paragraph I have sitting beside me Reunion Plans issued for "study and comment only" from 1947, 1949, 1952, and 1953. Also, in 1955 both northern and southern denominations published a joint hymnbook with the Reformed Church in America, with input from much smaller northern United Presbyterian Church and southern Associate Reformed Presbyterian Church. (This was a radical change for the Associate Reformed, which up till this time still sang only metrical psalms in the Calvinistic tradition.) This is the hymnbook we still use in the church I serve today.

But the dreams of those committed to reunion were shattered in 1958 when the southern denomination failed to reach the three quarters majority needed. Some became convinced that the huge majority needed would never be gained without doing something radical to tweak the vote. By the mid-1960s union churches were permitted in the south, churches which belonged to both northern and southern streams. "A Presbytery may permit *one* (emphasis mine) of its constituent churches to enter into a 'federated' or 'union' relationship with a particular church of another Reformed body under the specific terms of an agreement entered into by the highest court of each denomination." (Chapter 31, Book Of Church Order, 1964.) But what if that program were expanded to allow union presbyteries? This way presbyteries in the former border states of the Confederacy and other areas with congregations from either denomination in close proximity to each other could have the union experience. It also meant that the next time the vote for reunion came up, as it invariably would, pastors and elders not examined by southern standards would be voting for reunion within the southern bloc. This change to the southern Book of Church Order was approved at the 1969 General Assembly meeting in Mobile, Alabama. The text of the amendment read in part:

> A Presbytery of this Church may unite with a Presbytery or Classis of the United Presbyterian Church in the United States of America, the Reformed Church in America, or another Reformed body to form a union Presbytery (Classis) with the approval of the Synod of jurisdiction of which the Presbytery (Classis) is a part...The purpose of this union shall be a furtherance of a united witness and mission, the administration of a single program of nurture, sustenance, and growth of the churches within the union Presbytery (Classis), and the oversight of all churches within its bounds by a union Presbytery (Classis), which will hold title to the properties of the uniting judicatories and provide the functions and fulfill the duties of a Presbytery (Classis), as specified in the Constitution of each Church. (Chapter 32, The Book Of Church Order)

Many southern evangelicals had come to oppose reunion in these years because they believed the northern denomination to be less committed to theological orthodoxy than they were. At the same time, some southern conservatives opposed it because it would mean accepting African-American elders and pastors as equals in their presbyteries. (In those days most black Presbyterian churches in the south belonged to the northern denomination, though there were a few exceptions to this rule.) Regardless of their motives, some southern Presbyterians challenged the legality of a change to the Book of Church Order to allow for union presbyteries by a simple majority vote instead of the three quarters vote needed for all other things related to reunion. The General Assembly Permanent Judicial Commission, whose decision, like that of the American Supreme Court, is final, ruled that this simply was a change to denominational polity. The fact that this change made reunion much more likely was ignored by the Judicial Commission.

A few years ago the former Presbytery Executive of one of the union presbyteries wrote a book, telling of his experiences in the 1970s. "What insights can the modern Presbyterian Church learn from this period in our history?" queried the catalogue in which the book was offered for sale. "I can tell you the lesson of union presbyteries," I joked with my father, who had lived through this period in the southern denomination. "If you can't win, cheat!"

Nowhere is the "if you can't win, cheat" ethic displayed more clearly, however, than in the imposition of a denominational trust clause upon the property of individual churches within the new denomination when it was formed in 1983. The property trust was a huge point of contention for southern churches; the northern denomination had this specifically in its constitution, but the southerners did not. Even with the advent of union presbyteries, the threat of presbyteries voting against reunion, simply because elders were afraid that they would no longer own their church property, was of real concern to those who had worked so long and hard for one denomination.

Occasionally an old southern Presbyterian, usually a pastor, will challenge me on this point. "It was always understood that the property of the churches was held in trust for the entire denomination," they say. Elders never say anything like that! Implication always is a dangerous place to stand in a legal contract; what matters is what is written, not the "understandings" or promises which accompanied the deed. An actual reading of the property chapter in the Book of Church Order from 1981 proves there was no trust clause until the final year of the existence of southern stream. This is so important that it is worth reprinting in its entirety.

Chapter 6
Incorporation and Property of a Particular Church

6-1 FOR AN UNINCORPORATED CHURCH

A particular church which is not incorporated, desiring to elect trustees, may select from its confirmed membership trustees or officers of like nature who shall have the power and authority to buy, sell, or mortgage property for the church, to accept and execute deeds as such trustees, to hold and defend titles to the same, to manage any permanent special funds entrusted to them for the furtherance of the purposes of the church. In the fulfillment of their duties such trustees shall be subject always to the authority, and shall act solely under the instructions of the congregation which they serve as trustees. The powers and duties of such trustees must not infringe upon the powers or duties of the Session or of the Board of Deacons. Such trustees shall be elected in regularly constituted congregational meetings.

6-2 FOR AN INCORPORATED CHURCH

If a particular church is incorporated, the provisions of its charter and by-laws must always be in accord with the Constitution of the Presbyterian Church in the United States. If the congregation is an incorporated body, all the members on the confirmed roll of that church shall be members of the corporation. The officers of the corporation, whether they be given the title "Trustee" or some other title, shall be elected from among the members of the corporation in a regularly constituted congregational meeting. The powers and duties of such officers must not infringe upon the powers and duties of the Session or the Board of Deacons. All funds collected for the support and expense of the church and for the benevolent purposes of the church shall be controlled and disbursed by the Session and the Board of Deacons as their relative authorities may from time to time be established and defined. To the officers of the corporation may be given by the charter and by-laws of the corporation any or all of the following responsibilities: the buying, selling, and mortgaging of the property for the church, the acquiring and conveying title to such property, the holding and defending title to the same, the managing of any permanent special funds entrusted to them for the furtherance of the purposes of the church, provided that such duties do not infringe upon the powers and duties of the Session or of the Board of Deacons. In buying, selling, and mortgaging real property such officers shall act solely under the authority of the corporation, granted in a duly commissioned meeting of the corporation.

6-3   If a church is dissolved by the Presbytery, or otherwise ceases to exist, *and no disposition has been made of its property* (emphasis mine), those who hold the title to the property shall deliver, convey and transfer to the Presbytery of which the church was a member, or to the authorized agents of the Presbytery, all property of the church; and the receipt and acquittance of the Presbytery, or its proper representatives, shall be a full and compete discharge of all liabilities of such persons holding the property of the church. The Presbytery receiving such property shall apply the same of the proceeds thereof at its discretion.

The preceding words are almost identical to those found in the 1964 Book of Church Order; interestingly, the 1950 edition of the Book of Church Order, the earliest version I have, has no chapter on *property*. Paragraph 6-3 above does appear in its entirety in 1950 in the section on congregational meetings (paragraph 164), with slight changes of verb tenses ("If a church shall be dissolved" as opposed to "If a church is dissolved"), almost as if property were an afterthought. Yet even here, the presbytery gets the property only if the congregation has not made other arrangements. And do note: There is NO trust clause.

If the trust was always understood in the south, why was it necessary to add it to the property chapter one year before reunion? According to those who agreed with this change at the time, it was necessary to bring property standards in the south in line with those in the north. If that is true, then why was it also necessary to add a closing paragraph to the original 1983 Book of Order, the first edition for the new denomination, making property standards different? This is how the section begins:

All property held by or for a particular church, a presbytery, a synod, the General Assembly, or the Presbyterian Church (U.S.A.), whether legal title is lodged in a corporation, a trustee or trustees, or an unincorporated association, and whether the property is used in programs of a particular church or of a more inclusive governing body or retained for the production of income, is held in trust nevertheless for the use and benefit of the Presbyterian Church (U.S.A.)…Whenever a particular church is formally dissolved by the presbytery, or has become extinct by reason of the dispersal of its members, the abandonment of its work, or other cause, such property as it may have shall be held, used, and applied for such uses, purposes, and trusts as the presbytery may direct, limit, and appoint, or such property may sold or disposed of as the presbytery may direct, in conformity with the *Constitution of the Presbyterian Church (U.S.A.)*. (G-8.0201, G-8.0401)

The "exemption" establishing different property standards is the final paragraph the property chapter, and reads as follows:

The provisions of this chapter shall apply to all particular churches of the Presbyterian Church (U.S.A.) except that any church which was not subject to a similar provision of the Constitution of the church of which it was a part, prior to the reunion of the Presbyterian Church in the United States and the United Presbyterian Church in the United States of America to form the Presbyterian Church (U.S.A.), shall be excused from that provision of this chapter if the congregation shall, within a period of eight years following the establishment of the Presbyterian Church (U.S.A.), vote to be exempt from such provision in a regularly called meeting and shall thereafter notify the presbytery of which is it a constituent church of such vote. The particular church to be so exempt shall hold title to its property and exercise its privileges of incorporation and property ownership *under the provisions of the Constitution to which it was subject immediately prior to the establishment of the Presbyterian*

Church (U.S.A.). (emphasis mine) This paragraph may not be amended. (G-8.0701)

Please note that last sentence; you will not read anything like it anywhere else in presbyterian theology or polity! The Westminster Standards may be and have been amended. The Book of Order is amended regularly, as often as the General Assembly meets. No previous assembly, be it session, presbytery, synod, or General Assembly, can bind the actions of a future one; no court of the Church can make a decision and place it in stone so that it can never be changed in the future. Yet here in G-8.0701, in 1983, church property rights were placed in stone for southern churches, forever. Even after a major polity re-write in 2011, and two decades after any church could assert its property rights under this provision, this unchangeable paragraph exists as G-4.0208. Why? The only answer must be, because it was necessary in order to calm southern fears about losing their property in 1983. Without this, reunion would not have happened.

But also note the previous sentence in that block quotation. When a church exempted itself from the property chapter of the new denomination, it was then held "under the provisions of the Constitution to which it was subject immediately prior to the establishment of the Presbyterian Church (U.S.A.)." Many, many southern churches exercised this right; when I arrived at my first call in 1988, I discovered that it had held its congregational meeting one month after the reunion in 1983. Though the exemption was good for eight years, expiring in 1991, that congregation waited only weeks to exercise this special, unchangeable right. Why would they do this? It was because they had been told that this action would guarantee that their property would remain in their possession. I was told the very same thing in my seminary polity class in 1987. But that was not true.

It is important to note the wording of the unamendable paragraph; the property of exemption congregations would then be held under the provisions of their old constitution as it was at the time of reunion, not as it was only a year previous and going back for decades. Most of the elders voting to join the new denomination would not have known about those changes; neither would they have known the exact wording of the 1982/1983 version of the Book of Church Order. It is telling to note that the unamendable paragraph refers to a document unavailable to most people after 1983; this was before the internet, and the only way to get a copy was to order one from denominational offices in Atlanta, Georgia, in the brief months between its publication and the presbytery votes for or against reunion, which also began in 1982.

The only reason I have a copy of the 1982/1983 edition of the Book of Church Order is because I had a friend, the former Stated Clerk of our presbytery, who was a bit of a packrat and a polity wonk, who was willing to share his copy with me. (Fred went to be with the Lord in September of 2012, just days before I completed the rough draft of this book. He never got to read it.) My guess is that the vast majority of Presbyterians have never seen one. For this reason, I present the full terms under which southern property rights were "saved" at the time of reunion, for those who used the property exemption of the unamendable paragraph. This may be a shock to some reading these words, but your church property does not belong to you after all, in spite of your efforts.

Chapter 6
Church Property

6-1   If a particular church is not incorporated, it may, at a regularly constituted congregational meeting, elect certain of its confirmed members as trustees, to hold title to property in trust for the benefit of the particular church and of the Presbyterian Church in the United States. The trustees have power and authority to buy, sell or mortgage property for the church, to accept and execute deeds and to manage any permanent special funds entrusted to them for church purposes. In buying, selling or mortgaging real property, the trustees shall act under the instructions of the congregation adopted in a regularly constituted meeting. Their powers and duties cannot infringe upon the powers or duties of the Session or the Board of Deacons. The trustees do not hold title to personal property or have responsibility for it except to the extent expressly given to them.

6-2   If a particular church is incorporated, the provisions of its charter and bylaws must be in accord with the Constitution of the Presbyterian Church in the United States. All of its confirmed members on the active roll are members of the corporation. The officers of the corporation, by whatever name they are given, shall be elected from the confirmed members of the corporation in a regularly constituted congregational meeting. The officers of the corporation may be given any or all of the following responsibilities: holding title to church property for the benefit of the corporation and the Presbyterian Church in the United States; acquiring and conveying title to the property; buying, selling and mortgaging the property of the church; and managing any permanent funds entrusted to them for church purposes. In buying, selling and mortgaging real property, the officers shall act under the authority of the corporation granted in a duly constituted meeting of the corporation. Powers and duties of the officers cannot infringe upon the powers and duties of the Session or the Board of Deacons, who maintain control and disbursement of all funds collected for the support and expense of the church and for the benevolent purposes of the church.

6-3   *All property held by or for a particular church, whether legal title is lodged in a corporation, a trustee or trustees, or an unincorporated association, and whether the property is used in programs of the particular church or retained for the production of income is held in trust nevertheless for the use and benefit of the Presbyterian Church in the United States.* (emphasis mine)

6-4   If a particular church is dissolved by the Presbytery, attempts by either majority or unanimous vote to withdraw from the Presbyterian Church in the United States, or otherwise ceases to exist or function as a member of the Presbyterian Church in the United States, any property that it may have shall be within the control of the Presbytery and may be held for designated purposes or sold or disposed of in such a manner as the Presbytery, in its discretion, may direct.

6-5 The relationship to the Presbyterian Church in the United States of a particular church can be severed only by constitutional action on the part of the Presbytery (4-2). If there is a schism within the membership of a particular church and the Presbytery is unable to effect a reconciliation or a division into separate churches within the Presbyterian Church in the United States (see 16-7), the Presbytery shall determine if one of the factions is entitled to the property because it is identified by the Presbytery as the true church within the Presbyterian Church in the United States. This determination does not depend upon which faction received the majority vote within the particular church at the time of the schism.

6-6 Nothing in this chapter shall be construed to render a particular church, church court, or its property liable for the debt or obligations of any other church court.

6-7 Nothing in this chapter shall be construed to limit the power of Presbytery to receive and dismiss churches with their property, provided such requests are made in proper order.

6-8 Nothing in this chapter shall be construed to require a particular church to seek or obtain the consent or approval of any church court above the level of the particular church in order to buy, sell or mortgage the property of that particular church in the conduct of its affairs as a church of the PCUS.

6-9 The provisions of 14-5 and 14-6, and other sections in this Constitution setting forth the manner in which decisions are made, renewed and corrected within the Presbyterian Church in the United States, are applicable to all matters relating to property.

6-10 This Chapter is declaratory of principles to which the Presbyterian Church in the United States and its antecedent church bodies have adhered from the inception of the presbyterian form of church government.

Last things first, the final paragraph, 6-10, is demonstrably untrue. In fact, since colonial times Presbyterian churches held their properties in many different ways. For example, according to its deed, should the church I served in rural North Carolina ever cease to exist, the land will revert to the heirs of the Smith family, who donated their land to the congregation for its building in 1903. Many churches in the rural south have such reversionary clauses, and never in their wildest dreams did those who donated the land imagine they were giving it in perpetuity to a denomination miles and decades away.

Compare and contrast the different versions of the property chapter as it existed in 1982 and 1983. Suddenly a presbytery, which the year before had only the codified, explicit right to deal with property if the church ceased to exist AND no provision for the property had been made, now had the right to seize the property of any church attempting to leave the denomination without following proper procedure. It also had the right, only granted in 1982, to give the property to a minority of the members in a congregational dispute since their loyalty to the denomination was the one criterion by which the "true church" could be measured. (See Chapter 19, The Biblical Case For Separation, to appreciate the "true" irony of such a definition.) More troublingly, here and only here is it declared that the church property does not belong to the individual congregations, but is held in trust for the denomination. That was never in the constitution before the summer of 1982, and a few months later the voting for reunion began.

Even the wording of the unamendable paragraph is written to cover up the new reality: the exempted church "shall hold title to its property...". How many southerners read that phrase and stopped there, thinking the matter solved, without considering "under the provisions of the Constitution to which it was subject immediately prior to the establishment of the Presbyterian Church (U.S.A.)"? Most of them did not have a copy of that final edition of the southern Book of Church Order when they started to vote. For most of them, it would have been like reading through the fine print of a contract; do you always do that when buying a car or a house? No, they just decided to trust what they had been told, and in doing so signed away the birthright of their property.

Do not tell me that the southern elders understood for what they were voting, lulled into a sense of security by the unamendable paragraph. Even the pastors did not understand completely. Two decades later, sitting in a meeting of our presbytery council, I thought we might have to call an ambulance for a pastor who discovered that his congregation did not own its property. "But I was there in 1982," he sputtered. "Jim Andrews (Stated Clerk of the southern denomination at the time) promised us that property would be no hindrance to reunion, that it had been taken care of!" And I guess that, in a way, it was; just not the way this pastor had thought it "taken care of". And he was no novice to things Presbyterian. He had been a pastor for over a decade by 1983. He had not moved from place to place in the intervening years; he knew the presbytery leadership, and was part of the presbytery leadership. If anyone should have known, it was this man. But that day in presbytery council, all the current Presbytery Executive could say to him was, "I'm sorry. I can't go by what Jim Andrews told you then. I can only go by what is written in the constitution now." And what is not written, since the unamendable paragraph refers to a property chapter mostly unprinted since 1982.

What, after all, were thousands of southern churches trying to accomplish in the new denomination by declaring the exception allowed them under the property chapter of the Book of Order between 1983 and 1991? Without a doubt, they were trying to say, "Our property is not held in trust for a denomination, it belongs to us." But that is not what happened. What in fact did that declaration get them that is different from other PC(USA) churches, legally? It is found in paragraph 6-8 from 1982; they are allowed to "to buy, sell or mortgage the property" of the church without seeking the approval of their presbyteries so long as it is doing so while remaining in the denomination, to which the property still ultimately belongs. That's it. Nothing more is granted. It seems like a mighty small gain to deserve the super-extraordinary promise of an unamendable paragraph.

There is only one reason to explain the inclusion of the unamendable paragraph just months after the previous chapter to which it referred was changed; it was a necessary deception to bring about the required three quarters of southern presbyteries voting for reunion in 1983. Union presbyteries on their own could not accomplish it. The lesson of those who justify the means by the end, is always, "If you can't win, cheat, because you surely are right."

It is important to note here that in 2012 many civil courts are ruling that the property trust clause of the PC (USA) constitution is not binding upon the churches. They are finding, in some parts of the country at least, that a trust cannot be set up by its beneficiary without the express consent of the other party. In other words, though the denomination has declared that all property of all churches ultimately belongs to it, unless the church itself amends its charter or deed to declare the same thing, that may not be the case. Of course, given Paul's instructions in 1 Corinthians 6, Christians ought to avoid suing each other in secular courts. At this point the best thing to do is to sit down with presbytery representatives and hammer out an agreement by which a church may leave with its property, as the presbytery also is empowered to do. And then we remain transparent and keep our promises. This is what we have done in my presbytery. (See Chapter 20)

With the previous paragraph I had hoped that I had said all that was needed in an already long and complicated chapter. But I was wrong. On October 30, 2012, the General Assembly Permanent Judicial Commission, beyond which there is no appeal in Presbyterian polity, released a ruling with threatened to turn on its head every gracious dismissal policy adopted by any presbytery within the denomination. In the case of *Wilber Tom, David Hawbecker and Thomas Conrad vs. The Presbytery of San Francisco*, the GAPJC ruled that the presbytery had erred by releasing Community Presbyterian Church in Danville, CA, to the Evangelical Presbyterian Church under the terms of a presbytery dismissal policy adopted unanimously by the Presbytery of San Francisco in 2009. Under that agreement, the church agreed to pay the presbytery a lump sum of $108,640, plus an annual commitment of $42,500 for targeted PCUSA missionaries, ministries, and ministers, to be paid quarterly for the five years following the church's dismissal. But this was not enough for Louisville. In its decision the GAPJC acknowledged that, while it cannot undo the actions of San Francisco Presbytery at this point, it now would "exercise its declaratory authority to provide guidance to lower councils and *to prevent future violations* (emphasis mine)." The decision continued, "When a congregation seeks dismissal…it is the responsibility of the presbytery to fulfill its fiduciary duty under the Trust Clause. This fiduciary duty requires that the presbytery exercise due diligence regarding the value of the property of the congregation seeking dismissal. Due diligence, of necessity, includes not only an evaluation of the spiritual needs of the congregation and its circumstances but also financial analysis of the value of the property at stake. Payments for per capita or mission obligations are not satisfactory substitutes for the separate evaluation of the property held in trust."

What more can I say? Will this ruling void the gracious dismissal policy passed unanimously by my own presbytery in 2009? (See Chapter 20) What would qualify as "financial analysis", and how would such information be applied to the dismissal process? At this time it is too early for anyone to know. How would the GAPJC's ruling be enforced in a cash-strapped denomination? The presbyteries don't have funds for multiple, drawn out legal battles in civil courts against departing congregations. Neither do the synods. Would the General Assembly offices sue presbyteries? I do not know. But as the denomination collapses, this much is clear to me: the dogs are snarling over the scraps. I simply will repeat what I said in chapter 2: "Ironically, Religious Liberalism inherently must know that there is no unity in diversity apart from the limits brought by the fundamentals, because in practical application it seeks to impose a non-theological unity from above, through political constructs and maneuvers, intimidation and black-balling, and the embracing of the political agendas of secular liberalism."

CHAPTER SIXTEEN: JURIMANDERING

I was ordained as a pastor in 1988 by Wilmington Presbytery. It had 76 churches. It was a left-over of the old southern denomination, and on the chopping block. As I mentioned in the previous chapter, most African-American churches in the south at the time of reunion belonged to the northern denomination. However, few churches of the southern denomination were in the north. Because of this, after the victory of reunion in 1983, the overlapping presbyteries of the two denominations in the south had to be reorganized. The northern presbyteries pretty much remained as they were.

Somewhere along the way it was decided that the ten southern presbyteries of North Carolina should be merged with the corresponding northern presbyteries to form five mega-presbyteries in the state. The churches were not happy! What about our traditions? What about our camps? What about our presbytery offices? One of the more humorous realities of the months following official reorganization in 1989 was that Camp Kirkwood, located outside Burgaw, NC, and Camp Monroe, located near Laurinburg, NC, saw a large increase of giving from area Presbyterians who had not been there in years – as the only soon to be remaining vestiges of Wilmington and Fayetteville Presbyteries, respectively, nostalgia became a windfall for them!

As hard as this reorganization may have been for the larger southern presbyteries, how much more difficult must it have been for the African-American churches of the northern presbyteries? The new presbytery four older ones were forced to form had 193 churches. Wilmington brought 75 of its 76, one being moved north to the mega New Hope Presbytery. Fayetteville brought 90 of its 100, the other ten being combined with the new Charlotte Presbytery. But between the two smaller northern presbyteries, Cape Fear and Yadkin, there were only 28 churches. These Presbyterians, whose ancestors had been told by the ancestors of their new white colleagues in ministry that they would be happier associating with a different denomination than that of the PCUS, now went from being the only people in their presbyteries to being about 15% of the presbytery.

And percentages were not the only change. For example, by this time southern presbyteries were used to streamlining business in their meetings by having the details hammered out in committee meetings. The corresponding northern presbyteries were used to fighting it out on the floor of the larger, plenary sessions. The practical result of this was that black Presbyterians came to presbytery meetings ready to argue, only to find that the white Presbyterians had already done the arguing and settled the issue. This was not the recipe for a smooth transition!

Because I originally volunteered to work wherever the presbytery nominating committee thought I was needed, I quickly wound up on what many considered the worst assignment for a new pastor, Sessional Records. It was a thankless, pencil-pushing job, sort of like ancient foot-washing, reserved for the youngest and most inexperienced of servants! But because I was willing to do it, I became its chair in one year, and got a seat on Presbytery Council. (A presbytery or synod council, or even the General Assembly Council, functions like a session in a local congregation, the smaller body guiding the larger one. However, all its actions must be approved by the full presbytery, synod, or GA; sessions do not need approval from their congregations. In this sense, these three higher councils serve more like corporate steering committees, made up of chairs from the other presbytery committees, plus staff personnel.) It was an eye-opening experience for me at the tender age of 27! And I saw firsthand the conflict brewing between black and white leadership.

Around 1990 a young white seminary graduate came into our presbytery, and the nominating committee, as had been the procedure up until that time, rubber-stamped the people he requested to be on his commission to ordain and install. I had done the same thing myself in 1988; my father and an old college professor, an ordained Methodist minister, were included in my commission to ordain and install. But things were different now; I don't think there were any African-American churches in Wilmington Presbytery, but there were at least 29 in Coastal Carolina. No one from those churches was included on the commission for the young white seminary graduate in 1990. On the floor of the presbytery meeting no one thought about this; the original commission suggested by the young man and approved by the nominating committee, then was approved by the entire presbytery without discussion.

But the Black Caucus of the presbytery was not happy. Business as usual would not be acceptable, and they demanded a special called meeting of presbytery to form a new commission, which would include "racial/ethnic" members. The meeting was called. (This was not a difficult task; according to the Book of Order of the time, "The moderator shall call a special meeting at the request...of two ministers and two elders, the elders being of different churches.") In preparation for the meeting, the nominating committee prepared a new slate of pastors and elders to make up the new commission; with it elected, the meeting adjourned, having accomplished the purpose for which it was called.

There was just one problem: there still were no African-American members on the new commission! Bear in mind, the presbytery was huge and newly formed; none of us knew everybody. But the nominating committee, run by an old Presbyterian who apparently did not like having his work second-guessed, had placed the names of an American Indian, a pastor native to the country of India, and a Latino on the new commission. They were, after all, "racial/ethnic". In my later report on this to Presbytery Council, I wrote, "How could this not be perceived as anything but saying to the Black Caucus, 'We will do what you say, but not what you want.'?" Of course, when the truth came out, unhappiness among the black leadership became outrage. However, the young man in question was not warned of the crisis, and went ahead with his service of ordination and installation. Then he promptly married a couple who had been waiting for the church finally to get a preacher.

The Black Caucus filed a remedial complaint with the Synod Permanent Judicial Commission, and I was elected with two other people to the "Committee of Council" representing the presbytery in the case. One of them wanted to argue that the complaint should be thrown out on a technicality; the Caucus had failed to file the complaint within the required timeframe by a few days. But the other two of us insisted that this was wrong. "No," I said, "we're going to go before the PJC and say, 'We were a bad presbytery. Slap us on the wrist if you must. But don't set aside this young man's ordination, ESPECIALLY when he just married some folks.'" Mr. Technicality failed to make it to the hearing, and before it convened the other member and I sat down with the representative from the Black Caucus to explain the situation. We had learned that there was no problem with the young pastor; the preacher he had requested for his commission was a black woman pastor from the Methodist Church. The three of us became friends that day, and the PJC did censure the presbytery without setting aside the pastor's ordination.

Given the difficulties encountered by jamming together four presbyteries, why did reorganization in the south not simply leave the existing southern presbyteries in place and integrate the African-American congregations now within their geographical bounds? Though I do not remember how many of Yadkin or Cape Fear churches existed within the bounds of Wilmington, since Wilmington only lost one of its 76 churches, it pretty much existed as it always had, except now pushed together with its historic rival, Fayetteville Presbytery. (Think Duke and The University of North Carolina having to share the same gymnasium, and you'll get the idea.) What would happen to the much smaller Black Caucus as the giants wrestled in the sandbox in the 1990s? Did they get the attention they needed? My guess is that they would say they did not.

So what was the purpose of forming five giant presbyteries where there had once been ten in the old southern denomination? The best argument I have heard for it was that many of the African-American congregations had certain churches to which they had looked for leadership. If southern presbytery lines had severed those ties, it would have been much more difficult for those congregations to acclimate to the new denomination. Less persuasive but more prominent in the arguments after 1983 was that bigger would be better. With mega-presbyteries in North Carolina, there would be less duplication of efforts and more consolidation of bureaucracies to (you guessed it) do more mission. Certainly mega-presbyteries would be able to hire two or three executives, plus a large staff to accomplish the work of the Church. In my work with Sessional Records, I got to meet a lot of folks on the Fayetteville side of Coastal Carolina Presbytery. At that time, our committee would go out annually to pre-arranged meeting places to assist clerks in their records keeping. Sometimes they would complain about the size of presbytery, and I would say, "That's true, but if we weren't together, I wouldn't know you now!" And when I said that, I was thinking geographically, not numerically. There are plenty of much bigger presbyteries in the western part of the United States. Kansas has two; one is in the northern half of the state, and one is in the southern half.

But the North Carolina mega-presbyteries have come at a steep price. They have robbed most of the churches of any sense of ownership in the larger body. For example, Coastal Carolina's Sessional Records Committee under my leadership was meeting in small churches in part because we knew they were too small to host a meeting of presbytery any more. My current church's sanctuary is large enough to hold a meeting of our mega-presbytery, but we never have hosted one because we only have four adult bathrooms (two of each) and no elevator to assist people from the sanctuary level down to the Fellowship Hall. And the physical plant of my church is much larger than that of most of our churches.

So, what was the true purpose of mega-presbyteries? People who have been around a lot longer than I have are convinced that one purpose was to water-down the conservative southern vote in national referendums, a variation on the union presbytery "if you can't win, cheat" tactic. While I do not usually subscribe to conspiracy theories, one cannot deny that whenever there has been a national referendum on any changes to the constitution since 1989, where there would have been ten or more North Carolina presbyteries voting in the past, now there are only five. And each presbytery gets one vote in such referendums. For example, New Castle Presbytery, in the geographical north and on the Delmarva peninsula, has 53 churches. Coastal Carolina has about 190. Salem has about 150. In New England some presbyteries have about 30 churches. So, as I have said on the floor of Synod, is a North Carolina vote worth only one third, or one fifth, or even less than a northern vote? The practical answer is yes, and bureaucrats hate to have the question raised.

Sometimes I have been challenged on this "because national referendums are supposed to be like the Senate, not the House."

But this is not true. The American bicameral system does not come from Presbyterianism, it comes from England's House of Lords and House of Commons. And the idea that each state automatically gets only two senators, while its population determines the number of its congressmen in the House of Representatives, comes from Benjamin Franklin at the Constitutional Convention in Philadelphia in 1787; Franklin was many things, but a Presbyterian he was not! Fairness demands that the mega-presbyteries of the South be broken up so there is a parity of size with small population presbyteries in other sections of the country. But no one is addressing this need at the national level.

Another practical train wreck of mega-presbyteries is that the right hand does not know what the left hand is doing. The old adage is true that knowledge is power, and the only folks who really know what is going on are the people who meet regularly with presbytery staff. When I rotated off Synod Council in 2007 I also lost my ex-officio seat on our Presbytery Council. That lower council has itself gotten smaller, and much more easy for bureaucrats to manage since the days I served. Up through at least 2006, Presbytery Council had 30-40 members. In 2007 the presbytery adopted a new "neighborhood" organization. Council has been reduced to 11 members, plus staff; as I write this two people on Council are married to each other, as if input from the 150 churches were not already small enough.

The time has come to put an end to mega-presbyteries, at least in North Carolina. If helping the northern African-American churches adapt to the change of being numerical minorities within the southern white majority presbyteries truly was the goal, after more than twenty years it either has been reached or it never will be. However, those who benefit from the system as it is, like presbytery executives, are entrenched now in such a way that changing the status quo will be very difficult unless the churches themselves rise up and insist that business as usual is no longer acceptable.

A few years ago, while still on Presbytery Council, the problem of churches not giving financial support to presbytery came up when staff positions were going to have to be cut; after all, people have a hard time supporting something in which they feel they have no ownership. However, in the main presbytery meeting a commissioner made a motion that representatives should be sent first to those churches which had not sent money, to understand the problem before those staff jobs were eliminated. Most people on Council did not want to go, but I always have enjoyed going to the churches, I always did it with Sessional Records, and I already had a good relationship with people in the two churches to which I volunteered to go.

Both were very productive and informative meetings. One church was theologically evangelical, and concerned about the direction of the denomination; the other was sociologically conservative, and did not feel the presbytery shared their values. But both commented, as I had heard many times in Sessional Records meetings through the years, that the presbytery was too big. I included this in my report.

A month or so later I was included by accident in an e-mail exchange between one of the secretaries at presbytery office and the presbytery executive. She was asking him why the churches' comments about making the presbytery smaller were being omitted from the official report, which was to be presented to the entire presbytery in October. His answer was that they needed to consider the source of that information (me!), and that he found it very hard to believe that churches would come up with this critique on their own. Needless to say, that made me angry. At the October meeting, after we had heard once again about how tight money was and how difficult it is to govern such a large presbytery, I stood up and made a motion that we petition Synod to break us up into two or three presbyteries. This was without any warning, without any reports for the commissioners to consider, and there was no way it could pass. But when a sizable minority then voted "YES!", my point was made.

In recent years I have focused much more on the needs of my congregation, and let the presbytery falter on its own, without my interference. However, writing this book has brought many frustrations of past years to mind, along with the desire to see some of the necessary changes made to help the denomination which I am leaving. While it seems unlikely that my weak words will cause a shift back to theological fundamentals and away from orthopraxy, or back to confessionalism, accountability could begin to be restored as churches throw off the shackles of mega-presbyteries, presbytery executives, and presbytery staffs.

At the April 2012 meeting of my presbytery, after listening once again to the litany of problems faced because of budget shortfalls, the chair of the Finance Committee actually was off the podium and halfway to his seat, and the Moderator moving on to new business, before I could get to a microphone to address the situation. "Madame Moderator, I would like to make a comment to the Chair of Finance." He dutifully returned to the microphone, and I continued. "Last January I attended the organizational meeting of ECO, the Evangelical Covenant Order of Presbyterians, in Orlando, Florida. One of the really good ideas they presented was to have no more than 25 or 30 churches per presbytery. I believe that in our discussion of financial difficulties, we should seriously consider asking Synod to break us up into five presbyteries of 30 churches each. Now, I know that presbyteries so small would not be able to afford executives and the current staff. But all a presbytery that small would need is a Stated Clerk and a filing cabinet in a back room of one of the churches to hold the paperwork. That may seem sort of radical to us today, but it was a system which worked very well for our ancestors prior to World War 2. We could even sell the current presbytery office and divide the funds between the new presbyteries." And then I sat down.

I have a good friend who serves on the session of a nearby Presbyterian church. She told me that at their next meeting, when their pastor reported what I had said, the other elders said, "That's a good idea." And prior to the July 2012 meeting churches were asked to respond to a series of questions, including, "How could the ministry of the presbytery be better accomplished?" I wrote that breaking it up into 5 presbyteries would be better. But here's the thing – making the presbytery smaller, with fewer churches, was the most common response I read from all the churches. The desire is there. Hopefully the action will follow now.

CHAPTER SEVENTEEN: ECCLESIASTICAL DEFIANCE IS ECCLESIASTICAL ASSAULT

As my own church has grappled with the possibility of leaving the PC(USA) for another Reformed body, I have been given the daunting task of trying to explain what is wrong now, and how it happened. Certainly this book is part of that explanation. But because it is so complicated, one meeting of information was not enough to cover everything people need to know to make an informed decision. As the old teaching adage goes, the mind can only absorb what the seat can bear. To that end, our session called a series of three congregational meetings simply for the purpose of educating the people in the pews.

The first meeting dealt with theological concerns. The second meeting focused on polity. The third meeting was on ethics, especially orthopraxy, doing the right thing, as an essential of Religious Liberalism. After the second meeting, an Elder came up to me and asked, "Why are we doing all this? Why are we bogging down in polity? That's a word I've never even heard before! Can't you just explain it in one sentence?" I had to think about this for a few minutes. Finally I said, "We're trying to build a case as to why some of us believe it is time to leave the PC(USA). If I had to boil it down to one sentence, it would be something like this – The PC(USA) has abandoned theological essentials in favor of ethical ones, and its polity has been so undermined that there is no accountability, so it is very unlikely that we ever will be able to return it to its theological roots." "That I can understand," she replied.

Of course, if I had to boil it down to one story, I would just tell this one. I am not going to reveal the name of the presbytery involved, though anyone who has been paying attention to Presbyterian stuff in the last decade probably already knows which one it is. Certainly their leadership will know of whom I am speaking. But this is what happens when theology is abandoned, orthopraxy is embraced, and no one is willing to hold anyone accountable. It is the convoluted and shameful story of "Rogue" Presbytery and its use of presbyterian government to defy the plain teaching of scripture and the will of the vast majority of the denomination. If it seems complicated, that's because it is; exhaustion of those struggling for basic fairness seems to be one of the goals. I readily apologize for all the detail necessary to tell this story accurately, and, should you find your eyes drooping within the next few pages, I give you permission simply to move on to the next chapter. But first you must read the next paragraph!

What's so wrong with defiance if you don't agree with a rule, if you think it is immoral or unjust? Indeed, Civil Disobedience has a long and noble history in American life. But, unlike the State, the Church has no means of enforcing majority rule. Physical enforcement only comes when Christians sue each other in civil courts and the government comes to the aid of the winning party. However, lawsuits between Christians are strongly discouraged by the Apostle Paul in 1 Corinthians 6. When the Church is acting like the Church, its members act in good faith with one another, even with those with whom they disagree. Make no mistake about it: Ecclesiastical Defiance is Ecclesiastical Assault, from which there is no practical defense. For this reason, the proper course in denominations is for the minority to submit in good faith to the will of the majority. Those of the minority troubled by the majority decision should still have the freedom to work unmolested to change the opinion of the majority enough to where they become the majority. (Certainly this right exists in the PC(USA).) They have the freedom to withhold funds. They also have the freedom to leave, a freedom being exercised by myself and many others in the minority today, using the legal processes available to us within the denomination. Had Rogue Presbytery and its enabling allies of the Synod and General Assembly Offices forsaken defiance and pursued the course of submission to fidelity and chastity while working for changes in the written standard between 1997 and 2011, this chapter would not be necessary. They could have fought to win the hearts and minds of their opponents through mutual respect and reasoned argument. Instead, they bludgeoned the majority into submission to the will of their elite and unassailable minority. When they seek to assign blame for the break-up of large parts of the PC(USA) in the years ahead, they need look no further than themselves. When people are assaulted repeatedly they tend to want to move out of that neighborhood.

It's even more likely to happen when those charged with defending law-abiding citizens refuse to do their duty, and instead congratulate law-breakers for their bravery.

The story of Rogue Presbytery's defiance begins, for my purposes, in 1997 when the PC(USA) adopted language in its constitution which attempted to address the moral problem of ordaining actively gay individuals with a political solution. Like the disaster of prohibition in the 1920s, that "noble experiment" pushed by Religious Liberalism to address the social problems of alcoholism, it could not last for long. The words of "Amendment B", as it continued to be called by its opponents for the decade and a half of its inclusion, as if it really didn't become a part of the constitution by repeated majority votes, were these: "Those who are called to office in the church are to lead a life in obedience to Scripture and in conformity to the historic confessional standards of the church. Among these standards is the requirement to live either in fidelity within the covenant of marriage between a man and a woman (W-4.9001), or in chastity in singleness. Persons refusing to repent of any self-acknowledged practice which the confessions call sin shall not be ordained/or installed as deacons, elders, or ministers of the Word and Sacrament." (G-6.0106b) Without a doubt, this was not the best wording for which one might have hoped. Focusing standards upon practices "which the confessions call sin" rather than focusing scripture itself led to all sorts of hysterical rantings from opponents. Some combed the older confessions for archaic language. (I heard one mockingly complain that Westminster's condemnation of "allowing, tolerating, keeping of stews, and resorting to them", "stews" being another word for "brothel" in 1647, condemned all churches today which sold Brunswick Stew at fundraisers!) Some focused on minor sins to which humans might be prone, like being careless in our duties to God, or being indiscreet; some emphasized "eye of the beholder" sins, like immodesty in apparel or idleness. Some found sins identified in past centuries, but not considered sinful today, such as "the making of any representation of God…either inwardly in our mind, or outwardly in any kind of image…" (Larger Catechism Answer #109). Some even went so far as to "self-acknowledge" these practices and demand that church permanent judicial commissions take action against them. At least no PJC joined in the mockery by taking up such "challenges". And there were others who complained that this wording of "Amendment B" elevated the confessions above scripture, as if anything actually said in the Bible really mattered to them!

One of the best aspects of G-1.0106b's wording was that it did not single out homosexual behavior for condemnation. Instead, it held officers, whether they perceived themselves as being gay or straight, to the same standard: sexual fidelity in marriage, or chastity in singleness. The definition of marriage referenced in the fidelity/chastity standard, paragraph W-4.9001 in a different section of the Book of Order, includes the sentences, "Marriage is a civil contract between a man and a woman. For Christians marriage is a covenant through which a man and a woman are called to live out together before God their lives of discipleship. In a service of Christian marriage a lifelong commitment is made by a woman and a man to each other, publically witnessed and acknowledged by the community of faith."

It is significant to note that the General Assembly in 2012 was asked to change the wording of this paragraph from "between a man and a woman" to "between two people", thus allowing for gay marriage. Gay marriage is the next battleground for gay normalization advocates. Up through 2012 the General Assembly Permanent Judicial Commission's ruling on this matter has been that, since the definition of marriage exists as between a man and a woman in the Presbyterian Constitution, Presbyterian pastors are not permitted to officiate at gay union services while calling them marriages. Historically, dissenters have had the right actively to support, passively to submit, or peaceably to withdraw; but open defiance of the majority's will never has been an option. This standard is found in the 1758 Plan of Union between the Synods of New York and Philadelphia: "…when any matter is determined by a major vote, every member shall either actively concur with or passively submit to such determination; or if his conscience permit him to do neither, he shall…peaceably withdraw from our communion without attempting to make any schism." Defiance is not supposed to be an option. The Stated Clerk of the General Assembly reaffirmed in a letter dated August 21, 2002, that defiance is not an option for Presbyterians.

This was necessary because in 2002 pastors were performing gay marriage services already, and some pastors were revealing themselves to be involved in homosexual relationships.

In 2012, when the General Assembly of the PC(USA) chose not to change the definition of marriage from "a man and a woman" to "two people", opting instead for a two year study of the issue and moving the final vote to 2014, some pastors vowed "ecclesiastical disobedience" as they continued to perform gay wedding services. In fact, the original Vice-Moderator of the 2012 General Assembly had herself performed such a ceremony only months before; once the truth of her defiance was known she resigned from the position 36 hours after being elected. The defiant are unquestionably and openly breaking their ordination vows, yet they do so without fear of censure; they will not be reprimanded by their presbyteries, and they will not be defrocked, unlike many who are charged with schism. (See Chapter 20) Rogue Presbytery is one of those which helped to set the stage for this bizarre and unfair turn of events.

In 1999 a new pastor came into Rogue Presbytery, declaring from the beginning that he was gay and living with another man. He did not come to pastor a church, but to lead an organization within Rogue Presbytery dedicated to gay ordination, That All May Freely Serve. Already the Stated Clerk of Rogue had signed the original incorporation papers for the organization, and "TAMFS" had its own office in the presbytery office building. Intent upon forcing the issue, the gay pastor openly declared his defiance on the floor of the 2001 General Assembly, and repeatedly on-line.

At this point an Elder, who was a lawyer in the Washington, D.C., area also, brought charges against the gay pastor within his Rogue Presbytery, citing violation of ordination vows, and, oddly enough, heresy. (This layman obviously did not realize that heresy as an offense is a lost cause in a denomination without theological essentials and with an orthopraxy of inclusivity.) Once the original complaint was received by the presbytery's stated clerk, the procedure which he had to follow was spelled out in Chapter X of the Discipline section of the Book of Order. D-10.0103 said, "Upon receipt of a written statement of an alleged offense, the…clerk of presbytery, without taking further inquiry, shall then report to the governing body only that an offense has been alleged without naming the accused or the nature of the alleged offense, and refer the statement immediately to an investigating committee." Ordinarily the Stated Clerk would make this report at a meeting of presbytery, and, at the same time, name an investigating committee, which the presbytery then would approve.

An Investigating Committee in the Presbyterian Church is like a grand jury in the American criminal court system. They review the evidence in a case and decide whether it is enough to warrant a trial. If they do not find enough evidence, the case is closed. Now, remember that the Stated Clerk of Rogue Presbytery also was the incorporator for That All May Freely Serve in his presbytery, where the gay pastor now was working, in the same office building as the presbytery office. This clerk named a four member Investigating Committee. Three of the four either were members of That All May Freely Serve, or had made financial contributions to it! Not surprisingly, they found no grounds for a Disciplinary Case.

By this time it was 2002, and I was reading about this gross violation of majority rule in the denominational press. I called a friend, who at the time was the Synod Executive, and asked what might be done from that level to correct Rogue Presbytery's defiance. He said, "Well, I can't do anything, but if I were to receive a letter from a pastor requesting that an Administrative Review be conducted concerning Rogue Presbytery's handling of this situation, I would have to form a committee." I said, "I'll have the letter in the mail to you this week."

Since the Investigating Committee of Rogue Presbytery had found no grounds for a case, the case had never made it to the presbytery Permanent Judicial Commission. Had this happened, as in the American criminal court system, the losing side could have appealed to the next higher court, the Synod PJC; the losing side at that level could have appealed to the General Assembly PJC. However, the disciplinary case against the openly gay pastor had died in the amazingly biased Investigating Committee.

Thus, Administrative Review was the only option left open to the Synod. "Administrative Review is the supervision of lower governing bodies by higher governing bodies within the whole system of government of the church for the maintenance of its peace, unity, and purity." (D-1.0200) Administrative Review was being pushed from the Office of the General Assembly's Stated Clerk also; in the same August 21, 2002, letter reiterating that defiance of the constitution is not an option, he encouraged governing bodies to use the administrative review process, one with which most of us were unfamiliar, instead of the judicial process. The Clerk's office did not give details on how this should be done. But it was a way forward, a way to do something, so the current Synod Executive began working on it. At its November 2002 meeting, Synod Council voted to elect an Administrative Review Committee (ARC), to be named by the Executive, a man I knew who was greatly troubled by Rogue Presbytery's illegal and unfair defiance.

But my friend was completing his work in the Synod as well, and soon moved on. In January 2003, when the charge to the Administrative Review Committee was presented to and approved by Synod Council, it was through another man with deep roots in the Synod. Since he plays such a large part in this section of the story, I will refer to him as "Reverend Synod". He also was very much in favor of gay ordination, and as I learned subsequently, part of that "if you can't win, cheat" school of church politics which led to reunion in 1983.

In addition to this change, something odd had happened between November 2002 and January 2003. The Book of Order was very specific as to the scope of the review. The higher governing body "shall determine" five things: a. The proceedings have been correctly recorded; b. The proceedings have been regular and in accordance with the Constitution; c. The proceedings have been prudent and equitable; d. The proceedings have been faithful to the mission of the whole church; e. The lawful injunctions of a higher governing body have been obeyed. In the six weeks between the two meetings someone had opened a Book of Order to this list, and omitted the last two requirements. No one ever admitted to doing this. The Administrative Review Committee also was informed that it could not look into the judicial aspects of the specific pastor's case, which of course was why the Committee was supposed to have been formed, as an alternative method of getting at the problem. Though later I came to appreciate why administrative review could not be substituted for judicial review, at this early phase almost no one understood how it should be done. Because of poor instruction from denominational headquarters and someone deleting two of the five required areas of review, the charge to the Administrative Review Committee was incomplete, and the Council never was informed that sections of the job description had been erased.

Thus hobbled, the Review went forward for a year and was incomplete. When they made their report to Synod Council in October of 2003, they reported that all was well because 1) the proceedings had been correctly recorded; 2) the proceedings had been regular and in accordance with the Constitution of the PC(USA); and 3) the proceedings had been prudent and equitable. The committee never considered any facts about what the pastor had said. Whenever such facts were brought up, they were ruled "out of order" because this was a judicial aspect of the case, not administrative. Even more troubling was this assertion: since the pastor had not been ordained or installed into a church by Rogue Presbytery, and since he had not participated in the ordination or installation of anyone else violating the constitution in that presbytery, he himself was not in violation of the constitution's fidelity in marriage or chastity in singleness requirement. This opened a whole new set of potential problems, because it meant that fidelity and chastity need not apply to any pastor, in any presbytery, serving in an uninstalled or validated ministry, or who was retired, or who was a member-at-large. At the same time, every person in these special non-congregation based categories of pastor would have the same voice and vote on the floor of presbytery, and in its committees, as pastors serving churches. The Council was told that it could not amend the report, it could only accept or reject this year's worth of worthless, and perhaps even harmful, work. It was accepted with one dissenting vote, my own.

In the weeks which followed I did some investigating of my own, calling people and asking questions. It was at this point that I discovered that the two final required areas of investigation had been omitted, that the proceedings have been faithful to the mission of the whole church, and that the lawful injunctions of a higher governing body have been obeyed, which would include enforcement by Rogue Presbytery of the fidelity or chastity standard of the constitution. This was enough to revisit the report received in October.

I e-mailed the Council Moderator, a position now filled by Reverend Synod, and shared with him my findings about the insufficiency of an administrative review which omitted two of the five required areas. I asked him to call a special meeting of the Council to appoint a new review committee which would consider all five areas. When he did not respond, I knew he would not do it; I learned subsequently that his intention was to put this off until the next stated meeting of Synod Council, in March of 2004. So I called some friends on Council (yes, I actually work well with people when they do what they are supposed to do), and forced a called meeting of Council for December.

When we got there, Reverend Synod already had prepared a written motion calling for the rescinding of the acceptance of the first Administrative Review Committee report from October, and the appointment of a new committee to look into all five areas. One of the executives from another presbytery was there, acting as parliamentarian, and he told the Council that all five areas had to be investigated. At this point Reverend Synod asked me to make the motion for the new committee, and it passed with one dissenting vote, from a pastor from another presbytery closely allied with Rogue. After this, another vote was taken in a different matter, extending the time allowed for Rogue Presbytery and its ally presbytery to prepare to buy property the Synod owned and was selling within the geographic bounds of Rogue.

In the first few days of 2004 an e-mail was sent out from the Synod office telling us that a called meeting of Council was needed for 2:00 PM on Tuesday, January 20th, to act on a communication from Rogue Presbytery regarding the action we had taken in December. Reverend Synod was in charge of getting the preliminaries together for this meeting, the purpose of which was vague. I assumed it had something to do with the property matter, an ongoing headache for more than a decade.

But on Friday afternoon, January 16th, just before the long Martin Luther King holiday weekend, the Council was informed that the purpose of the meeting was to rescind our actions in December in forming a new review committee, and to reaccept the original report from October. Attached was a letter from Rogue Presbytery threatening to bring charges against the Council with the General Assembly PJC if the new review committee was not stopped. Because of the holiday, I could not contact the office of the denomination's Stated Clerk in Louisville until Tuesday morning. I did contact a friend in my own presbytery who was serving on the General Assembly Advisory Committee on the Constitution. She told me something I had never heard in over 18 months of working on dealing with Rogue Presbytery administratively instead of through the denomination's judicial system: Administrative Review cannot focus on individuals, but only on the process used by governing bodies, making sure that the rules are applied equally. Nobody had understood this: not me, not my Synod Executive friend, not the original review committee, not Reverend Synod, and not even Rogue Presbytery. It almost seemed that the Stated Clerk's Office in Louisville, which had originally suggested this route, was trying simply to drag out the process as long as possible through most people's unfamiliarity with administrative review, hoping that I and others like me would get exhausted and go away before any resolution was accomplished. And even if that wasn't their intention, eventually that's exactly what happened.

That Tuesday morning, January 20th, I finally got in touch via e-mail with the Director of Constitutional Services of the Office of the General Assembly, the man who originally had informed my Synod Executive friend about administrative review in 2002. Later he would become known for authoring the draconian Louisville papers, which suggested that presbyteries play hardball with churches attempting to leave for other Reformed bodies by pre-emptively filing property claims in civil courts; he also gave advice on the type of wording presbyteries should use in their arguments which would make the presbyterian system seem more hierarchical, like that of the Episcopalians. For my book I simply will call him "The Director". The written proposal from the Synod executive committee which I had received on Friday,

January 16th, referred to him specifically. "(The Director) has said that of the five tasks listed for Administrative Review Committees/Commissions in the Book of Order (G-9.0409), it is not mandatory for the higher governing body to inquire into all five areas."

These are the actual e-mails from Tuesday morning, January 20th:

> Me: I'm a member of the Council of the Synod...and need your help. We're having a conference call this afternoon to reconsider our actions regarding the (Rogue) Presbytery ARC, and part of the information being put forward by our Moderator...makes no sense to me. Please look over this motion, particularly 3 A., in which you are quoted as saying that the 5 areas of inquiry in a (sic) Administrative Review, which the Book of Order says are "shalls", are actually "mays". I just spoke with...about this, and he thinks there must be some misunderstanding. Can you help me? And could you please give me an answer before our meeting at 2:00 PM Eastern Time this afternoon? Thank you!
>
> The Director: The operative "may" is in G-9.0408. It is within the discretion of a higher governing body to do administrative review, or not. It is also within the discretion of the higher governing body to determine the scope of that review. In the case of the synod's first committee that scope was very narrow.
> It is only if irregular actions are found that G-9.0409 comes into play. The "shall" in that section refers to making the determination, not to any of the 5 items that the higher governing body may review.
> The synod could accept its special committee's analysis and recommendations, or it could start over, as it apparently has chosen to do. But if there is not a determination of "irregularities or delinquencies" there may be nothing more to be done.
> The substantive problem with the intended subject of this particular review is that the Book of Order basically assigns the "faithful mission of the whole church" authority and responsibility to the two members of the

presbytery's PJC (D-10.0303e). If you look at D-10.0303c you will find that the two criteria those two PJC members are to use is "whether principles of church discipline will be preserved by the decision of the investigating committee not to file charges."

The original committee's charge was more aimed at the appointment, makeup and training of (Rogue)'s investigating committee. I do not believe that charge violates the Book of Order. But looking into whether the investigating committee carried out "the faithful mission of the whole church" would almost by necessity run up against the presbytery PJC's determination on "discipline be preserved by a decision not to file"

There is a line of GA PJC cases that prohibit the use of Remedial cases to challenge problems (delinquencies or irregularities) in discipline. Since the Synod does not have standing to file a Remedial case against one of its own presbyteries (D-6.0202), those cases are not directly applicable, nor binding. However the same logic (that review of disciplinary process is limited to review within the disciplinary process) would apply in cases of Administrative Review.

It is not that the Synod cannot review (Rogue)'s action regarding its dealings with (the defiant pastor), it is that it cannot undertake a review of a decision our Constitution places in the hands of another body (the presbytery's PJC members). The Synod could surely undertake a review of (Rogue)'s general dealings with (the defiant pastor) (validation of his ministry in the first place, supervision since), but I believe the current approach is unlikely to survive judicial scrutiny.

Hope the above is responsive, if not acceptable. Peace. (The Director)

Two very important pieces of information were contained in this e-mail. 1) A new Administrative Review Committee would have to focus on general proceedings, like the Validation process for ministers not working in churches. I will explain how that works a bit later. Ironically, had Rogue Presbytery and Reverend

Synod simply let the original second review go forward, the best I could have hoped for would have been a result which got over into the disciplinary process, as the Director warned, and the General Assembly PJC would have overturned the Synod's actions. 2) The Director's interpretation of "shall" and "may" regarding what the review could entail made no sense whatsoever to me or anyone else with whom I shared it. His own words handed me what I needed to force the Synod to begin to do its duty in the face of a leadership which wanted simply to make this go away.

The "may" to which the Director referred is found in G-9.0408, "If a higher governing body learns at any time of any irregularity or delinquency by a lower governing body, it *may* (emphasis mine) require the governing body to produce any records and take appropriate action." In other words, the higher governing body "may" decide to require the review, or it may not. But once the decision to go ahead has been made, then the "shall" kicks in, the required part. G-9.0409 says, "In reviewing the proceedings of a lower governing body, the higher governing body *shall* (emphasis mine) determine…whether:", and then the five areas are listed. Remember this. It becomes important soon!

The called meeting of Synod Council on Tuesday, January 20th, at 2:00 pm was not a face to face meeting, but a conference call. The executive committee of Council, headed by Reverend Synod, who had written the proposal for the second review one month earlier, now called for rescinding the December decision and readopting the original report received in October. The Council, which voted one way in October, and another in December, now voted to reverse itself again in January, all at the direction of Reverend Synod. To the credit of the members, however, the smell of a rat somewhere must have been detected; instead of voting almost unanimously this time, as it had in the earlier votes, there were eight yes votes, four no votes, and three abstentions. Prior to the vote I explained to the Council very clearly that if this action were taken, I would be working to have a special called meeting of the entire Synod body, not just the Council, to have the larger group decide, not just the bureaucrats and allies of Rogue Presbytery who dominated Council, whether or not a new review was needed. And I would do it as soon as possible.

Forcing a called meeting today would be impossible, since the Synod Council became the Synod body for one meeting per year beginning in 2007; there is no larger body to which one might appeal now. This makes the Synod much more easy to control, and supports the status quo. Even in 2004 it was harder to force a called meeting than it would have been in earlier years, as the number of commissioners was reduced through the years. But the procedure was listed in G-12.0201 in 2004, the chapter on the Synod. The second sentence of that paragraph says, "The moderator shall call a special meeting at the request or with the concurrence of three ministers and three elders, representing at least three presbyteries, *all of whom must have been commissioners to the last preceding stated meeting of the synod.* (emphasis mine)" It was a much smaller pool from which to draw than someone would have had even a decade earlier, so I wound up calling folks I really didn't know, trying to convince them that this problem was serious enough to warrant the time and cost of a called meeting. It took some doing, but it got done. The meeting was called for March 27th, 2004.

The meeting itself lasted three hours, and had its contentious moments. The new Executive of Rogue Presbytery complained that he had hoped relations with the Synod would have been better than this. Apparently no one had ever told him that defying the rule of law and threatening court action to allow the continuance of defying the rule of law was not the best way to win friends and influence people. He also said that the fact we were meeting that day seemed "stupid," which probably did not help his cause. Another pastor in Rogue Presbytery complained about the three reversals of the Synod Council. One of the most outrageous moments for me was when a commissioner directly asked Reverend Synod, "Why did the Council vote one way in October, another way in December, and another way in January?" He answered, "We did not know what to do. We were just trying to buy some time." He finally admitted that he had been acting in bad faith, at least since December. Providentially, I never had to work with this man again after that day; I would not have known what to say to him, and whatever came to mind would not have been kind.

Key to my argument that day was the Book of Order itself. I had copies of the section in question passed to the commissioners, as well as the very important Preface page in its beginning, which included these definitions: "In this Book of Order (1) SHALL and IS TO BE/ARE TO BE signify practice that is mandated. (2) SHOULD signifies practice that is strongly recommended. (3) IS APPROPRIATE signifies practice that is commended as suitable. (4) MAY signifies practice that is permissible but not required." I asked the commissioners to look at the words before them, and vote accordingly; were we going to abide by the constitution, or not?

I also decided I needed to address the argument by the Director, the one sure to be brought up by Synod leadership. "The Director says that 'shall' means 'may'. Now, he's supposed to be the expert on the constitution. But I can tell you that he is wrong. I can tell you he is wrong because I can speak the English language, as my mother taught it to me. Look at these definitions. 'Shall' is mandated. The only 'may' here is whether or not the higher governing body decides to conduct a review or not, but once it does, the 'shall' takes effect. And I can't help but think, maybe we ought to send the Director the bill for this meeting, since his advice is what made it necessary."

One of the most cogent arguments that day came from an Elder. "I look at the Book of Order," she said. "That's all I know to do. I see only three of the five things being done. To me, it is very simple. It says it should be done. Now we have time to rectify the situation. We can do it right away. To me, it's a no-brainer."

In the end, we won the day. The Synod body itself voted 19 to 14 to have a new Administrative Review Committee. This one looked into all five areas. This one found problems with the validation process in Rogue Presbytery. It met regularly with Rogue Presbytery in the years which followed.

But nothing changed. The defiant pastor continued to have his ministry validated every year through 2007, when I rotated off Council for the last time. In the interim, 2004-2007, whenever I tried to remind Synod leadership of their responsibilities in dealing with Rogue Presbytery, they stonewalled. I even tried having another called meeting to address the issue, but I could not get a third pastor commissioner to agree. Then I was gone from the Synod, and focused on my congregation. By the end of 2011, with the fidelity in marriage or chastity in singleness requirement now removed, the defiant pastor had been moved from the list of Validated ministries of Rogue Presbytery to a Member-At-Large, as he sought a call to pastor a congregation.

Validated ministries were defined in G-6.0203 in the Book of Order as "ministers…designated as educators, chaplains, pastoral counselors, campus ministers, missionaries, partners in mission, evangelists, administrators, social workers, consultants, or other specific tasks appropriate to the ministry of the church…". Each year each pastor engaged in a validated ministry must have his or her status reviewed. G-11.0403 gave these "shall" requirements:

A presbytery *shall* (emphasis here mine, and throughout the quotation) determine the ministers of the Word and Sacrament who shall be its continuing members. In making this determination the presbytery *shall* be guided by written criteria developed by the presbytery for validation of ministries within its bounds. These criteria *shall* be based upon the description of the nature of ordained office found in G-6.0100 and G-6.0200 and the following standards:

a. The ministry of continuing members *shall* be in demonstrable conformity with the mission of God's people in the world as set forth in Holy Scripture, The Book of Confessions, and the Book of Order of this church.
b. The ministry *shall* be one that serves others, aids others, and enabled the ministries of others.
c. The ministry *shall* give evidence of theologically informed fidelity to God's Word. This will normally require the Master of Divinity degree or its equivalent and the completion of the requirements for ordination set forth in G-14.0482.
d. The ministry *shall* be carried on in accountability for its character and conduct to the presbytery and to organizations, agencies, and institutions.

e. The ministry *shall* include responsible participation in the deliberations and work of the presbytery and in the worship and service of a congregation.

Personally, I do not see how the defiant pastor's validated ministry passed most of these requirements year after year after year. But Rogue Presbytery never had a problem with the disconnect. Ecclesiastical Defiance is Ecclesiastical Assault, from which there is no practical defense.

Before I completed my time on Synod Council, I asked the Synod's treasurer to give me a rough estimate of the financial cost to Synod for trying to get Rogue Presbytery to cease its defiance. She quickly calculated that it was more than $38,000 thus far. That is an outrage. As the years dragged on I came to believe that Rogue Presbytery would need to be treated eventually by the Synod in the same way that a presbytery would deal with a church displaying similar defiance. Its Presbytery Council should have been dissolved, just like a Session can be dissolved by its presbytery, and replaced with an Administrative Commission to run things until proper, faithful leadership could be found. Nothing less would have stopped their system-wide defiance. But Synod leadership, intent on enabling the defiance because most of them agreed with gay ordination, would have nothing to do with that. Justice delayed, and delayed, and delayed, with no intention of correction, is justice denied.

The system is so corrupted, so without accountability, that it is very unlikely that those committed to the biblical essentials of the faith will ever be able to return it to theological integrity. Religious Liberalism, a different religion that sometimes uses biblical wording, is now firmly entrenched in the PC(USA), and impossible to oust by human effort. But I console myself in the knowledge that this different religion of inclusivity and orthopraxy that I call Religious Liberalism, will fail. The Christian Gospel will prevail.

CHAPTER EIGHTEEN: WHY RELIGIOUS LIBERALISM WILL FAIL

Religious Liberalism will fail. It will not be able to stand the test of time. Look at modern Europe, once the bastion of Christianity, now a spiritual dead zone. Religious Liberalism, which has its origins in the work of the German theologian Freidrich Scheiermacher, will fail because it already has failed on that continent. The progression is clear: Religious Liberalism to Materialism to disillusionment to some type of religious conversion. Right now the fields of Europe are ripe for harvesting by Islam.

In chapter 11 of his letter to the Romans, Paul gives the theological reason for majority Jewish rejection of Jesus as the Messiah: a partial hardening has come upon Jews to make them jealous as Gentiles enter the Kingdom of God, and once the full number of Gentiles comes in, then the full number of Jews will follow. I have always thought there was a sociological reason for first century Jewish resistance to the Messiahship of Jesus as well: you mean I'm going to have one of those Gentile Christians sitting by me in worship, and eating next to me at meals, and calling on my daughter? For centuries it had been drilled into the heads of Jews by God – Remain separate from Gentiles! The northern and southern kingdoms had not listened, and had both been punished by exile. Even in the time of Ezra and Nehemiah, post-Babylonian exile, the Jews were intermarrying with Gentiles for political purposes. But finally they understood. It became a way of life, remaining separate from Gentiles. Then Jesus came, and after His resurrection, when He was recognized by some as the promised Messiah, the sin-sacrifice for all who repent and believe, the need to remain separate was gone. In fact, to insist on Gentile conversion to Judaism in addition to conversion to Christ would be tantamount to saying, "Jesus did not do enough." But He did do enough!

This argument, whether or not Gentiles had to become Jews in addition to becoming Christians, was the first major argument within the Church. The Jerusalem Council of Acts chapter 15 attempted to resolve it, and yet this was the same problem threatening to destroy the churches of Galatia in Paul's later letter of the same name. Just as there were many reasons why first century Jews did not accept Jesus en masse, there are many reasons Religious Liberalism will fail. The Church would be foolish to embrace it simply to broaden its appeal. Ultimately, it appeals to no one.

Leading with my strongest argument, Religious Liberalism will fail because it is not true. Whatever else I say in this chapter is academic since this approach, to Christianity in particular and to religion in general, is false. By its very nature, Religious Liberalism discounts the idea of truth and falsehood, preferring to be all things to all people, to be, to borrow a phrase from Free Masonry, Pure Religion, uncluttered by specific essential doctrine. Like the white abolitionists of the 1850s, Religious Liberalism ignores the words of the Bible in favor of a vague religious mandate driven by an essential of inclusivity at any cost. "Look," said a colleague who should have known better, "the first century Jewish Christians had to accept the first century Gentile Christians, and so twenty-first century Christians must accept homosexual practice," ignoring the fact that inclusion of the Gentiles had been prophesied through much of the Old Testament; he also was confusing a person's ontological state with a person's behavior. At the same time, he ignored the words of scripture which condemn sinful behaviors, as well as those which warn against false teaching. Not only is Religious Liberalism not true, it is not even honest. It uses the same words as historical, biblical Christianity, but gives them different meanings which are clear to the initiated, but misleading to everyone else.

Religious liberalism also will fail because it arrogantly and wrongly assumes it is the next phase of Christianity. In the minds of its adherents, just as the Protestant Reformation brought new life to the Church by breaking the exclusive claim of a tradition-bound Roman Catholicism to Christianity in the west, now Religious Liberalism is breaking the hold of the idolatry of the Bible, a book which people worship instead of worshipping God. As I write this, I recall something my old preaching professor, Elizabeth Achtemeier, said in class one day – "The words of scripture give me my freedom as a woman. When you start messing with those words, you're messing with my freedom!"

Religious Liberalism is not the next phase of Christianity; if it were, how could it be so ineffective at winning converts? Why are Europe and North America not experiencing revivals on par with the Great Awakenings of centuries past, spearheaded by the "mainstream" denominations which have come to champion it? In fact, the exact opposite is true. The "mainstreams" are dying, and unbelief is rampant. And why shouldn't it be? How can a religious movement which looks, sounds, and smells just like its secular counterparts hold any appeal for a culture weary of what it already knows? What appeal can such a religious movement have as it devolves into works righteousness, when contrasted with a mirror secular culture which demands no work at all? The Reformation changed the world because it changed the hearts and minds of people who were hearing the clear call of the gospel in the words of the Bible itself. The Reformation offered hope which only comes from Jesus Christ, God reaching down to save a sinful and broken humanity. But cut off from scripture, Religious Liberalism can mimic only the dysfunctional culture from which it has sprung; it certainly cannot rise above it, or offer any hope for this life or the next. Why bother to convert when there is no change, and where there is no power or message or will to do so? As he already is, the unbeliever has what Religious Liberalism claims to offer. Why go to the trouble of attending church, or giving time, talent, or money when the basic message is, "Be nice by including everybody."? Put another way, if the death and resurrection of Jesus Christ is not the most important event in history, if it may not even have happened, and if it does not define who I am to the core of my being, why bother?

Religious Liberalism will fail because it assumes that the Bible is a culturally bound book, created by human beings reaching up and imagining God. Recently a leader from our presbytery visiting the church privately told two Elders and me that this is his understanding of the Bible. I'm not making this up or exaggerating. "The Bible was written by people thousands of years ago, resting on a hillside, looking at the stars and trying to make sense of it all. But God is bigger than that. All that matters it that Jesus died and rose again; beyond that I don't care." How one would know that Jesus died for our sins and rose again apart from scripture, however, was not explained.

The more I study the Bible, the more I am amazed by it. How could a book written over 2000 years by forty different authors from many different walks of life, writing in two or three different languages on three different continents, hold together so well, so beautifully? How can such a book still move the souls of people who read and hear it 2000 years later, all over the world? It is only possible if one Holy Spirit inspired them all as they wrote, and if that same Spirit still speaks through these words today.

Those who claim that the Bible is simply a man-made document should compare it with other documents and dogmas which we know are man-made. Sometimes when I am explaining this to teenagers I say that if my dog could imagine a god, he probably would project himself upon the clouds: like me, just bigger. Since he is a poodle, he probably would think of a Saint Bernard in the sky! Isn't this exactly what we see in Greek, Roman, and Egyptian mythology? The gods are like us, just stronger, and they don't die. They come in pairs, male and female. They are bound to their land, and their worship is connected to patriotism; that's why Egyptian gods are worshipped in Egypt, and Greek gods in Greece. They sometimes make mistakes, and they sometimes are petty and cruel. A comparable Jewish "mythology" would have the Lord linked with a Lady, like Baal and Asherah of the Canaanite religion. It certainly would not claim that eventually all the peoples of the world would come to worship our God, especially when the nation was under the thumb of a mighty empire like that of Babylon or Persia. Instead, when the Jews were carted off to captivity, they would have acted just like the foreigners who were moved into Samaria by the Assyrians a century earlier; they would learn the ways of the god of that land, and perhaps mix aspects of Yahweh worship in with that of their new divine masters. (That's probably what did happen with the much more sophisticated refugees from the northern kingdom conquered by the Assyrians, already accustomed to pagan influences. Within a century, they ceased to exist as distinct descendants of Abraham, and we are left with legends of the mysterious Ten Lost Tribes of Israel.) For the survivors of the destruction of the southern kingdom, Judah, their adherence to and belief in the God who created the heavens and the earth, who brought them out of Egypt, who eventually would bring their children out of Babylon, was what made them weird and what made them present to be sent home after seventy years of captivity.

Or consider the Trinity. The Old Testament is sure there is only one God; the Shema, the central affirmation of Judaism found in Deuteronomy 6:4 (Hear, O Israel, the Lord is our God, the Lord is one.), is very clear about this, and the false gods of the Gentiles are regularly mocked in its pages. At the same time, the plurality of God's triune nature is hinted at in several places: Genesis 1:26 (Let Us make man in Our own image…); the Wisdom Song of Proverbs 8, where a mysterious companion, Wisdom (female because the Hebrew word for wisdom, Hokmah, is feminine) helps the Lord create the world and eventually comes down to earth (John is very clear that this is Jesus in the first verses of his gospel); or even the fact that the generic Hebrew reference to the Lord as God, Elohim, has a plural ending ("im", as in one cherub, two cherubim) while always using singular verbs. The purpose for these Old Testament oddities becomes clear with the revelation of the New Testament that there is one God who exists simultaneously in three persons: Father, Son, and Holy Spirit.

Truthfully, I don't understand the Trinity; it is beyond my experience. And I find this completely reassuring. When the true God reveals Himself, there should be something about Him that I cannot understand. After all, He's infinite, and I am not. Returning to my dog illustration, there are things in my life which are far beyond my poodle's ability to comprehend. He does not know why I leave or where I go when I am at work. He does not understand that if he only can get the refrigerator door open, he can eat the same food I eat. At this moment, as he sleeps by my feet, he has no idea why I am staring at a little screen and making these clicking noises. My life is far beyond his. And God is much more beyond me than I am beyond my dog. The Trinity is not a belief a human being would imagine while lying on the hills of Palestine, gazing at the stars. Only self-revelation by the one true God can account for it. Scripture is not man-made. It is God-breathed; it is inspired.

Religious Liberalism will fail because it assumes that orthodox Christians are xenophobic, afraid of the stranger and things unfamiliar. Nothing could be further from the truth. Convinced of God's providence, the orthodox Christian can and will walk into new situations, expecting to receive a blessing from a loving heavenly Father. For example, I work with children all the time; surprises abound, and not always pleasant ones!

In 2003 I became convinced that God was urging me to learn Spanish because so many Latinos were moving into our community; in the space of one decade, the Hispanic population had increased by 500%! Though I had taken the language for two years in college in the 1980s, and I could read some Spanish, up till then I never could speak it. This was because, when I had graduated from high school, I had toured for a year with a singing group which included several Swedes, and they taught me a very basic form of the spoken Swedish language. I don't know how it works for others who are multi-lingual, but my brain does not have English, Swedish, and Spanish filing systems; it has the native language file and the foreign language file. Therefore, when I tried to speak Spanish in college, I could not complete a sentence without throwing in Swedish words. It was very frustrating, and finally I gave up trying to speak Spanish at all.

But Swedes were not filling our community, Latinos were, and God kept pushing me. Twice in the space of a year I took a week-long Spanish immersion class at our local community college, and began watching the news in Spanish every morning. Despierta America on Univision, with the wonderful news woman Neida Sandoval, who spoke clearly and slowly, was my show of choice. And it worked. While my Spanish is far from that of a native speaker, I can carry on a business-level conversation today. And I cannot speak a simple sentence in Swedish now without throwing in Spanish words!

Soon after building up my Spanish abilities I attended a meeting of our presbytery council; because there was going to be some lag time around lunch, I also brought a copy of our local Spanish paper, La Voz (The Voice), to read. Through my community college classes I had become good friends with the editor, and she had asked me to write a regular column for La Voz. I did, and it was called "Palabras Del Gringo Viejo" (Words of the Old Gringo). I must say that my Spanish is not publication worthy; I wrote in English, and she translated for me! But I enjoyed reading her rendering of my words, as well as reading the other columns and news items.

As I waited for the presbytery council to begin, I read my paper. A retired pastor well-known for her progressive views walked by, then stopped and came back to me. "You can't really read that, can you?" she asked. "Of course," I replied. I guess she could not. It seemed incomprehensible to her that I, who cared so deeply about theological orthodoxy, would not be too xenophobic to avoid learning Spanish. She assumed I would be sympathetic with those whose bumper stickers read, "If you come to America, learn English!" In fact, when friends have made such comments to me, I typically respond, "People should learn English. But it's hard to learn. Historically, first-generation immigrants who come here struggle with the language and the culture, usually settling in ethnic neighborhoods. Their children, raised here, are the ones who are completely Americanized, and speak English well. In the meantime, we would do well to be able to communicate with everyone we can." When I realized that Pastor Progressive only could deal with me as a one-dimensional stereotype, I urged all my orthodox friends to learn Spanish. "It drives liberals crazy!"

Oh my, what would she do if she knew about all my African-American friends and mentors, including those who attend our church and those who have preached here? What would she say about the black woman with whom I went to high school, a friend who now is a lawyer in Washington, D.C.? In 2012, even though we had not seen each other face to face in over 30 years, Cecelia made a special trip to Burlington to worship with us and then have lunch with one of our teenagers, a black girl who also was considering a career in law. What a terrific time we had; I thought they might encourage one another, and they did. Now, in the interest of full disclosure, I have to admit that we did run into one problem that day: one of the church's Elders was terribly disappointed to learn that Cecelia and her family live in D.C., and so were unable to become members! Afterward, in the fall of 2012, she volunteered to proof-read, and then extensively edit, the manuscript for this book. Only true friends do things like that! Biblically informed, orthodox Christianity has nothing to fear from the stranger; it embraces the adventure of the different, knowing that its firm foundation will withstand any challenges, from without and within, and that non-fundamentals, non-essentials, always must be open to change.

Religious Liberalism will fail because it assumes that all orthodox Christians hate homosexuals. Of course, there are orthodox Christians who do hate homosexuals; that is a sin for which and from which we must repent. Our schizophrenic culture is not much help in this matter. While the media champion the cause of normalization of gay life-styles, the teen expression of disdain, "That is so gay," has arisen from secular sources, not religious ones. With no moral compass or corrective device, such chaos will reign. Christians have no excuse for the hatred of homosexuals when we consider the full witness of scripture. While there are Old Testament passages which condemn homosexual practice, Christians must read the Old Testament in light of the New. After all, while there are holy wars of annihilation in the Old Testament, no Christian theologian ever has argued that God wants every man, woman, and child of the enemy, combatants and civilians, killed.

The word of the New Testament on homosexuality is neither that of permissiveness nor violent oppression, contrary to the opinions of Religious Liberals. The deciding passage is Romans, chapter 1, in which Paul is explaining how everyone is a sinner, guilty first of idolatry, the sin from which all others flow. The behaviors mentioned in the verses following are merely symptoms of the original idolatry. The first one is homosexual behavior. And yet the "depraved mind" to which God has given over all idolaters (all people) leads to many other sinful desires and behaviors; among them are murder, gossip, and being disobedient to one's parents. (Obviously, Paul is thinking, at least in part, about the Ten Commandments.) Taken literally from this text, homosexual behavior is no better than murder, but no worse than gossip. Though Christians may be concerned for those who engage in it, and resist the culture's tide which seeks to normalize it along with all other sexual anarchy, our most responsible and fair response is to see it as being no different than heterosexual couples living together without being married. Most churches have non-married couples living together in the 21st century. We do not bar them from church attendance; instead, we build relationships with them from which we can encourage them to submit their lives more and more to God's revealed will. All Christians have had to learn this same lesson throughout our lives. This is the option which rejects both permissiveness and oppression.

Religious Liberalism will fail because it cannot compete with a Bible in the common language which can be read by anyone. The Reformers understood the power of the Word in the 1600s, and earlier; so did the oppressive Roman Catholic hierarchy, which made translation of the Bible from the original languages or Latin a capital offense. Many people died for making those translations, and for distributing them. (As late as the mid-1800s it was still illegal to have a Bible in Spanish in Mexico; early Presbyterian missions to Mexico involved the smuggling of Spanish Bibles.) American colonists also understood this, especially in New England. The purpose of our educational system, which began in that part of the country, was to teach children to read so they could read their own Bibles. Then they would not have to depend upon religious professionals for their entire spiritual formation. It was understood as a defense against tyranny.

A few years ago a married couple began attending our church; she was from the United States, and he had been born and raised in Mexico. Even more interesting to me was the fact that she had been raised a Unitarian-Universalist, and her brother was a pastor in that faith, while he had been raised Roman Catholic, and his brother was a priest! They became members, and immediately became involved in our evening Bible study program.

I asked her how it had happened that she rejected the extremely liberal positions of the Unitarian-Universalist religion, which most orthodox believers hold to be outside the Christian faith. It is the poster-child of Religious Liberalism. Her answer amazed me. As a nurse working in North Carolina, she wanted to be able to communicate with her patients who spoke only Spanish, and so enrolled in a Spanish immersion program in Mexico for a few weeks. Once she returned to the United States, she began attending a Bible Study in Spanish at a local church, to help her remember what she had learned; the Bible Study was taught by the man she eventually married! "When I read the Bible in Spanish, simply reading the actual words, it by-passed all the Unitarian-Universalist spin on the meaning of the words in English. I could no longer believe what they taught me it said because I was reading what it said for myself."

Religious Liberalism as a religion will fail. The Presbyterian Church (USA) is foolish to hitch its slowing wagon to this dying horse. And it is not simply being foolish; it is being unfaithful to Jesus Christ.

CHAPTER NINETEEN: THE BIBLICAL CASE FOR SEPARATION

From sitting under my father's teaching throughout my teens I knew there were serious problems within our denomination. It was not that Dad complained about things going on at presbytery meetings; in fact, I believe he probably sheltered us and the congregations more than he should have from national shenanigans, like the equalization of funds (an infuriating 1960s denominational policy which siphoned off money given by congregations for mission work, and then redirected it to aid underfunded and unpopular political activism, beloved by denominational leadership) and union presbyteries. But every now and then I might overhear him talking with my mother about some pastor coming into presbytery whose theology was not biblical, not evangelical, and not even Reformed. "Why didn't you say something?" I remember asking him once. "Son, you have to pick your battles," he replied. "If you get a reputation for just being opposed to everything, no one will listen to you."

Also, in our local congregation the books of Francis Schaeffer were held out as commendable critiques of secular culture and its influence on the Church since the Enlightenment. I remember watching the film series he created in the 1970s during our Sunday evening services, both "How Shall We Then Live", and his pro-life project with later-to-be Surgeon General C. Everett Koop, "Whatever Happened To The Human Race?". My university History Honors project in 1985 was a 113 page paper entitled, "The Authors Who Shaped The Jesus Movement", beginning with David Wilkerson and ending with Francis Schaeffer. (Ironically, the one seminary history professor with whom I shared this paper could not believe I had chosen the five authors whose work I examined, and so did not bother to read it. Even if the book had sold tens of thousands of copies, or was available through the very successful college ministries of Inter-Varsity or Campus Crusade for Christ, since it was not part of his elite academic experience, he was not interested. And his specialty was missions!)

But as I went to seminary, it became clear very quickly that if something was from the 20th century but wasn't Barth, Brunner, or the Niebuhrs, or one of the newer special interest theologies (feminist, progressive, liberation, etc.), it did not count. Schaeffer, held up to me by my church as an example of practical Reformed theology at work in the modern world, did not count. One hilarious experience I had in those days was with my delightful, Swiss-born professor, Matthais Rissi. Dr. Rissi was a good man, and even though he was a universalist, stating that Jesus said that if He was lifted up, He would draw all people to Himself, and so He shall, he nonetheless believed without a doubt that Jesus was God incarnate, had died for sins, and had risen from death. He did not believe hell would last forever, but it was a pretty bad place, and you didn't want to go there, as you surely would apart from Jesus. I appreciated his genuine faith, in addition to his refusal to take himself too seriously. He taught the class in Philippians I took in May of 1987, and one day, as I was walking out of class, listening to my Walkman tape player (the forerunner to i-Pods, kids) with headphones, he stopped me and commented that I seemed to like music a lot. Yes, I said. I happened to be listening to Mark Heard's Victims Of The Age cassette at the time, and sensing an opportunity to tweak my professor, I said, "You know, this guy was a student of Francis Schaeffer's at La Bri." Dr. Rissi's eyes got really big, and he said, "Oh, you don't read him, do you? That man was bad. That man was demonic. That man did more to divide the southern Presbyterian Church than any other." He wasn't angry, he was just concerned for me. So I replied that I appreciated Schaeffer's insights into western civilization and philosophies, and that I found his earlier work more helpful than his later writings. "So," I reassured him, "I don't believe everything he says. But I don't believe everything you say either!" And this man, with all his degrees and training, who might have taken great offense, instead brightened up and laughed long and loud with me, his student. I also said that I didn't think I really belonged in our denomination, that I probably belonged in one of the smaller, more orthodox denominations. No, he insisted, I had a place in this denomination. And I did for many years.

One of the themes drilled into my head for those many years within the orthodox camp of the PC(USA) is that you don't leave. The Religious Liberals say the same thing, but for different reasons, such as "I used to be like you and I can no more deny you than I can deny myself," or some other comment which sounds affirming, but actually is quite condescending. Sometimes Religious Liberals and bureaucrats like to reference Calvin, who condemned schism as a great sin; when they do this, I like to remind them that Calvin also said that the true Church exists where the Word is rightly proclaimed, and the sacraments rightly administered. Can they really assure me that the Word is rightly proclaimed in a denomination where belief in Jesus' resurrection is optional? Are the sacraments rightly administered when the Atonement, the moment commemorated in the meal, is optional? And (this usually ends the discussion), are they saying that the PC(USA) is the one true Church? (Calvinists always condemned this claim by the Roman Catholic Church, and have never held that we are the one true Church in 500 years of existence!) We simply believe that we are a part of the one true Church, the Church Universal, the Church Invisible, God's people in all times and places, ultimately known only by Him. This is illustrated historically by the fact that in colonial times, in New England, many towns either had a Congregational church or a Presbyterian one. Since both were Calvinistic in doctrine, neither felt it necessary to add another Reformed body to that community based simply on the difference in the form of government.

The argument against separation from the orthodox side has always been much more compelling for me. It is, "The prophets of the Old Testament cried out against the idolatry and sin of their generations, insisting, 'Thus saith the Lord!' Even if no one listened to them, at least they would know that a prophet had been among them. And at no point did Jeremiah or Isaiah or any of the prophets say, 'Come, let us leave and form a new, pure nation.'" And that's true. That argument kept me in line for decades, and I quietly expressed my dismay to friends who in that time have chosen to leave, reminding them of the prophets' refusal to do so, as well as the fact that their leaving would weaken those of us who remained.

Beyond this, there is no perfect denomination. While the PC(USA), my denomination, was fighting about sexuality over the past three decades, one of the small denominations which had left us was embroiled in another controversy: must pastors believe and teach that the days of creation described in Genesis, chapter one, were 24 periods of time? Haven't we done this before, in the 1920s? Is this really essential? Ironically, in that denomination the conservatives willingly admitted that "yom" can mean more than a 24 hour period of time, but, they continued, since the writers of the Westminster Confession of Faith in 1647 believed that these were 24 hour days, a person agreeing to the essential teaching of the Westminster Standards would also have to adopt the prevailing view of 1647. In other words, Confession, clearly a man-made document, is more important than scripture. And the Westminster Divines spun in their graves. To their credit, that denomination decided against requiring belief in 24 hour days of creation. At the same time, I have no desire to be caught up in that type of family fighting.

A few years ago I had the privilege to attend a local presbytery meeting of another Reformed denomination. What a joy it was to listen to a young pastor give the biblical argument for why that denomination excludes women from the offices of pastor or elder. It is not that I agreed with him; I did not. But at least the Bible, chapters and verses, was being cited for his position. Why can my own presbytery not ask new pastors to explain their own theological positions from scripture, citing chapters and verses? Since the vast majority of Christians around the world do not ordain women, nor have they throughout history, why do we? (For my answer to this question, see Chapter 7.) Instead, our "floor examination" is an informal meet and greet, with few difficult questions, and jeers for those who disrupt the flow of an already business-filled, though rarely Spirit-filled, meeting, by asking about deeper matters.

At that same meeting I ran into an old friend from seminary days; since graduation he had become convinced that the ordination of women was wrong, and renounced his PC(USA) ordination, being welcomed into the other Reformed body. He introduced me to a young man who was attending presbytery with him, either a youth pastor or an associate pastor of some kind, and went on to say that this man hated to come to presbytery meetings because of the tendency of some to pontificate. My friend said, "I told him, 'Hey, any time you fill a room with folks with this much education, you're always going to find an a**-hole. I'm just happy we don't have any heretics!'" A few years later this same friend led the charge to remove from their denominational seminary some of the professors who had been part of the Constitutional Presbyterians group with me, the same ones who had objected to my "Westminster alone" position, because they were Barthians. And this makes me wonder; would I be the subject of such a censure and removal if I joined this group, with whom I have a lot in common, when they learn I do not share their view on women's ordination? Would I be willing to risk my livelihood with that possibility looming over me? So, not only did the prophets not advocate leaving, but leaving also can be dangerous. Better the Ahabs and Jezebels I know.

The choice to leave is difficult. But I no longer believe it is unbiblical. Recently my father shared with me the fact that his mother, my grandmother, who had been a missionary to the mountains of Virginia in her 20s (where she met my grandfather!), had a discipline of reading three chapters of the Bible a day, plus five chapters on Sunday. This way, the entire Bible can be read in a year. Fascinated, I started following her example in 2010. Yes, I have read it all before. But I need to be reminded, and the Lord always shows me something new that I haven't noticed before, or points out something I have forgotten.

Ahijah the Shilonite is one of those obscure prophets found in two chapters of the Bible. If you blink, you will miss him. But what he does in 1 Kings 11 is amazing. He does not call for the faithful of Israel to depart with him to form a new nation. Instead, he delivers the word from God to Jeraboam, son of Nebat, that God wishes to punish the descendants of King Solomon for that king's idolatry, and offers a new kingship to Jeraboam, and an eternal dynasty like that of David, to Jeraboam. God Himself is behind the splitting of His people into the nations of Judah and Ephraim (or Israel), the southern and northern kingdoms. It is not a schism, it is God's judgment, and a promise of blessing if only Jeraboam will trust the Lord and obey Him like David did.

Let me refresh your memories of this story. Just as God made an eternal covenant with Abraham, that He would bless him and make him into a great nation from whom all the families of the world would be blessed (ultimately fulfilled through the death and resurrection of Jesus), so God made an eternal covenant with David to create an eternal dynasty ruling that great nation descended from Abraham, with David's descendant forever on its throne. This also is fulfilled ultimately through Jesus. David's son, Solomon, started well. We are told that at his birth, the Lord loved him. (2 Samuel 12:24) He obeyed his father's wishes regarding unfinished business when he became king, and he humbly asked God for wisdom instead of riches or a long life, and was rewarded with all three. He built the magnificent first temple, and humbly admitted in his prayer of dedication that not even this building can house the God who fills heaven, and "the highest heaven". We also are told that gold was so common in the days of Solomon that silver had no value! God's material blessings were poured out abundantly upon David's first direct descendant.

But we are told that Solomon also was a ladies' man, and that he took many foreign wives, 700 in all, plus 300 concubines. 1 Kings 11 tells us that in his old age they turned his heart away from serving the Lord, and that he began to serve other gods as well. He allowed his pagan wives to construct new altars to their gods on the mountain east of Jerusalem, including one for Molech, whose worship included the sacrifices of children. Because of this, God raised up adversaries against Solomon, including Jeraboam, son of Nebat, and swore that He would tear away a part of the kingdom from Solomon's son in the future. He would not remove all of the tribes from David's descendants, but the coming punishment would mean losing most of them.

Jeroboam had been a valiant warrior, trusted by Solomon. According to 1 Kings 11, Ahijah the prophet went to see Jeraboam alone in a field one day; Ahijah was wearing a new cloak. The prophet took off his cloak and tore it into twelve pieces, then commanded the warrior to take ten of the pieces for himself. "Thus says the LORD, the God of Israel, 'Behold, I will tear the kingdom out of the hand of Solomon and give you ten tribes…'" And the Lord, through Ahijah, went on to offer Jeraboam the same covenant David had, an eternal dynasty, if only the rebel king will follow Him faithfully. When Solomon learned that this had happened, he sought to kill Jeraboam, and the young man fled to Egypt until the old king finally died.

The rest of the story is better known. Solomon's newly crowned son, Rehoboam, was asked by an assembly of the people to lower their taxes since the temple now was built. He requested for three days to consider the matter. In that time his father's advisors urged him to lower the tax burden, but his friends, the advisors with whom he had grown up, disagreed. In one of the most testosterone driven pieces of advice ever recorded in literature, they said he must answer, "My little finger is thicker than my father's loins! Whereas he loaded you with a heavy yoke, I will add to your yoke! He disciplined you with whips, but I will discipline you with scorpions!" Rehoboam listened to his friends, and their answer was his answer. The northern tribes answered, "Bye!" Only Judah, the tribe of David, and little Benjamin, remained faithful to David's heir. The others called for Jeroboam, lately returned from Egypt, and made him their king. And when Rehoboam raised a huge army to force the seceding tribes back into the union, another prophet, Shemariah, spoke up and reminded the people that this division was the prophesied will of God. The army of Judah and Benjamin went back home.

I think the reason most of us have missed this powerful account of God's division of Israel into two nations is that the story of the independent northern kingdom did not end well. Immediately after the southern armies stopped threatening the new ten-tribe confederation, we read that Jeraboam decided he could not trust the Lord to keep His promises. The Lord had made very clear in Deuteronomy that worship was to be centralized "at the place where I indicate" in order to guard against pagan influences. The place God had chosen was Jerusalem, where the temple had been built. Jeraboam decided that if the people continued to worship in Jerusalem, soon "the heart of this people will return to their lord, even Rehoboam, king of Judah; and they will kill me and return to Rehoboam, king of Judah." Out of fear Jeraboam developed a plan of action, to build new temples within the northern kingdom: at Bethel near Jerusalem, where Jacob had once had the vision of the heavenly staircase, and in the far north, at Dan. He also instituted a feast to compete with the feast in Jerusalem on the fifteenth day of the eighth month. Though Jeraboam was condemned by the prophets for his actions, including Ahijah, through whom God had offered an eternal covenant, the king never repented of his actions. His dynasty died with his son, Nadab, two years into his reign when he was assassinated by Baasha, who then ruled in his place. And for the rest of the history of Israel, regardless of the good one of their kings might do, all their kings are considered evil because they continued in the "sin of Jeraboam, son of Nebat"; they continued to worship at Bethel and Dan, and other high places, thus opening the way for the syncretism with paganism of the Assyrian captivity and the rise of the Samaritans.

It ended poorly because of human sinfulness and fear, but it began gloriously, as the will of God and punishment for Solomon's idolatry. Today, by its actions, the Presbyterian Church (USA) is bowing at the idol of contemporary, secular American culture, and that idol is the obelisk. Our leaving will not be schismatic, it will be prophetic as the Lord builds something new "to the north". Those of us who go must do all we can to make sure that our Jeraboams remain faithful to Gods purpose, establishing clear and biblical theology, as well as meaningful accountability.

Writing these last few pages has proven revelatory for me. Just as Solomon was willing to compromise faithfulness to the Lord and sacrifice the children for the sake of political alliances (the main purpose of marrying foreign princesses), so the PC(USA) has done in deleting sexual standards. On April 9th, 2011, as I stood to speak on the floor of our presbytery, I had decided not to attempt a theological argument which would only sway the supporters of fidelity in marriage and chastity in singleness. I had determined to make an emotional plea, not for biblical faithfulness, but for the sake of our children. Throwing dignity to the wind, I walked around all that morning wearing around my neck an eight by ten photograph of the five kids comprising our youth group, dear teenagers with whom I worked every week. When I stood, I began with words from the Confession of 1967.

> "Anarchy in sexual relationships is a symptom of man's alienation from God, his neighbor, and himself...The

church, as the household of God, is called to lead men out of this alienation into the responsible freedom of the new life in Christ." (Confession of 1967, 9.47 BoC) Mr. Moderator, this is a picture of my current core youth group, two boys and three girls. Two are black, three are white. You and I never knew the sexual pressure these teens face today, from television, from the internet, and from peers; the two thirteen year olds in the picture have been praying in Bible Study for a 12 year old friend who is pregnant, though she's not sure which of two guys is the father. Of the five, only one lives with both of his (biological) parents. In the face of this sexual anarchy, I try to teach them that God's will for His children is chastity in singleness, and fidelity in marriage, which is between one man and one woman, a picture of Christ and the Church. But how can I teach this in a denomination which refuses to hold our ordained officers to the same standard? How will I be able to teach this if our own presbytery refuses to uphold that standard? I don't know. But I do know this: I will do whatever is necessary to protect the children entrusted to my care from the sexual anarchy which pervades our secular society. My elders and I also will protect the congregation entrusted by God to our care. I pray that you, the elders and pastors of churches in _____ Presbytery, will do the same by voting against this amendment which invites sexual anarchy into our denomination and into our congregations.

My plea fell upon deaf ears. For the sake of bowing at the altar of our culture's sexually permissive attitudes and the misguided understanding of homosexual behavior as an ontological condition comparable to race or eye-color, my church's children were to be sacrificed. It was a moment impossible to forget, and difficult to forgive. If most of Solomon's kingdom could be snatched away for such an offense, surely the cost to the Presbyterian Church (USA) could be, and should be, the loss of hundreds of congregations still faithful to the Lord. There is a biblical case for separation.

CHAPTER TWENTY: ECCLESIASTICAL McCARTHYISM – "YOU ARE SCHISMATICS!"

In a denomination which tolerates open heresy from the pulpit and the seminary podium, one might think any idea is allowed. After all, it has gone without a single heresy trial in almost sixty years, and has no list of essential beliefs. However, this is not the case. Like the communist-baiters of the 1950s, one charge alone, without any proof or trial, can be used at best to blackball a pastor, or at worst to remove him or her from office. That charge is schism. For those unfamiliar with the word, a schism is a split, a division. The Great Schism of Church history divided the western and eastern sections of the Church into the Roman Catholic Church and the Eastern Orthodox Church respectively. That occurred in 1054 AD, and the rift never has healed. Within the PC(USA), the charge of schism is used to support the status quo. It is the refuge of bureaucrats, whose main concern is peace at any price to keep dollars rolling in, regardless of belief or behavior. It is the logical conclusion to the "theology divides, mission unites" mantra.

In the spring of 2002 I was serving on Synod Council when our representative on General Assembly Council, a retired pastor in his 70s, made a report regarding the loss of funds being sent to the national denomination, resulting in down-sizing and lay-offs. "The problem is two-fold," he announced to us. "The defeat of Amendment O," which would have prohibited gay union services on local church property (see page 59), "is part of it. A lot of churches are upset about this. And the second thing is this CONFESSING CHURCH MOVEMENT!" He practically spat the words.

The Confessing Church Movement was a shot across the bow of the denomination, a warning that many, many local congregations were upset about the tolerance, as well as the embracing, of Religious Liberalism as a viable alternative to historic, biblical Christianity. Mirroring the actions of the Confessing Churches in Nazi Germany prior to World War 2, brave churches which rejected the notion of "German Christianity" in the 1930s and the idea that the Church has any Lord other than Jesus Christ, and certainly not the State, the 21st century movement was very organic within the PC(USA). On March 2, 2001, Summit Presbyterian Church in Butler, PA, had published its statement, claiming as its own three historic positions of Christianity under attack within the culture and the denomination. 1) The Bible is the Word of God. 2) Jesus Christ is the only way of salvation. 3) Among the behaviors to which Christians are called is limiting sexual contact either to fidelity in marriage, which is between one man and one woman, or chastity in singleness. Then one of the largest congregations in the country, First Presbyterian in Orlando, FL, issued the same statement. Soon a floodgate opened, and nearly one tenth of the denomination's churches, about 1,100 out of 11,000, confessed these same three truths as a witness to the world. No one knew what would happen next; would this lead to a new, "Confessing" denomination?

That's what the retired pastor feared and hated. He ranted for a few minutes about those terrible Confessing Church people, saying that he did not even want to sit at a table with one of them. After he calmed down, the moderator asked if there were any comments or questions from the group. I spoke up, "Madam Moderator, I just want to say that I am a member of the Confessing Church. My church was one of the first 100 Confessing Churches. I have served faithfully in the PC(USA). I have served my congregations and in my presbyteries. I have served on this Council faithfully. And I will leave this table when someone picks me up and throws me out." Could have heard a pin drop after that! Not surprisingly, Reverend Synod had my comments expunged from the record by directing the secretary to omit them from the minutes to be approved at the following meeting. I didn't care; we all knew what had been said.

But that was not the end of the confrontation. After the meeting concluded I wound up standing in the bathroom next to our General Assembly Council representative, urinal by urinal. "Tom, I don't understand why you are so angry about the Confessing Church Movement." He hemmed and hawed as we washed our hands, but got out of the bathroom without saying much. Providentially, he and I wound up in line next to each other a few minutes later, waiting to get the supper provided by the Synod office. "Tom, I really want to understand why you are so angry. What is wrong with churches standing up for what we believe?"

"I've seen it happen before," he shouted, wagging his finger. "I saw it happen in 1973 with the PCA! (The Presbyterian Church in America) And I saw it happen again in 1981 with the EPC! (The Evangelical Presbyterian Church) These people are all the same! They lie!" I replied, "I'm not them. I was 10 when the PCA formed. I turned 19 in 1981." How can anyone argue with that? He said, "I...I...I don't want to talk to you!" With that, he raced from the building and never came back that evening. I guess he bought some supper on the way home.

The experience of many southern Presbyterian pastors aged 64 and older is colored by rifts and splits within the old southern denomination in the years leading up to reunion in 1983. They lost a lot of friends from seminary days, and, like most family fights, the rage and hurt of those perceived betrayals burn deeply into the psyches of those who lived through that time. My heart goes out to pastors scarred by past splits. At the same time, I have to wonder, what about the concerns of the pastors and churches which left to form the PCA and the EPC? Were all their concerns unfounded? If so, why is it that the larger denominations have lumbered on into exactly the same problems of unbelief prophesied by the Machens and the Schaeffers and the Kennedys of those days? Is it possible that the PC(USA) and its predecessor denominations have kept splitting because those pastors and elders who remained have failed to address the concerns which caused those earlier splits?

The Confessing Church Movement about which my angry friend was so concerned in 2002 became a flash in the pan, not a full-blown denominational split. Without any elected leaders and without an agenda beyond simply voicing faithfulness to central doctrines and behaviors of the Christian faith perceived as being under attack within the denomination, no follow-up action occurred. Because of this, institutional loyalists, lulled into a sense that the crisis had passed, returned to their "theology divides, mission unites" position for another decade. Religious Liberals became convinced that if nothing happened in 2002, nothing would happen once they finally cleared the way for the current cultural cause de jour, allowing the ordination of sexually active gay pastors, elders, and deacons. But the institutional loyalists and Religious Liberals were wrong in their assessment of the Confessing Church Movement. For those of us who were a part of it, it had an important message: there are still thousands in this denomination who have not bowed to Baal. If a split ever were to happen, though we might go quietly, we would not go alone.

I recently received a form letter from my presbytery's Committee on Ministry which articulated the status quo position quite clearly. "The Committee on Ministry…believes it important to express its sincere hope and firm expectation that your pastoral leadership will be faithful to the ordination vow you took to uphold the peace, purity, and <u>unity</u> (emphasis theirs) of the Church." There are two blazing ironies in this single sentence. One, the order is changed for their purposes. Officers vow to uphold the peace, unity, and purity of the Church, not the peace, purity, and unity. When I teach this to officers and new members, who promise to uphold the purity and peace of the church in the traditional vows which our church still uses, I tell them that the only time we disturb the peace and unity of Church is when the purity is at stake, not our own preferences and egos. As to the second irony, when at any time in the quarter century of my presbytery's existence has its Committee on Ministry sent out a letter to a pastor reminding him or her of the vow to uphold the purity of the Church? I'm not aware of it ever happening. Unity and peace seem to matter a lot to bureaucrats. Purity, not so much.

The letter continued, "The COM believes that our denomination is not apostate, and bears the marks of the True Church which John Calvin outlined." As I said in the previous chapter, these are the Word being rightly proclaimed and the sacraments being rightly administered. "Rightly", correctly, has no definition in a denomination which consciously and continually refuses to enumerate Essential Tenets; that being the case, how would the Committee on Ministry apply Calvin's standard? Apparently preaching and sacraments only are correct if they lead to unity above all else, regardless of truth, regardless of God's revelation in scripture.

Returning to the letter, "Our Westminster Confession acknowledges that 'The Purest churches under heaven are subject both to mixture and error.' (XXVII, 5) No denomination composed of human beings will ever be perfect." What a wonderful example of the buffet approach to confessionalism I wrote about at the end of Chapter 13, The Nature and Role of a Confession of Faith! What is the rest of the very same sentence in Chapter 27, paragraph 5? "...and some have degenerated as to become apparently no churches of Christ. Nevertheless there shall always be a Church on earth, to worship God according to his will." Unless the PC(USA) is itself the sole true Church on earth, or even the sole expression of the Reformed faith, and if it has "degenerated as to become apparently no church of Christ" as a denomination, should not a congregation be free to affiliate with a different, more faithful part of the Church? The answer is yes. The Presbyterian answer always has been yes. I will talk about that momentarily. First, though, let us consider Westminster's view of the True Church.

Citing the Westminster Confession of Faith as the model for the marks of the True Church is unwise for those who would stop with John Calvin's definition. Written in 1647, Westminster is heavily influenced by Scottish Presbyterianism, and as such, by John Knox. Knox had a third mark of the True Church: Discipline also will be applied.

A favorite phrase of Religious Liberals within the PC(USA) is "Freedom of Conscience". Chapter one of our Book of Order, our form of government, even cherry-picks the phrase from Westminster, "God alone is Lord of the conscience, and hath left it free from the doctrines and commandments of men which are in anything contrary to his Word, or beside it, in matters of faith or worship." Most Religious Liberals do not even mean this much, however, when they use the phrase. In my experience, they simply are declaring, in the words of Jiminy Cricket, that they will let their conscience be their guide! In fact, in a June 21, 2012, letter from Saint Andrews Presbyterian Church of Santa Barbara, California, challenging its presbytery's plan to form a union presbytery with the newly formed ECO: A Covenant Order of Evangelical Presbyterians denomination on the grounds it will promote schism, the session wrote that ECO's listing of essential tenets and requirement that officers adhere to them "violates (the) *fundamental* (ironic emphasis once again mine) theological conviction that God alone is Lord of the conscience and that freedom of conscience in the interpretation of Scripture must be maintained." Freedom of conscience in the interpretation of scripture? No confession of faith grants this, and certainly not Westminster, from which the phrase comes! Westminster says that our conscience is "free from the doctrines and commandments of men which are in anything contrary to (God's) Word, or beside it in matters of faith or worship." (Book of Confessions, 6.109) No one is free to go against the words of the Word! But for Saint Andrews, Santa Barbara, freedom of conscience means "fundamentally" that anything goes when it comes to doctrine, regardless of the Bible's words. Historically speaking, this is an odd position for Presbyterians, though not odd at all in the 21st century PC(USA).

What does Westminster say about the abuse of Christian freedom and the disciplinary response of the Church to those who abuse that freedom? "God alone is Lord of the conscience" is the beginning of paragraph 2 in Chapter 22. Paragraph 3 begins this way: "They who, upon the pretense of Christian liberty, do practice any sin, or cherish any lust, do thereby destroy the end (the purpose) of Christian liberty...", which is the ability to serve God all the days of our lives. Paragraph 4 continues by explaining that those who oppose lawful Church authority (which is subject to the authority of scripture) are resisting God. "And for their publishing such...erroneous opinions or practices as...are destructive to the external peace and order which Christ hath established in the church...they may be lawfully called to account, and proceeded against by the censures of the Church." The true Church will apply discipline, according to The Westminster Standards. But the PC(USA) has not applied discipline for theological shenanigans since the 1950s.

Ironically, only the "schismatics" of today, those who care deeply about biblical integrity in theology and are willing to fight for it, live under the threat of being "proceeded against by the censures of the Church." Theological heretics, especially those serving in callings away from the local congregation, are safe, and often commended for their original thinking. Those who accept and champion the sexual ethics of the culture against those revealed in scripture are protected by their bureaucratic allies, who are themselves often removed from practical accountability. While the Reformers always maintained that the Church can exist in places where it sometimes is more invisible, it is difficult to deny that of the marks of the True Church set down by Calvin and Knox continue to fade badly within this denomination.

When Presbyterian leaders raise the charge of schism as the worst sin, I answer, "Then why has the ability of a congregation to be dismissed to another Reformed denomination been part of the constitution of the Presbyterian Church for decades?" When I was ordained in 1988, Chapter XV in The Book Of Order, on ecumenical relationships, said this: "When a particular church of another denomination requests that it be received by a presbytery of this denomination, the presbytery shall verify that the church has been regularly dismissed by the governing body of jurisdiction, and the advice of the highest governing body of that denomination has been received, and shall then receive the church in accord with its responsibilities and powers. Similar procedures shall be followed in dismissing a particular church from this denomination to another." (G-15.0203) Those words went unchanged in the denomination's constitution until 2011, when the denomination adopted a new Form of Government. But still the schismatic hunters have no leg on which to stand. Now it says, "After consultation with the congregation involved in joint witness and the next higher council or governing body of the other denomination involved, a presbytery may receive a congregation from or transfer a congregation to a denomination with which the Presbyterian Church (U.S.A.) is in full communion or correspondence when it determines that the strategy for mission of that congregation is better served by such a transfer." If leaving the PC(USA) is such a terrible sin, why does the PC(USA)'s own constitution allow for it? Certainly it is not because of the hardness of the hearts of those who want to leave! Certainly, at least in part, it is because Presbyterian denominations never, ever have claimed to be the one true Church. Schism means breaking fellowship with the one true Church. Leaving for another denomination does not mean, it never has meant, leaving the one true Church. Those of us who are leaving are not schismatics, regardless of what our hysterical friends believe or say. We simply are being regrafted by God into a healthy branch of the vine.

As I type these words in 2012 I still am a member of the PC(USA), certainly blackballed to the point that no one even will have me on a presbytery committee, and purposely skipped over as a commissioner to our General Assembly, but still allowed to serve my congregation, though I speak openly about my plans to leave while the congregation considers its own affiliation. A decade ago I would not have had this freedom. In all likelihood, if I had spoken openly of leaving back then, for the congregation or me personally, the Committee on Ministry would have removed me as pastor, and perhaps even dissolved the Session, appointing a commission of the presbytery to run the church until suitable leadership, committed to remaining, could be found. That's the way it often was done in the aftermath of the formations of the PCA in 1973 and the EPC in 1981. And in the middle of the first decade of the 21st century, harsh measures of padlocking church doors and filing injunctions in civil court against "schismatic" congregations were secretly suggested from the General Assembly Stated Clerk's Office in the now infamous "Louisville Papers"; that scandal is our own denomination's equivalent of Watergate! But the questionable "trust" clause of Chapter 8 in the Book of Order (See Chapter 15) also posited the use, sale, or transfer of property with the presbyteries, not the General Assembly. Though somebody in Kentucky might wish me removed today, my presbytery has final say over my disposition. Events within the presbytery in 2008 have given me the freedom to be honest.

I still remember the day, July 19, 2008, because after the presbytery meeting I gathered with our church band, Veracity, still wearing my dress shirt and tie, for what would be our final group photographs. One of them wound up on the back of our last CD, Moving On, and I do look, well, cocky, in part because I had just won a rare victory on the floor of the meeting. That day the presbytery had committed itself to authoring what became its gracious dismissal policy. And though I could not have known it in 2008, the victory would be even sweeter a year later when the policy which my actions began and which I helped to write would be adopted unanimously by the presbytery, with no dissenting votes. That almost never happens.

That morning the presbytery received a report from the commissioners who attended the 2008 General Assembly, which had just met that June in San Jose, California. During the report it was mentioned that some presbyteries had declared themselves "G-6.0106b free zones"; this was the paragraph requiring fidelity in marriage and chastity in singleness for pastors, elders, and deacons finally removed in 2011. But in 2008 it was a part of the constitution of the denomination. Those who did not agree with it were free to work for change, but defiance was not an option. At least it was not supposed to be an option. A small minority of presbyteries, convinced of their own wisdom, had taken it upon themselves to hold up a middle finger to the rest of the denomination. They were openly defying the majority, and protecting their own members from prosecution in church courts. (See Chapter 17)

That morning I had had enough. When the commissioners' report was concluded I got to a microphone and put a motion on the floor 1) that our presbytery declare itself a "Chapter 8 free zone"; 2) that our presbytery declare that none of the church property within its bounds is held in trust for the denomination; and 3) that our presbytery declare that all the property of the member churches belongs to those churches. Chapter 8, of course, was the Property Chapter. Knowing that most southern churches still were operating under the misinformation that they owned their property, and what a sore subject it had been prior to reunion, I expected a second to the motion right away, and I got it.

I spoke to the motion. "Mr. Moderator, next summer I'm going to be marrying a little girl who grew up in our church to her fiancé. Her great-grandfather bought the land on which our building is located, in 1950, and when he bought it, he did not buy it for _____ Presbytery or a denomination, he bought it for our congregation. He gave it to our congregation. It does not belong to anyone else."

Had we gone to a vote at that moment, it probably would have passed. But lunchtime had arrived, so the vote was delayed until after the meal. During that break the Stated Clerk of the presbytery came up to me and said, "Powell, I think your motion is illegal." "Of course it is," I replied. "That's the point." It was no different than what the "G-6.0106b free zone" presbyteries were doing without fear of censure. But this was something which would terrify the Louisville bureaucrats; their sure response would expose the double standard. I hadn't thought of anything beyond that.

Providentially, another pastor, a good friend, approached me during the break as well. He had been thinking a lot about the impending crisis when fidelity and chastity finally would be stripped away and many churches would need to leave the denomination in order to survive. "This is an opportunity," he said, "to get the presbytery to develop and adopt a gracious dismissal policy, as the General Assembly just urged the presbyteries to do in June. If you will let me bring in a substitute motion as an answer to your motion, I think that will satisfy everyone. We can get something we really need out of this." Thinking strategically instead of tactically has never been my strong suit. I thank God for wise friends like Steve Moss. I quickly agreed. So did the entire presbytery. They even saw fit to put Steve and me on the committee to draft the new policy.

The gracious dismissal policy we created wound up serving as a model for most North Carolina presbyteries, as well as several others beyond our state. In it the presbytery vowed not to initiate civil court cases against churches considering leaving for another Reformed body. It also vowed not to take court action against pastors, officers, or members in those churches so long as the policy is followed. It was written in such a way that openness and honesty were promoted.

And it was fair; no wonder it received a unanimous vote! First, a time of attempted reconciliation with the troubled congregation would take place, to address its concerns; if that was deemed unsatisfactory, a resolution team then would be appointed by the presbytery to find a way forward through dismissal. Two thirds of the congregation needed to be present for a vote, and two thirds would have to vote to leave in order to go. If 90% or more voted to leave, the church could go with its property. If the vote to leave was between 66% and 89%, the church would owe the presbytery the percentage by which the congregation had voted to stay, and a payment plan would be worked out, but they still could go with their property. And I will say here and now that the presbytery has been even more gracious in practice than the policy required or I expected, not insisting on as much money from departing churches as allowed by the policy.

As a final note to this story, my Presbytery Executive later told me that when the Executive in one of the "G-6.0106b free zone" presbyteries heard about the policy we had adopted, that man lamented that such a document ever was needed. I said, "The next time you see him, you tell him I said that it is because of him and his presbytery, and presbyteries like them, that this document was needed." The injustice of disregarding majority rule has driven churches away as surely as theological anarchy and ethical relativism. Who then are the true schismatics, breaking with fairness, with the plain meaning of words, with the authority of scripture, and with the Church Universal in the name of inclusivity?

CHAPTER TWENTY-ONE: THE GLORY OF THE CHURCH UNIVERSAL, MILITANT AND TRIUMPHANT

Today, the Church is one of the most maligned institutions in the western hemisphere. Certainly there are many things, both historical and contemporary, about which the Church should be ashamed. But by and large I must say that the Church is a force for good in society. It is light and salt in a world darkened and made bland by sin. It is not yet a perfect Bride. But it is the Beloved of Christ, and He will perfect her. His faithful people are commanded to be part of her many times throughout scripture. I have written much in this book about the things with which I disagree in my denomination. But I still believe the Church to be a glorious thing and something to celebrate.

It annoys me when I hear people saying they "don't like organized religion". I have found this either to be the hiding place for people who want to make up their own religion, based on feelings or nature worship, or to be a refuge for practical but quiet atheists and agnostics who don't want to be known as opposing belief in God. What, you prefer a chaotic religion? No, in fact, what they seem to want is a tailor-made religion which asks little but brings assurance upon demand. It really is based only upon gazing into oneself, and clamoring for comfort.

Of course, not liking organized religion has deep roots in American mythology and practice. One of my favorite examples of this comes from Daniel Boone, who claimed that he knew it was time to move further west whenever he discovered wagon tracks within five miles of his house. "Getting too crowded around here!" Mormonism and Russellism are two practical attempts of Americans not trusting organized religion and inventing their own. It even has been argued that two modern, secular examples of "religious" experiences are found among fans at sporting events and music concerts; while there is a sense of belonging, there is no demand for anything beyond a good time.

However, while "Lone Ranger" Christianity is acceptable in American culture, there is no example of it to be found in the New Testament. Even Paul, with a reputation for being a loner and a personality like sandpaper to some, still coordinated his efforts with the churches. He repeatedly brought funds from Gentile churches to the poor mother church in Jerusalem, and submitted to the wisdom of the Jerusalem elders when they ordered him to go through a Jewish ritual with other Jewish Christians, as well as ordering him to pay for it himself! (Acts 21:22-24)

What has been accomplished by non-organized anything, anywhere and at any time in the world? Nothing beyond momentary good feelings or catharsis. How has a chaotic approach changed anything for the better in any meaningful way? What has anarchy in anything contributed to society, to groups or to individuals? I know there are non-religious people who have changed the world, at least for a time, including practical atheists Stalin, Mao, and Hitler; but you still have to admit, they were organized! What non-organized movement, secular or religious, can claim for itself the world-changing, life-bettering accomplishments of the Christian Church over two millennia and longer? As I like to remind my youth group, our most effective local charity is Allied Churches, not Allied Atheists!

Of course, the true value of the Church cannot be measured simply in temporal terms, as non-believers are wont to judge. Like the ancient Jews, it has been entrusted with the oracles of God, and the proclamation of the gospel. And as important as the Bible has been to Western Civilization, the message of eternal life has eternal consequences. It is the preaching of that Word which the Holy Spirit uses primarily as the means of convincing and converting sinners, of saving us from the fires of hell, and for building us up into the image of Jesus Himself. Truth matters beyond what the senses can discern!

Why should you and I be involved in a church? The beginning of the answer is found in the 20th chapter of Exodus, in the Ten Commandments. The fourth commandment says, "Remember the Sabbath Day, to keep it holy. Six days you shall labor and do all your work, but the seventh day is a Sabbath to the LORD, your God. In it you shall not do any work, you or your son or your daughter, your male or your female servant, or your cattle, or your sojourner within your gates. For in six days the LORD made the heavens and the earth, the sea, and all that is in them, and rested on the Sabbath day; therefore the LORD blessed the Sabbath day and made it holy." God wants His people to take one day off in seven from doing the things they must do to keep food on the table. Why? So we will remember that He is God, and we are not. If we want to please Him, we will remember the Sabbath Day; the benefits are ours, not His!

Calvinists believe there are three uses for the Commandments: 1) to convict us of sin and let us know our need for a Savior; 2) to order society; 3) to guide the individual Christian in the ordering of his or her life in the process of sanctification. When it comes to sanctification, that lifelong process by which we are made more and more like Christ, perfection is not the point. Jesus has already lived the Law perfectly, and His righteousness is imputed to us when we are justified, when we are saved. At no time in this life will we come close to living the Law perfectly, even when we are at our best. And we often are not at our best. No, trying to order our lives according to God's Law is simply an offering of love to Him.

I illustrate it for the congregation like this. I am not the perfect husband. There are things which I do today, even after 28 years of marriage, which absolutely drive my wife nuts. I can't seem to remember to shut cupboard doors. I leave the lights on in rooms that I have left. I cannot help but clutch the handle over the passenger window and stomp the floor when she drives! But because I genuinely love her, I try to do things which please her. I cook. I wash dishes. I vacuum. I take out the trash. And sometimes I even make the bed, poorly. Even though I am not the perfect husband, I try, and if I did not try, someone would have the right to observe that I don't seem to love her very much.

So it is with our relationship with God. We cannot lose our salvation (Calvinists believe that once you are saved, you always are saved, citing John 10:27-29), so fear is not our motivation for doing good. Our motivation is thankfulness. Since we cannot lose our salvation, if we do not try to live in a way that is pleasing to Him, perhaps we are not thankful, and perhaps have not been saved in the first place. If this is the case for you, if you are not living for Jesus out of thankfulness, today is the day to surrender your will to the will of Him who loves you so much that He died for you. Conversion is not a matter of feelings or the intellect. Conversion is a matter of the will. Are you willing to submit all you understand of yourself to all that you understand of Jesus, as much as possible? Trying to live the commandments, trying to be like Jesus, and getting better at doing them over time, is one of the ways the Holy Spirit assures us that we truly belong to the Lord.

A pastor friend of mine recently wondered out loud as to when the Jews began to link Sabbath rest with Sabbath worship. This is a great question, and I don't know that the Old Testament answers the question directly. However, I speculate that, at least in part, it may have begun during the reign of King Jehoshaphat, who, according to 2 Chronicles 17:7, sent officials, Levites, and priests out into the cities of Judah in the third year of his reign. "And they taught in Judah, having the book of the Law of the LORD with them; and they went throughout all the cities of Judah and taught among the people." (2 Chronicles 17:9) Prior to this, temple worship in Jerusalem was the main emphasis in the Old Testament religion; in fact, private worship "on the high places" was seen as a dangerous thing because it invited pagan influences into Judah. But the destruction of the temple by the Babylonians in 587 BC, along with seventy years of exile, meant that the type of worship and teaching done during Jehoshaphat's reforms would be necessary, as well as ingrained in the Jewish mindset. Certainly the fact that the chronicler emphasized this story, untold in 1 Kings, means that this type of worship, able to be performed weekly in synagogues with or without a temple, was being held up as a model for post-exile Jews. Dispersion Jews, scattered all around the eastern Mediterranean Sea, followed the same pattern with their synagogues.

Christians are called to be disciples of Jesus, literally students of Jesus. What pattern did He set? The definitive verse is Luke 4:16, "And He came to Nazareth, where He had been brought up; and as was His custom, He entered the synagogue on the Sabbath, and stood up to read." It was Jesus' custom to go to synagogue on the Sabbath Day, Saturday on our calendars. We should do the same. Why do most Christians worship on Sunday instead of Saturday? Because this is the day Jesus rose again. Think about that for a moment. Why would the early Christians, who were all raised as Jews and all had worshipped on the seventh day of the week in keeping with the commandment, suddenly change to worshipping on the first day of the week? It was happening early on; Eutychus fell from the rafters and died, only to be revived by Paul, during a service on the first day of the week (Acts 20:7ff), while John sees the vision of Revelation during worship on the Lord's Day, Sunday (Revelation 1:10). Sunday worship is one of the best external evidences for the historical events of Easter, and Jesus' rising from death. The only reason first century Jewish converts to Christianity would have done this would be if something as paradigm shifting as creation itself, the thing remembered by the commandment, a new creation, had occurred on that day. Jesus ushered in the beginning of the Day of the Lord, promised in the Old Testament, when He rose again.

"And let us consider how to stimulate one another to love and good deeds, not forsaking our own assembling together, as is the habit of some, but encouraging one another; and all the more, as you see the day drawing near." (Hebrews 10:24+25) "If someone says, 'I love God,' and hates his brother, he is a liar; for the one who does not love his brother, whom he has seen, cannot love God whom he has not seen." (1 John 4:20) It can't be much more clear than this! It is the Lord's will that His people gather weekly to worship Him and build up one another in the faith. Church membership or attendance does not make one a Christian. But a Christian, under ordinary circumstances, will seek regular worship and fellowship with other believers. This is not to say that a non-church attending Christian is unsaved, but that, apart from other believers, he or she is not being as effective a witness to Christ in the world as he or she could be. If you can get there, you should get there, at least weekly. This is God's plainly revealed will.

As I mentioned in Chapter 9, the purpose of spiritual gifts is the mutual building up of other believers. Paul wrote about this extensively in 1 Corinthians 12-14, and to a somewhat lesser degree in Romans 12 and Ephesians 4. The Corinthian discussion is particularly fascinating, especially given the context readily apparent from the letter itself. The church in Corinth was a mess, without a doubt. Paul wrote it at least three, maybe four times, and after his death the Roman church sent the non-canonical letter known as 1 Clement to the Corinthians, urging them to clean up their act! In that congregation there were factions lining up behind their favorite preachers against the others, there was gross sexual immorality, there were members suing each other in court, there were people coming to communion drunk, etc. And, in an ancient version of a modern conflict, there were some who spoke in tongues, languages of spiritual ecstasy, during the worship service, while there were others who did not; the tongue-talkers said the ones who did not also did not have the Holy Spirit, while the ones who did not counter-charged, "You don't even know what you are saying! You might be saying, 'Jesus is accursed!'" (1 Corinthians 12:3)

Paul begins this section of the letter by saying that no one speaking by the Spirit of God says, "Jesus is accursed," and no one can say, "Jesus is Lord," except by the Holy Spirit. Of course, a parrot could repeat the words; here Paul is talking about someone who has submitted to the Lordship of Christ, who has other gifts of the Spirit, but who does not speak in a language of spiritual ecstasy. Having established these facts, Paul then goes on to discuss the nature and purpose of spiritual gifts. It is not about you. It is about you using your gifts to build up the faith of your brothers and sisters in the Lord, and your faith being built up by them using their gifts. The gifts themselves are given by the Holy Spirit, and nobody has them all. The only way to experience the fullness of the Holy Spirit through His gifts is to be around other believers whose gifts are different from your own.

Paul actually writes, "But to each one is given the manifestation of the Spirit for the common good." (1 Corinthians 12:7) How can there be a common good if we keep to ourselves? Yes, working with other Christians, with other PEOPLE, can be difficult at times! Why else would Paul feel the need to stop in the middle of his discussion of spiritual gifts to talk about agape love, the kind which only comes from God and for which human beings can only be conduits, like pipes through which water flows? When Paul writes about speaking in the tongues of men and angels but not having agape love, or how this kind of love bears all things, believes all things, hopes all things, and endures all things, do you think he's merely talking about you and Jesus strolling through the garden where nobody else will be? Yes, a personal, individual relationship with Jesus is essential; God has no grandchildren! But the context of the much beloved 1 Corinthians 13 is the agape love needed for being part of a body made up of frail and flawed people. And then Paul returns to the image of corporate worship for chapter 14!

John's gospel is an amazing, sometimes confusing, take on the person and work of Jesus. Sometimes he mixes up the order of events to emphasize Jesus as the Messiah. Sometimes he uses images of light and darkness to illustrate truth. And sometimes, when the other three gospels tell a particular story, John tells something else to make a point.

Nowhere is this more clear than in John, chapter 13. Here John tells a story that takes place on the night when Jesus was betrayed. What happened that night, before Jesus and the disciples went into the Garden of Gethsemane? Jesus instituted the Lord's Supper, communion, or Eucharist in some traditions. Most people know this. Even Paul knew about it; the one story he tells about Jesus' earthly ministry in his letters is this one. "For I received from the Lord what I also passed on to you: the Lord Jesus, on the night He was betrayed, took bread, and when He had given thanks, He said, 'This is My body, which is broken for you...'" (1 Corinthians 11:25ff) The writer of John's gospel also knows about the Lord's Supper; otherwise, Jesus' discussion of eating His flesh and drinking His blood in chapter 6, and the misunderstanding which accompanies it, makes no sense.

But when the time comes to tell the best-known story of Jesus' ministry in the first century Church, John skips it almost entirely. He gets them to the table, and then Jesus gets up, gets out of his clothes, wraps a towel around Himself, and begins to wash the disciples' feet. This is the lowest service a slave would perform, reserved for children and unskilled labor. Peter especially does not want this; only when Jesus declares that if Peter does not allow this, he can have no part in Jesus, does he submit. When Jesus is done, He says that He has given the example as the teacher, and now the disciples should wash one another. Later that evening Jesus gives His new commandment, that they display agape love toward one another. That's how it's done, serving each other in the Church.

And John never describes what happened at the table as far as the meal, or the bread and the wine go. This is because he is showing his readers through this story what it means to "discern" the body of the Lord; remember, Paul wrote that everyone who takes part in communion should examine himself before coming to the table, because he who partakes without discerning the body of the Lord eats and drinks judgment to himself. To receive communion the right way, we must be serving other Christians.

Think about that in light of Jesus washing the disciples' feet. There is no job beneath the dignity of a Christian to perform, especially in service to other believers. And I almost think it would have been easier for Peter to be ordered by Jesus to wash the feet of the other disciples than it was for Peter to receive the washing from Jesus. It takes humility to serve someone. It also takes humility to allow someone to serve you. That's part of the glory of the Church. This type of humiliation does not happen apart from the other believers with whom we share the process of sanctification, becoming more like Jesus.

In fact, the two basic attitudes Christians are called to develop in the New Testament are thankfulness to God, and humility before other Christians. While I suppose the first might be cultivated to a certain extent apart from a congregation (though it would be enhanced within the congregation, I believe), humility before other Christians will not happen apart from being around them and serving them, with all their warts and ours! Paul writes, "Do nothing from selfishness or empty conceit, but with humility of mind let each of you regard one another as more important than himself; do not merely look out for your own personal interests, but also for the interests of others. Have this attitude in yourselves which was also in Christ Jesus, who, although He existed in the form of God, did not regard equality with God a thing to be grasped, but emptied Himself…" (Philippians 2:3-7a) You can't be looking out for the interests of others if there are no others.

One of the best arguments for being part of a congregation is found in the actual words of the New Testament. The word we translate as "saint" in English is "hagion" in Greek. Its root meaning is holy. A saint is a holy one, which is to say, someone who has been set apart for God's own use.

Roman Catholicism and Greek Orthodoxy latched on to the concept of "holy one" and through the centuries re-interpreted a "saint" as a really good person, almost perfect. But that is not the New Testament usage of the word. In the New Testament no individual is ever referred to as "Saint" somebody. While the titles of New Testament books in older translations might be "The Gospel of Saint Matthew" or "The Epistle of Saint Paul to the Romans", the actual texts of those books have no such designations. Luke calls Paul Paul. Paul himself calls Peter by the Aramaic word for rock, the actual nickname given to the apostle by Jesus, Cephas. Not Saint Cephas, just Cephas, "Rocky"!

No individual is called a saint in the text of the New Testament, but groups of Christians, congregations, are regularly referred to by the writers as "saints" in the plural, holy ones. Even the incredibly dysfunctional church of Corinth is greeted as saints. The biblical use of the word indicates that we are holy, set apart for God's use, as we remain together in congregations. It's not that one cannot be a believer in Christ while keeping to himself; the proverbial Christian marooned on a deserted island would be saved. Justification is a solo proposition. But sanctification, that process by which we become more like Jesus, is done in groups. After all, as Jesus said after washing the disciples' feet, "By this all people will know that you are My disciples, if you have love for one another." (John 13:35) In order to become effective Christians, we must be around other Christians we can love, not because they are always so loveable, but because this is Jesus' command. In an increasingly individualistic society, that a diverse group of people should come together regularly, connected not by biology or history or race or common interests, but by a commitment to the Lord Jesus Christ, this is a powerful witness to the power of the Holy Spirit in our lives.

I have heard this reality wonderfully illustrated by a charcoal fire. When a fire is going among the bricks, all the pieces share the fire and burn together. If you take one out, its flame goes out. If you put it back in, the flame returns, shared by the others. The hymn We Are God's People expresses it like this: "We die alone, for on its own each ember loses fire/ Yet joined in one the flame burns on/ To give light and warmth, and to inspire."

My wife was raised in an independent Baptist church which believed the doctrines taught by the ancient Apostles' Creed, but did not recite it or the Nicene Creed in worship. The first time she came to visit in my home church, after the benediction she wanted to know, "What's all this about believing the Holy Catholic Church?" She had been taught that Roman Catholics were not Christians because of extra-biblical traditions like the veneration of saints, transubstantiation, and the Pope. And I had to teach her then that the name "Catholic" was in the creeds 700 years before the Latin side of the Church started calling itself "Catholic" against the Greek Orthodox. Catholic means "universal"; the Holy Catholic Church is not the Roman Catholic denomination, but it is God's people in all times and places.

The ancient imagery for this Universal Church is glorious. The Church Militant is the part which is on earth at this moment, fighting the good fight, finishing the course, and keeping the faith. The Church Triumphant is the part which now rests in the presence of Jesus, beholding His face in glory. When Christians die we leave the Church Militant for the Church Triumphant; both groups are alive and united by our faith in Jesus. The hymn "The Church's One Foundation" puts it like this: "Yet she on earth hath union with God, the Three in One/ And mystic sweet communion with those whose rest is won/ O happy ones and holy, Lord give us grace that we/ Like them, the meek and lowly, on high may dwell with Thee."

That's a long way from church as merely a gathering of friends. It's a long way from the caricatures of "church" found in culture. It's a long way from a voluntary service organization to which you may or may not desire to belong. It is the body of Christ, His powerful witness in a broken and bleeding world.

CHAPTER TWENTY-TWO: TRADITIONAL VS CONTEMPORARY

"There's something about the massive sound of a distorted guitar that I REALLY like!" The year was 1982, and I was trying to explain to my father, who had minored in music at Wheaton College while supplementing his income by playing organ in Chicago churches, why I like heavy metal music. I didn't expect him to understand. Recently he had asked me why a great blues rock vocalist I liked had to sound like he was in pain while singing.

Instead, Dad's eyes sort of lit up, and he exclaimed, "Like the massive sound of a pipe organ!" Well, yeah. A few months later I was telling this story to a friend, a retired Air Force colonel. His eyes lit up, and he exclaimed, "Like the massive sound of a B-52 engine!" Again, well, yeah. Maybe men never move completely beyond our need for massive toys and loud bangs! It's just that the need expresses itself differently to each one.

I point this out because, at first glance, I would seem to be a prime candidate for championing contemporary worship styles within the Church. The seminal massive guitar sound for me is exemplified by the Marshall-stacked, Gibson guitar-birthed drive of Strutter, the second track on 1975's Kiss Alive! album. In 1977 and again in 1978 my high school rock band did entire concerts dressed as Kiss, complete with me breathing fire and throwing up blood. (Except when my father was in attendance!) To this day, I love blues based hard rock; not only do I still listen to it, I write, record, and perform it. Sans makeup.

But I do not care for most contemporary Christian music or worship styles. The music is easy enough to explain. Most of what the contemporary Christian music industry coughs up today sounds like it came off an assembly line: pasteurized, homogenized, and designed for mass consumption. I can say the same thing about most of the contemporary secular music industry as well. Most worship choruses strike me as bland, and certainly repetitious.

One of my favorite hymns is "O Sacred Head, Now Wounded," a gem from the Middle Ages. The final line is, "O make me Thine forever, and should I fainting be, Lord let me never, never outlive my love to Thee." Translation: Lord, if I begin to waver in my faith, please kill me before it's too late. This hymn will never become a positive and encouraging worship sing-along. And more's the pity. I could go on as well about over-production on a lot of modern Christian recordings, but for a guy with blues in the blood, what else would you expect? Most people don't like blues, so what I prefer musically is not what is going to appeal to the majority in a congregation.

However, this raises the question of the purpose of worship. Is it to make Christians feel good about ourselves? Is it to wrack us with feelings of guilt? Is it to be an emotional experience, or an intellectual exercise? Certainly all these things can happen in worship. But in the Reformed tradition, we believe that God reaches us primarily through our understanding. The central part of a worship service is the sermon; as I tell the kids in my youth group, it doesn't just seem like the longest part of the service, it IS the longest part of the service.

And for this reason, nothing else in the service should distract from the sermon. When I entered seminary at the age of 22, fresh out of college, my hair was longer than my wife's, several inches past my shoulders. I was trying to look like the Christian rockers I admired so much, like Larry Norman and Glenn Kaiser of Resurrection Band. About five months into seminary, realizing that I would be participating in a summer internship at a church, I decided it was time to cut the hair I had been growing for two and half years. My ministry was not going to be one of a rock and roller, but of a preacher. I realized that if people only looked at my hair, they would never hear the Word. That concept has followed me throughout my ministry. What we do in the worship service should follow the worship designs laid out in scripture, and should not distract from the preaching. Rock and roll is what I love, but I don't force it on my congregation.

While in seminary I had the joy of being taught preaching by Elizabeth Achtemeier, a powerful preacher in her own right. One day in class I asked her, "How do you know what is offensive?" She asked what I meant. I said that one of my favorite Christian rock songs has this line: "Gonorrhea on Valentine's Day (VD)/ And you're still looking for the perfect lay…Why don't you look into Jesus, He's got the answer." The class erupted before I got to the final line, and a classmate shouted out, "You've found what's offensive!" Once everyone had calmed down, I rephrased the question. "One of my favorite sermons is Jonathan Edwards' 'Sinners In The Hands Of An Angry God'. But some of the images that I find powerful in it are those which many people today would find merely offensive. How can we tell the difference?" Now that everyone understood what I was asking, Dr. Achtemeier replied, "This is why you have to know your congregation well to preach well to them."

The biggest complaint about Reformed worship from my contemporary friends and family is that it is boring. The biggest complaint I hear about contemporary worship from most Presbyterians is that it is not reverent. Do you see the trap here? What is reverent to some is boring to others, while what is exciting to some is irreverent to others. How do we know the difference? We must get to know the people with whom we worship, and tailor the worship experience to insure that, no matter what else happens, the preaching of the Word is plainly heard without distraction.

2003 was a difficult year for my ministry. I had been in my church for seven years, that time when things seem to fall apart for many ministers. (In fact, I had stayed in my first call for eight years, the last one being especially hard.) I sought the Lord with more focus, praying for His guidance. One of the things He seemed to say to me was, "Start a band with the youth group." "But Lord," I protested, "no one likes my music." "That's OK," He said, "we're going to use better music than yours!" About the same time I discovered an acoustic based Christian band out of Chicago called Seeds; their harmony-laden sound reminded me of the early Eagles. With the three teens who remained in the youth group, I put together the band: me on guitar, my son on bass, and the two girls singing lead and harmony. I added the second harmony, and we called ourselves Veracity. When we made our debut performance in the morning worship service, singing a Seeds song, an eighty-four year-old retired school teacher came up to me afterward, put her arm around me, and said, "I don't care if it had a guitar, it was still pretty!"

Even with this blessing, however, I was careful not to allow the teen band to eclipse the sermon. We sang occasionally in church, but never with the drummer we soon added, along with a teenage guitarist. Most of the time the youth band was an outreach band, playing full concerts in secular settings around the city. Coffee shops and street corners were our specialty.

Contemporary or traditional? Most people have a preference; I have the benefit of coming from both worlds. Veracity introduced contemporary music beyond the youth room; at the same time, the older members formed "The Revival Choir", and sang special selections of early 1900s revival hymns for anthems on occasion. Both now have lapsed, and a young man, with backgrounds in both southern gospel and contemporary praise and worship music, has redesigned the evening service for those who like something more up to date, with the blessing of the session. Through it all, the Word has been proclaimed clearly and without distraction. By easing our way into modern styles and respecting the preferences of everyone in the congregation, and by stressing the centrality of the Word all along, we have managed to avoid the divisive worship wars which have plagued many a congregation. How might that be done at your church?

The experience of the Reformers in the 16th Century is helpful to me. Zwingli banned all music and instruments from worship in Zurich. It should be noted that Ulrich Zwingli himself also was a musician, but he wanted no distraction from the proclamation of the Word; a quote I have heard attributed to him is "A church is four bare walls and a sermon." In Geneva, after considering the examples of scripture, Calvin brought back music, but with these three rules: no instruments; no harmony; lyrics based on scripture. It was from the stricture of these limitations that Presbyterians developed the discipline of writing metrical psalms, simple melodies with words based on the book of Psalms. In the 1955 Presbyterian Hymnbook the same metrical rendering of the words of Psalm 23 has three different melodies, a vestige of rules from the Reformation.

The best of the contemporary worship songs of the past fifty years, such as Seek Ye First, Psalm 5, and No Other, praise God and teach the Bible by using the actual words of scripture. No Christian ever should have a problem with that. Someone once asked Phil Keaggy why he did not introduce his songs with, "This is a song God gave to me," as many Christian artists did in the 1970s. He responded, "I'm not sure God would want credit for all my songs." When the words are from the Bible itself, we do not have to wonder whether or not they are inspired!

CHAPTER TWENTY-THREE: WHERE DO WE GO FROM HERE?

On February 2, 2011, a group of pastors from "tall steeple" churches in the PC(USA) wrote an open letter to the denomination which has come to be known as "The Deathly Ills" letter. Its first line read, "To say the Presbyterian Church (U.S.A.) is deathly ill is not editorializing but acknowledging reality," and then went on to declare, "How we got to this place is less important than how to move forward." Their proposition was radical for Presbyterians, and anticipated much of what I have written in this book: 1) Connect with like-minded congregations within the PC(USA), something already having been done through the years by groups such as The Presbyterian Coalition, Presbyterians For Renewal, and the old PCUS Covenant Fellowship; 2) Restructure and decentralize middle governing bodies, a proposal ultimately rejected by the Middle Governing Bodies Commission in 2012; 3) Form a new Reformed body. If that sounds like schism to you, well, the opponents of this letter certainly screamed it from the top of their tiny lungs. But by God's grace, the bureaucrats in Louisville did not act on such accusations, defrocking pastors and dissolving sessions as they would have done in years past. The signatories of the letter also invited all like-minded pastors and elders in the PC(USA) to join them for an organizational meeting in Minneapolis, MN, in August of 2011. I went. The place was packed with representatives from every single state in the United States, over 1900 people representing 852 congregations. The work begun there in August of 2011 led to the official formation of a new Reformed body, ECO: A Covenant Order of Evangelical Presbyterians, in January of 2012.

But I am getting ahead of myself! As I have already said in Chapter 9, Presbyterians by nature do not go independent; that would be like a Baptist church giving up baptism of adults by immersion for the "christening" of infants! Being part of a larger group of churches, that's what makes us distinctive, our connective and accountable governance within and beyond the local congregation. Having said this, when a Presbyterian church or pastor becomes convinced that it, he, or she can no longer remain faithful to Christ by remaining in the current denomination, the next immediate question is, "Where shall we/I go?" This question has occupied much of my thought since April of 2011.

The week after my presbytery voted overwhelmingly to remove ordination standards I called a friend who was the executive of the non-geographic PC(USA) Korean American presbytery which overlapped mine. We had gotten to know one another through our work together in the Synod. "Can we send a delegation to meet with you and representatives from your presbytery, and discuss the possibility of us being transferred from our presbytery to yours?" This was something that had been in the back of my mind for several years. The non-geographic, ethnic presbyteries in my denomination tend to be very orthodox. However, they also have few churches; this particular presbytery had about 30 congregations at the time. In my discussions with the Koreans through the years, they have always been open to having "American" churches join them. In my experience, having attended one Korean presbytery meeting, plus synod dealings, they are a very gracious people; during the meeting, which was held entirely in the Korean language, a pastor sat with me and another Synod representative, quietly and patiently translating for us the entire time. They know that the Korean presbyteries have much to offer orthodox American churches, and that the American churches can help them, both financially and in their secondary task of smoothly transitioning an immigrant community into American society by the second generation.

I was not surprised when he immediately agreed to meet with me and a delegation from our session. We gathered at a Korean church most centralized for the two groups, each driving two or three hours to get there. Together we were treated to a wonderful lunch of Korean dishes served at church in the senior center for elderly Koreans, whose children were at work. My hope at the time was that our congregation would be willing and able to transfer presbyteries. It would have been a good exchange for all.

Transferring presbyteries within the denomination is the easiest change for a Presbyterian church to make, especially when a non-geographic presbytery with which it identifies theologically overlaps it. (Not all churches have this option, however; non-geographic ethnic presbyteries are few, and ordinarily are limited to the population which speaks a language besides English. Aside from the Koreans, I have had positive experiences with representatives from Lakota Presbytery, which is in the central United States and made up of members of that Native-American tribe, known commonly as the Sioux, a French word for snake. Needless to say, they don't like the insulting name by which most of us know them!) For a church, transferring from one presbytery to another avoids questions of property ownership and accusations of schism. At the time we were talking about this, my answer to Religious Liberals and bureaucrats who questioned my desire to make this change was, "We like Koreans. Don't you?"

One of the times I have been proudest of my son was in the summer of 2011 when he and I were visiting with my father. Though Dad understood where the church and I were coming from, he still had his doubts. "But son," he objected, "joining a Korean presbytery will be very difficult for an American congregation. There will be the language barrier. There will be cultural barriers." "But Grand-dad," piped in my son before I could say anything, "that's the point!" And it is! Like the bizarre flock of birds filled with hawks, doves, peacocks, ostriches, and turkeys, the very fact that such a diverse group of people could come together in spite of the differences which should keep them apart in a world where birds of a feather flock together, the common commitment to Jesus Christ, revealed in scripture, who died for our sins, is risen and returning, is powerful witness to a factious world that God is certainly among those Christians.

Alas, it was not to be. Ultimately, our congregation's leadership determined that remaining in the PC(USA) at all, even if we were to join our brothers and sisters in the Korean presbytery, would not be far enough away from the chaos of the denomination for many of our members. At the end of the day, they would be leaving the congregation if we stayed in the PC(USA) at all, and that was a loss the church could not afford, and perhaps not survive. One of the realities of more than a decade and a half of Reformed, biblically based preaching and teaching was that we had attracted new members committed to that way of thinking; most older members were already there! Now, when they saw clearly that their own denomination did not share this essential commitment, many wanted nothing to do with it. At the same time, I commend the Korean option to any churches now which must remain in the PC(USA) to survive, but are grieved by the decisions it has made and continues to make. They want you, and they need you. You can help each other.

I do want briefly to note here that for a short time in 2011 and 2012, as part of a General Assembly initiative to restructure the middle governing bodies (synods and presbyteries), there was talk of developing non-geographic presbyteries within the PC(USA) based on theology instead of language and culture. Some also fine-tuned the concept to hope for "overlay presbyteries", theologically based second presbyteries within the bounds of existing geographic presbyteries. The advantage of this would have been the simplicity of transfer from just one presbytery to just one other, in addition to remaining in the current denomination while being protected from the growing grasp of Religious Liberalism. According to the Book of Order, the minimum number of pastors and churches needed for forming a presbytery is twelve of each. (G-11.0102, old BoO) In mega-presbyteries, having well over one hundred churches already, such numbers would not have been difficult to find. But in 2012 the General Assembly Commission on Middle Governing Bodies, tasked with finding new ways of organizing presbyteries, refused to allow theologically based non-geographic presbyteries or overlay presbyteries. Some critics charged that this was a means of stifling theological diversity. Of course it was. For those committed to integrity in biblical interpretation and application, theological diversity never has been a goal. Theological diversity (read: heresy) is something to be opposed. Other denominational voices fretted that orthodox, non-geographic presbyteries in the south might use their right to release congregations with their properties as a means of pillaging the PC(USA) of property it had annexed unilaterally in 1982 and 1983. In truth, by 2012 the point had become moot for our congregation. If the church were to survive with the lion's share of our membership intact, we would have to leave the Presbyterian Church (U.S.A.) altogether.

The oldest of the alternative Reformed bodies available to our church in 2012 is the Associate Reformed Presbyterian Church. Historically speaking, this body is the sister of the PC(USA). While the denomination in which I was raised and ordained traces its founding in the United States to 1789, when its first General Assembly met in Philadelphia, the ARP was a separate group of Presbyterians distinct from The Established Presbyterian Church of Scotland when they arrived in America in 18th century, and they were organizing alongside the dominant Presbyterian brand of that time. Their first Synod was formed in 1782, also in Philadelphia. By 1900 most of their churches and presbyteries had been absorbed into the larger body of what would become the PC(USA), except for the Synod of the Carolinas, which had been granted separate status from the rest of the denomination in 1822.

I like the ARPs! Three of my seminary professors were from that denomination: Ken Morris, "Baby" Greek; Jim Mays, Old Testament; and John Leith, Theology. And just as their presence at an established PC(USA) seminary in the 1980s was no surprise, up until the 1970s pastors moved easily from churches in the old southern denomination (PCUS) to the ARPs and back again. My father, ordained in the PCUS, was offered a call to an ARP congregation in 1965; having only arrived at his church in Augusta, Georgia, the previous year, he respectfully declined. My own dealings with the local ARP congregation and its pastors have been wonderful here in Burlington.

But things have changed since the days of cheerful fraternity between the PCUS and the ARP. A major sticking point between the two denominations now is the ordination of women; the PC(USA) mandates such ordinations, and the ARP mandates that they not be ordained, as they have since colonial times. While I personally might be able to submit my understanding of women's ordination to the majority view of the ARP, working for change but not defying the will of the majority, I could not ask the Elders of my church who happen to be women to simply step aside once their three year term in office is completed, never to be elected to Active status again. While I seem to have a lot in common with the ARP, this is a deal-breaker.

The PCA is The Presbyterian Church in America. As I have already said, it was founded in 1973 in anticipation of the reunion between the southern and northern denominations which was being forced through at any cost. In 2012 it had more than 1450 churches and missions throughout the United States and Canada; it certainly was the largest of the alternative denominations available to our church, and had a congregation in Burlington with whom we already worshiped and fellowshipped regularly. In fact, that congregation, Northside Presbyterian Church, was organized by our church's pastor in the 1950s, and we have had more contact with them locally than we have with any PC(USA) congregation. Several of our older Elders have expressed a willingness to transfer to that denomination, as well as the ARP. It is unquestionably a dynamic and faithful denomination.

But women's ordination is even a bigger shibboleth in the PCA than in the ARP, perhaps because many experienced the "right foot of fellowship" when they were booted out of the PCUS in the 1970s for not accepting the mandate of female Elders, regardless of biblical interpretation. Many of their older pastors and elders remember the devastating votes of the late 1960s and early 1970s, and the refusal of the southern branch from which they sprang to exercise any discipline for theological deviation. And these people don't play. I have heard it said, "It is better to be a conservative in the PC(USA) than a liberal in the PCA," and to an extent, I believe it. I have no desire to be actively driven out of a new denomination any more than I have desired the tacit but firm shove from the old one. Perhaps I could be convinced otherwise; I have several good friends who are PCA pastors. But for the same reason that the ARP would not be a good fit for my church, our women elders, it is not a viable option for me while I remain its pastor.

There are other Presbyterian groups which exist, such as the Orthodox Presbyterian Church, which is the northern equivalent of the PCA; they left the northern denomination in the 1930s, along with Greshem Machen, following the Fundamentalist/Modernist Controversy of the 1920s, and adopted Westminster Seminary in Philadelphia as their alternative to Princeton Seminary. Their presence in North Carolina is very small, and they do not ordain women. There also is The Bible

Presbyterian Church, which broke with the OPC over the question of Dispensationalism in the late '30s; their view of end-times prophecy, and women's ordination, as well as an even smaller presence in North Carolina, would make them a poor fit for my congregation. However, there are two other denominations of Presbyterians in which I believe our congregation and I could find a home. They are the Evangelical Presbyterian Church and ECO: A Covenant Order of Evangelical Presbyterians.

The Evangelical Presbyterian Church (EPC) was formed in 1981, in part as a response to the impending reunion of the larger northern and southern streams of Presbyterianism in the United States; as previously stated, that reunion did take place, come hell or high water, in 1983. While many in the EPC held theological beliefs in common with the PCA, there were two major differences. First, the PCA held firmly to the belief of John Calvin and others in the Reformed family that the spiritual gift of speaking in tongues as described in the Bible ceased with the completion of the New Testament, having completed its function, along with the gifts of miraculous healings by the laying on of hands and raising dead people back to life. Many of the founders of the EPC believed the gift of speaking in tongues still to be a legitimate gift for the modern Church, through their own experiences or the experiences of their membership. Because of this, the PCA did not want these churches. If there were to be a denominational home for them, they would have to build it themselves. Secondly, once their new home was completed, the founders of the EPC rejected both the liberal mandate that women must be ordained by sessions and presbyteries, as well as the conservative mandate that women must *not* be ordained by sessions and presbyteries. They left this matter in the hands of the ordaining bodies.

While the controversy of speaking in tongues has quieted in recent years (EPC ministers say the matter rarely is addressed and the gift rarely is exercised in their presbytery meetings), the option of women's ordination instead of an insistence upon it has given rise to the idea that the EPC is not a good place for PC(USA) women Elders and Pastors. It has not helped that some churches within the EPC have chosen not to elect women as

Elders any more, including the congregation in which I grew up in Lynchburg, Virginia. (Ironically, the only other church I remember from my childhood joined the PCA decades ago; both of these churches left their more liberal denominations after my father stopped being their pastor!) Also, two of the eleven presbyteries within the EPC do not ordain or install women as pastors, and, while others are open to the possibility, most actually do not have women pastors yet. They are addressing the issue. They are making arrangements to allow churches which wish to call women pastors to switch to a neighboring presbytery should their own not ordain or install women. The presbytery to which our church would belong should it join the EPC does allow women pastors and has a female theological student under the care of presbytery, though currently no women are serving in this capacity. The women Elders of that presbytery do hold positions of power and influence at this time, in 2012. And since most PC(USA) churches leaving for another Reformed body this year in North Carolina are going to the EPC, the influence of women's leadership is certain to become stronger.

The EPC is a small denomination, with just under 400 congregations nationwide. However, they are dynamic in their commitment to the gospel and to church-planting; the number of EPC churches has almost doubled in ten years, and not just through transfer of PC(USA) congregations into their fold. Churches plant churches instead of presbyteries, as it was throughout pre-World War 2 American Presbyterianism. Part of the reason for this within the EPC has been the discovery that new believers are much more likely to join a new church plant instead of an established, older congregation. The idea of my church starting a store-front chapel in downtown or out in the county is very exciting to me, supported and initially peopled by members from our congregation. Also, the EPC constitution states that the churches, not the denomination, own their properties. There is no trust clause.

For me, another attractive aspect of the EPC is that they only have one confession of faith, The Westminster Standards. Their understanding of Westminster is classic Presbyterianism as well, not just a museum piece, but a "Here we stand, we can do no other, so help us God!" statement to the world as to what they believe and do. And it is written in pencil – already, since their forming in 1981, they have written new chapters on the Holy Spirit and the purpose of Missions. Beyond Westminster, the EPC has a listing of seven Essential Doctrines which stand in line with historic Reformed Christianity. Their denominational motto is "In Essentials – Unity, In Non-Essentials – Liberty, In All Things – Charity." They also have restored ordination vows from the old southern denomination to the way they were written in the 1950s (see Chapter 1), including the promise to inform the presbytery of one's own initiative if his or her views change.

Geographically, EPC presbyteries are huge. The Presbytery of the Mid-Atlantic, which overlaps our community geographically, has congregations in all of South Carolina, North Carolina, Virginia, and parts of West Virginia. And I have complained about having to drive only three hours from one end of my current presbytery to the other! However, numerically their sizes are far from the mega-presbyteries of the PC(USA). The Presbytery of the Mid-Atlantic had less than 60 congregations in 2012, though that number was expected to increase with more than 40 PC(USA) congregations within their bounds exploring the option of transferring to the EPC. Already there was talk about dividing the presbytery in two. And mercifully, they have no presbytery executives.

The EPC understands the havoc that no accountability has wrought throughout the PC(USA). To that end, pastors not serving churches, including retired pastors, have voice but no vote at presbytery meetings. This is not about disenfranchising anyone; it is about checks and balances, and knowledge of the corrupting influence of unbridled power.

ECO: A Covenant Order of Evangelical Presbyterians was unveiled at the Orlando Gathering of the Fellowship of Presbyterians in January of 2012, and I was in attendance with one of my Elders, in the front row. As a completely new denomination formed by churches who were in the PC(USA), the fingerprints of its predecessor denomination were much more obvious at its inception when compared with the other Reformed bodies of which I have spoken in this chapter. Women's ordination was guaranteed. The Book of Confessions was retained rather than a return to the Westminster Standards. The

Book of Order was retained as amended in 2010, prior to the adoption of the more permissive New Form of Government.

However, like the prohibitionist raised in the home of an alcoholic, their new rules addressed many of the same failings of the PC(USA) about which I have written, so much that I almost accused someone of borrowing my manuscript while I wasn't looking! ECO will have no vote for pastors not serving churches at their presbytery meetings. Their goal is to have no more than 20 churches in their presbyteries, thus promoting collegiality among pastors and eliminating the position of Presbytery Executive. Churches will be encouraged to find ways to take the gospel to the community rather than simply waiting for the community to show up at their doorsteps. Part of this will be accomplished through churches starting new churches, not presbyteries. From the beginning, they have made it clear that their churches will own their property, it will not be held in trust for the denomination. And, in spite of the adoption of a Book of Confessions, ECO has written and approved a list of Essential beliefs which reflect the historic Reformed understanding; perhaps this will over-ride the dusty museum effect the collection has inflicted upon the PC(USA). I hope so. At the August 2012 Gathering of the Fellowship and ECO participants were told that the Book of Confessions probably will be getting smaller in years to come, thus bringing a more clear articulation to the world of the faith proclaimed, so help us God.

One of the most interesting innovations of ECO is the re-introduction of the Narrative on the Health of Mission and Ministry (for Congregations) abandoned by the northern Presbyterian Church after 1925. Rather than focus on numbers, as the PC(USA) Annual Statistical Report has done as long as I have been a pastor, the Narrative encourages congregations to think and talk about the mission to which Jesus is calling them. Each year the Session will be asked to meet with sessions from other congregations to encourage and challenge one another to spread the gospel of our risen Lord, with discussion based upon the narratives presented.

Ten questions make up the Narrative:

1) How has the Holy Spirit been evident in your congregation in the past year; through conversions, growth in the fruit of the Spirit, or other transformational experiences that make disciples of Jesus Christ?
2) How has your congregation extended itself beyond its bounds through the establishment of new communities of worship and discipleship, expanding the Kingdom of God?
3) In what ways is your congregation seeking the welfare of the community to which you have been called; devoting itself to the poor, seeking justice, and living out the whole of the Great Commission?
4) How are you encouraging people to allow God's Word to shape their priorities and actions, and to nurture constant learning and the life of the mind?
5) How are you helping children and others new to the Christian faith to discover Jesus and grow in their understanding and love of God's Word?
6) Describe the moral expression of your congregation – are you more like the world, or more like participants in the values of the Kingdom of God?
7) How is your congregation intentionally unleashing the ministries of women, men, and people of different ethnic groups who are experiencing God's call?
8) How is the idea of ministry as the joy and calling of every disciple evident in your congregation? How are you equipping people to represent Jesus more effectively in their respective professions?
9) Illustrate the commitment of your congregation to global evangelism and discipleship, including examples of where you are engaged and with whom you are partnering.
10) How does your congregation understand commitment to the larger church throughout our connectional relationships within the Body of Christ?

The idea in asking these questions is not to punish or embarrass churches. It is to foster discussion and consideration of what might be attempted and accomplished for the glory of the Kingdom of Christ. It is to prevent congregations from being content with what they or their grandparents might have done in the past, and encourage them to press on to the new thing to which the Lord is calling them.

By mid-2012 there were about 100 churches either in or vying to join ECO. Two presbyteries had been formed, the Presbytery of the East and the Presbytery of the West, with the Mississippi River dividing them. The closest church to North Carolina was in Greenville, South Carolina, though two churches in Charlotte were considering joining the new denomination. Our church is considering ECO as well as the EPC. Though I have friends in the EPC and really don't know anyone in ECO, I believe I could be happy in either denomination.

CHAPTER TWENTY-FOUR: ANSWERING OBJECTIONS

As I have indicated before, on Monday, August 15th, 2011, I met with my presbytery's General Presbyter, and an Associate Executive Presbyter who I also consider to be a friend. This was not a meeting that I went into with any thought of anything being resolved. For me it was just an opportunity to vent, to let these two men know what I have been through, and am going through, as the pastor of a church in a presbytery without discipline, without instruction, without correction, without accountability, without the will to change any of these things, and, at least up till this moment for me, without pastoral care for pastors. The conversation was amiable, though honest. For them, I think, it was a time to get me to ask myself, "What really has changed now that ordination standards have been destandardized?" Unfortunately for them, my complaints had little to do with sexuality, and all to do with theology and accountability. The overwhelming vote to allow sexual anarchy within the Church had unequivocally laid bare for me the heresy and hypocrisy of the denomination; a phrase I found myself repeating over and over was, "I refuse to play this game anymore."

One of the first defenses they offer was this: We all can agree to submit to the Lordship of Jesus Christ. And I replied, "I refuse to play this game anymore." When I say Jesus Christ, I mean the pre-existent Son of God, "begotten of His Father before all worlds, God of God, Light of light, Very God of Very God; begotten, not made; being of one substance with the Father, by whom all things are made." These words are from the Nicene Creed. And I went on to say that I believe He was conceived in the womb of a virgin named Mary, that He died as the atoning sacrifice for our sins, that He rose again, and that He is coming back. "But that is not what many of our pastors and elders mean when they say they 'submit to the Lordship of Jesus Christ.'" And they couldn't deny this.

I went on. Speaking to the Presbytery Executive, I said, "I have pointed out to you the web site of one of the churches within our presbytery, a church which claims to be part of and which includes on its site a link to a group called The Center for Progressive Christianity. This group lists eight essential doctrines on their page, four of which are heresies, one which might be, and three which are fine, like 'We welcome all people to our church.' Guess what? We do too! Among the heresies is their essential teaching that Jesus is the way to salvation for Christians, but other religions are fine. They teach that the Lord's Supper symbolizes the bounty that God has for all people. That is not true. The Lord's Supper symbolizes Jesus' body broken and His blood poured out as our atoning sacrifice. I already have pointed this out to you, our presbytery executive. And you aren't going to do anything about it, are you?" His initial silence answered loudly enough.

He then suggested that if I was concerned, I should bring charges against the church myself. "No, I've already been down that rabbit trail with Rogue Presbytery. I will not waste another minute of my time or energy on our judicial process." And this was before I knew about the Kaseman ruling from 1981. I refuse to play this game anymore.

"But conservatives and liberals need each other," came the next argument. Have you heard this before? "Without conservatives we would blow up, and without liberals we would dry up," goes the saying. I responded, "No, Christian conservatives and Christian liberals need each other."

"My son just spent two months living in a commune in the inner city of Chicago, called Jesus People USA. I know the Jesus People well; I was first introduced to them in the 1980s through the music of one of their bands, Resurrection Band, and their literary magazine, Cornerstone. Our church band used to play music from their community. We have hosted two concerts from artists within that community.

"The Jesus People are liberal Christians. Their answer to social problems might be different from mine. But they believe the gospel. They believe that the Bible is God's Word, that Jesus was born of the virgin, that He died for our sins, that He rose again, and that He is coming back. Many people in the PC(USA) do not believe these things. They are outside my understanding of what is a Christian. They are not Christian liberals." They are Religious Liberals.

The Executives almost had run out of things to say. But not quite. "But what you believe is acceptable in our presbytery," they countered. "Yes, but it is not essential. These are essential beliefs for me and my congregation. I cannot remain with a denomination in which these essentials are merely some options among many."

At this point it had become very clear that nothing they said was going to shake my conviction that I could no longer pastor in the PC(USA) and retain any personal integrity. They did have one final question for me, which fit perfectly into the Religious Liberal essentials of orthopraxy and inclusivity. "Would you be willing to continue to work with us on missions of common interest?"

"Of course," I replied. "We work with Mormons all the time through Allied Churches, our local shelter and kitchen." In fact, I hope that our congregation will partner to help support some of the Hispanic ministries and churches which already exist within this presbytery, whether or not it stays, and whether or not I am the pastor.

Truthfully, the one appeal to remain which truly has tugged at my heart came from one of the Latino pastors in our presbytery. "Please don't go," he said. "We believe as you believe." And I know they do. Another Latino pastor commented after worshipping with us that the service reminded him of what he had grown up with in Mexico. "You even use the Westminster Shorter Catechism as a responsive reading, like we did," he said. Religious Liberalism has not seized South and Central America, or Africa, like it has Europe and the mainline denominations begun in Europe and transplanted to the United States and Canada. I would like to stay for my Latino friends; I would like to continue to work with them when I no longer am a pastor in the denomination of my birth. But our congregation cannot survive in the PC(USA) now. And I cannot stay. To my friend who said, "Please don't go," I said, "Come with us." But I don't think he believes they can survive outside the financial resources of the PC(USA), which does have deep pockets. My prayer is that our congregations will become closer in the years to come. The only reason that has not happened already is that the churches are in different cities.

For the most part, the Religious Liberals I know have remained silent as the congregation and I have been pondering whether or not to leave the PC(USA). One notable exception was a woman with whom I butted heads regularly through the years, even though we both have tried to be friends. At a presbytery meeting in the winter of 2012 she said she was sorry that I was leaving while my church was staying. I corrected her; my congregation had not made that decision one way or the other at that time, but was considering its options.

"I wish you would stay," she said to me. "We need your point of view." I thanked her. But this fits the Religious Liberal agenda. She wants me to stay, not because she wants me to have any power to implement my beliefs or impose them on the denomination (beliefs to which the denomination once was faithful), but because she wants that old way of thinking "included". I can be one of the Collection! "Here is our Feminist. Here is our Muslim. Here is our Wiccan. Here is our Liberation theologian. And here, rounding out the Collection, is the orthodox, historically Reformed Christian, or, as we like to call them, our Conservative." I have no interest in being part of the Collection, especially when just being there validates an essential of Religious Liberalism. "Look," says the Religious Liberal to another congregation troubled by the direction of the denomination. "We're OK! We have some of you too! If they don't have a problem with being part of this denomination, why should you?"

An Elder from another congregation expressed disbelief that we, as a congregation, should insist that Christian morality includes fidelity in marriage, which is a union between one man and one woman, or chastity in singleness. "This is going to be an increasingly minority position in America," he declared. "Gay marriage will become legal in our lifetime because the younger generation does not see this as any big deal." So shall we change the biblical definition of marriage to fit the culture? Shall we change our entire message to make it acceptable to the secular culture? People in the Presbyterian Church have been attempting that for a century, and look where it has gotten us.

I told this Elder that I had been preaching through the books of 1st and 2nd Chronicles that year. In the last decade, providentially, I have become fascinated with the eight books of the post-exile, written when the Jews returned to Judea following the Babylonian captivity. They are Ezra, Haggai, Zechariah, Nehemiah, Esther, Malachi, and the two books of the Chronicles. The Chronicles often are forgotten on this list because they do not talk about the post-exile period, as do the others. Instead, they retell the history of Judah from the priestly perspective, from the time of David till the Babylonian captivity in 587 BC. Often they are neglected by historians, including myself, because 1st and 2nd Samuel, and 1st and 2nd Kings, are the primary documents, written soon after the events described; the Chronicles are secondary documents written centuries after the fact, and use the earlier books as some of their sources. Why go with later sources instead of earlier ones more likely to be accurate? What I came to appreciate about the Chronicles in 2012 is that they were being written for Jews in the post-exile, when they were not the dominant culture, and when they were a small part of powerful empires. They were very much like the Christian Church in America and Europe today, scorned as backward, superstitious people. The message of the writer of the Chronicles was two-fold: 1) Here is where our ancestors went wrong, and 2) Now God's people MUST cling to Him and His revealed will even more closely. The Church cannot be the Church by adopting worldly attitudes and wisdom. We must remain weird. This is how minority cultures survive and thrive instead of being assimilated by the majority culture. It is the difference between the ten tribes which were lost and the three tribes which remained until the coming of Christ. We must remain faithful to the Lord, and not adopt society's attitudes, including that of sexual anarchy.

"In fact," I continued in my reply to the elder convinced that gay marriage would certainly come, "my biggest prayer for America is not that we will go back to the way it was," (after all, the past which held more stable families also held some pretty awful things, like Jim Crow and no voting rights for women or Native Americans), "but that the Lord will send Revival upon our nation." Revivals saved England from the violence of the revolutions of 1848, which swept through almost every other European country. "That's a word I don't hear very much anymore," he commented quietly. "I use it all the time." Our hope must be in the Lord. Whether He sees fit to send Revival or not, Christians who would truly be the light of the world and the salt of the earth, for which Jesus in His Sermon on the Mount, must conform our lives to His will revealed in scripture. Whether we live or whether we die, we belong to Him, not the world.

I realize that I have had many negative things to say about my PC(USA) presbytery in this book, things in which I take no delight, but which illustrate the greater problems in the denomination so well. At the same time, I have no doubt that many Presbyterians who choose to remain with that denomination love Jesus and will continue to try to give a faithful witness to Him while there. That's just not where He is calling me now. I've bled too much and hurt too much to continue. Plus, my congregation will not survive if it remains. (When I made this comment to a presbytery official, he sort of smirked and said, "Well, a lot of our congregations aren't going to survive anyway." How do you answer that?)

But I would not be honest in the picture I am painting if I did not also say that most of our current presbytery leadership has bent over backwards trying to help those of us who cannot remain to find our way forward free of barbs and unnecessary roadblocks. My Executive informed me that, should there be a lapse time between when the congregation leaves and when I leave, I am welcome to remain a member of presbytery in good standing for the sake of my health insurance and pension plan until the final transfer of credentials is complete. Likewise, all pastors who are leaving will be invited to attend meetings of this PC(USA) presbytery as corresponding members. In addition, as I have said, churches and pastors who leave will be welcome to work on mission projects of common interest, and members or pastors of departing congregations will be welcome to join remaining churches on mission trips. These are small concessions, but I personally appreciate them very deeply. I have heard horror stories of pastors leaving in recent years who have been threatened by their furious Executives, "If you ever come back, we know how to take care of you…" None of this has happened in my PC(USA) presbytery. Grace abounds.

Even so, strong differences remain. A retired pastor friend sat in on a meeting of our congregation as I explained my understanding of the ethical problems in the denomination, not specifically those dealing with sexual anarchy, but more generally, with an emphasis on orthopraxy as defined by the culture, not orthodox essentials. "But none of this matters to me," he objected. "My church and I just ignored the denomination; when they approved something with which we didn't agree, we just made a new rule for our church. We could be the church here, and not pay attention to the denomination." But that is not what I signed on for. I do not think that the way to be Presbyterian in the 21st Century is to become more Congregational. Plus, the denomination can only be ignored for a short time, until a new pastor must be found, or when the old one must be removed for reasons good or ill. Then the presbytery will vet the new pastor. What standards will they use? Will every evangelical congregation be able to find an evangelical pastor? Probably not.

According to the statistics of the denomination, in 1995 39% of the pastors enrolled in the pension plan were under the age of 45; I was one of them back then. By 2010 that number had plummeted to 23%. Several things must be happening. Young evangelicals either are not being allowed into the PC(USA), or, more likely, are choosing other churches and denominations where the gospel is clearly proclaimed. Young Religious Liberals either are choosing not to go into the ministry, leaving the ministry disheartened, or finding church work not connected with congregations. Ironically, in an era where Religious Liberalism has become the overriding power bloc in the PC(USA), Religious Liberals are failing to convert enough young people to care for the churches we have, let alone increase the number of churches or the number of people who attend.

Presbyteries cannot be ignored. They are the gatekeepers. In 1996, when I came to Westminster Church, I was approved by the pulpit committee, but rejected by the presbytery Examinations Committee the first time I met with it. This was not because of my commitment to theological essentials, but because I answered one of the examination questions stupidly. Each presbytery examines new pastors differently; this one had decided that it would emphasize the five areas of ordination exams: Open Book Bible Exegesis, Bible Content, Theological Competence, Worship and Sacraments, and Church Polity.

Unfortunately, no one had told this to me, so my written statement had omitted any reference to sacraments, ie., the Lord's Supper and Baptism. The committee focused on that.

All went well until someone asked, "Would you be willing to re-baptize someone?" I did not know that the presbytery had just been dealing with a pastor who had been doing this. I did know that Presbyterians do not re-baptize! But I also knew that the text many Presbyterians cite for this position, Ephesians 4:5, "...one Lord, one faith, one baptism...", is a proof text; Paul is not saying that Christians are only baptized once, but that we have one common baptism as Christians, along with one common faith in our one common Lord, Jesus Christ. For some reason at this point my mind reeled back to my seminary years when someone asked the question, "If a member of the congregation is on his deathbed and has become convinced that, for want of a bit more water on his head, he will be consigned to the fires of hell, would you be willing to splash some more as Pastoral Care?" Back then, in 1987, I had said that I might, though such action wouldn't really qualify as a baptism. And so suddenly, stupidly, in 1996 again I said I might, even though it was a different question! And I was summarily rejected. As I told folks later, some of the committee members might not have known the difference between the work of creation and the works of providence, but they all could count higher than one!

I was in agony. My wife had already given her notice at work, without any explanation that "my husband is taking a new job," since I had not told my original congregation (the WORST thing you can do is tell them that you are leaving, and then you don't), and in that small town the word would get around quickly. The committee was in agony too; they did not want to reject me, but I had answered incorrectly. My wife, well, she was not happy. "You always say Presbyterians don't re-baptize!" But the church's pulpit committee decided to stay with me, and the Examinations Committee for the presbytery agreed to meet with me once again a month later. That time I passed.

My point is this: ignoring the denomination is not an option for Presbyterians. Eventually the presbytery will come a-knocking. And we never were designed to be congregational. Accountability and collegiality are hallmarks of the Presbyterian

Church, along with the essentials of Scripture as God's Word, infallible in all matters of faith and practice, and Jesus Christ, completely God and completely human, born of a virgin, atoning sacrifice for sin, risen from death, and coming again.

Having used up my youth fighting to return the PC(USA) to historical and biblical integrity, I now simply hope to find a denominational home already committed to that theology, polity, and practice. We won't blend into the dominant culture. We will be weird. But we will reflect the love of Jesus to a broken and hurting world, to His glory alone. We will bind up the wounded, encourage the faltering, and always, always point to the cross and the empty tomb. Those touched by our ministries will continue that work when we are gone, and when what used to be the PC(USA) has become completely assimilated and indistinguishable from the darkness it inhabits, the Church Militant will be thriving. Then He will return, and the Church will become completely the Church Triumphant!

APPENDIX: CONFRONTING SEMINARY TRUSTEES, 1998

The following article originally was written by me and published in The Presbyterian Forum on-line publication in 1999. It is reprinted here with permission. I wrote this in my young and naïve phase of denominational engagement, when I actually thought that confronting problems face to face and explaining my position, and perhaps inspiring others to do the same, would lead to changes. But like dealing with Rogue Presbytery, because there was no practical means of holding the seminary accountable within the PC(USA), its leadership was able to put up with me until I got tired and went away. Nothing changed for the better.

THEOLOGICAL EDUCATION: HOW ONE CHURCH CAN MAKE A DIFFERENCE

"How can I make a difference?" Have you ever said that about the Presbyterian Church (USA)? How frustrating it can be, especially when attempts to return the denomination to its biblical and confessional roots get sidelined at presbytery, or clotheslined at General Assembly! The temptation we face is simply to ignore the denomination, to place our energy and effort in local ministries we trust. However, doing this can only bring disaster; we are a connectional Church, and abandoning the larger ministries and governing bodies will mean more frustration and heartache, if not outright schism.

Theological Education is a huge area problem in the PCUSA, though working for changes within the system seems a daunting task. After all, if John Leith and Jack Kingsbury seem unable to affect changes at Union Virginia, what can one little preacher or one little session do? Beyond this, who wants to challenge a seminary professor's teaching when you haven't sat in the class, and your knowledge of Schleiermacher is weak? Nobody likes to seem "intolerant", or even worse, ignorant.

I silently watched Union move away from orthodoxy for years, until Dr. Kingsbury was suspended from teaching in 1996, the only professor ever to be suspended there, and this on the questionable grounds of "intimidating" students. I wrote a letter of support for my former professor, one of the kindest and most humble I had known in my seminary years. In doing so I set off a chain of events which led to a meeting in November of 1998 at my church between our session and six trustees from Union, with input from representatives of several other churches in our Presbytery. The biggest names at Union were present: ... I write this article to say, "If we can do this, so can you." In fact, by the end of the meeting the trustees themselves were saying how much they had benefitted from this gathering, and how they should do it more. I pray that you will consider giving them the same opportunity we did, and that nationwide another nine theological institutions will enjoy such attention.

Step 1: Read John Leith's book, <u>Crisis In The Church</u>. Dr. Leith explains many problems in the seminary system, from teaching centered around religious studies departments in secular universities to independent Boards of Trustees who answer to no one directly. It will help you get started.

Step 2: Write some letters to the Trustees, respectfully voicing your concerns. Ask questions, present facts. Do not demand the firing of anyone, request more information.

Pastors probably need to begin the conversation with seminaries. Not only are we more familiar than most lay people with various theological debates and problems within the Church, we usually have some inside tracks through old professors and staff people at our alma maters. Write every member of the Board; sometimes negative letters are buried if only one or two people receive them. You will be sure to get some response if you write everyone, and you may even find trustees sympathetic with your concerns. (We did.) The list of trustees is a matter of public record, and can be acquired through the seminary.

Step 3: Keep a file of every letter you get from the seminary. This is an invaluable source of information for finding points of inconsistency over time. For example, it was helpful to answer the statement that only basic Reformed theology was taught in basic theology classes with a Theology I syllabus listing Rosemary Radford Ruether's <u>Sexism And God-Talk</u> as one of five texts. (2012 clarification – Ruether is a radical feminist whose denial of basic Christian beliefs, such as the Trinity and the Resurrection, places her not only outside Reformed theology, but outside historic Christianity's understanding of itself.

However, Religious Liberals like her.) Make a note of every other communication as well; on May 28, 1997, just after noon, we received a (hostile and deceptive – 2012) phone call from a person identifying herself as "a pastor in the Presbytery of West Virginia" who finally turned out to be a member of Union's staff living in Richmond!

Step 4: Involve your session. A church court has much more clout than an individual. Some first responses to my initial letter were rather condescending; when the session wrote a few months later, the condescending parties were much more polite. Your elders are a gift from God, and an often untapped resource. As you will see, it was the wisdom of the elders which saw these events through to the end. I also checked with them at every stage of the communication to make sure a righteous cause had not become my personal vendetta.

Step 5: Accept an invitation to go to the seminary with members of your session. Such an invitation to "come, see what we are doing," is, or at least was, a standard response from the seminary. I do not think they expected us to accept it. Once the invitation was accepted, conditions began to be added by the seminary. The president informed us that since the Board of Trustees has responsibility for examining the fitness of professors to teach, it was not our jurisdiction, and we could not ask what they personally believed. The elders saw this restriction as an opportunity, and requested an additional meeting with the Trustees. Besides meeting with the president on our Union trip, we attempted to meet with three professors, two of whom accepted our invitation, and a third who could not, though a phone call from me convinced her to write a letter to the session. The logistics of finding a date, finding a room, scheduling interviews, and rescheduling work took about two months.

Step 6: If necessary, involve your presbytery as a mediator. Even those who might not agree with or understand your concerns can recognize unfairness. Three days before we were to go to Union (and two days after the Trustees had met), the president called to postpone our meeting to the following week, which was, of course, impossible for our elders. His reason: he had to meet with other people who were big contributors to the seminary which, he said, we were not!

I was ready to quit. The elders said, "Inform presbytery," which I did. Our associate executive said, "He may not think much of Westminster's annual gift of $1100 to the 1% Fund (2012 – this 1990s fund was gathered voluntarily from the churches of the denomination with the suggestion that it be 1% of the total budget, and then was divided among all the seminaries), but when he considers what our presbytery gives, I believe he will reconsider." He advised me to write our presbytery council; they wrote the seminary in our behalf, only asking that we work out our differences. Suddenly, after three months of silence from the seminary, the Chair of the Board of Trustees began to answer our letters again.

Step 7: If seminary leadership will agree to meet at your church, invite other like-minded churches from your presbytery to attend. This time we invited them to come to us, and the elders told me to invite other sessions. This was essential for the success of the meeting. By the time the Trustees had arrived, several could not look at me without blood in their eyes, but when they heard similar concerns expressed by folks from whom they had never heard, cracks appeared in the armor. We also invited a representative from the presbytery office.

The meeting went from 11:00 AM to 3:00 PM, with an hour for lunch at 12:30. Our Clerk of Session acted as neutral moderator, inviting those with raised hands to speak. I spoke only twice, with eager pastors and elders allowing no gaps of silence between Trustees' answers and the next comment or question.

Step 8: Openly record the meeting. We did this because a trustee who could not be there requested a transcript. The objections of some trustees nearly stopped it; they were concerned that out-of-context quotations would be published. The tape was saved only by the timely comment from a lawyer turned preacher that recording would preserve the proper context. If a session votes to tape at a prior meeting, these objections should be avoided.

This was helpful later, when some attendees thought a blanket of confidentiality had been lowered over the entire meeting. The tapes proved otherwise; we had agreed not to distribute the videotape, and not to release individual quotations for publication to prevent out-of-context reporting. Never be sneaky in the name of truth; truth doesn't need the help of hidden agendas. However, do not be lulled by the "we're all just friends sitting around talking. I see no need to tape" tactic. "Friends" who do not know or trust each other, with such opposite views of the state of theological education, can only benefit from an exact record being kept of what is said.

Step 9: Feed them a good, free lunch, everybody together. We arranged for a local Greek restaurant to cater the meal. You would be amazed at the difference in the level of tension on that tape before and after lunch! Perhaps we did depart that meeting, if not as true friends, at least as not quite enemies. We certainly understood one another better.

So, what did we learn from the meeting? The trustees are convinced that Union is on the right course now, that the public relations problems they are having are just that, P.R. problems aggravated by biased reporting from publications like The Presbyterian Layman. The praises of John Leith were sung, and the course of the Presbyterian Coalition's Renewal of Theological Education mission statement was embraced; the Coalition was surprised to hear this! (One wonders how the Covenant Network of Presbyterians will react to this news, or what they would be told by Trustees at their own meeting.) (2012 – The Coalition was a special interest group of evangelicals, while the Covenant Network exists, even today, for the sole purpose of insuring the ordination of actively gay individuals.) I believed we changed no minds. However, I also believe the Trustees began to see their critics as having legitimate concerns; perhaps an avalanche of mail from and meetings with other churches nationwide would make an impression and bring about good change. Unlike churches, our seminaries' Boards of Directors have no one directly looking over their shoulders. Presbyteries don't, synods don't, and General Assembly doesn't or won't. But you can if you will try.

One Final Observation: Do not be afraid of seminary professors! This is a tough lesson for preachers to grasp. Professors have higher degrees than we do, they are sometimes internationally known, they are experts in areas about which we know little, and we think they taught us everything we do know!

But fewer and fewer of them have served a congregation for a significant amount of time; as John Leith used to say, "Ideas that wouldn't last two minutes in a church can last decades in a theological institution." They may know Calvin better, or Schleiermacher, but preachers know the Bible, and that's where our final authority rests! Don't allow the debate to end with Schleiermacher, end it with Paul! And you don't have to attend all their classes to know how they teach; read their books, since they don't publish what they don't believe.

Stonewall Jackson used to say, "Duty is ours, and consequences are God's." If theological education is going to change for the better in the PCUSA, individual pastors and sessions will have to accept the duty of scrutinizing our seminaries. Remember John Knox, at whose funeral it was said, "He feared God so much that he never feared Man."

2012 – With the meeting done, once I had transcribed the tapes and delivered copies of the manuscript to all interested parties, writing this article completed all I personally could do to try to bring the seminaries back to orthodoxy. I began to focus on other things, usually at the Synod level, as well as my duties within the congregation. As far as I know, no other church attempted to have such meetings with seminary trustees; it is easier simply not to send evangelical students to the established PC(USA) seminaries. Evangelical seminaries' graduates usually are acceptable to PC(USA) presbyteries; however, fewer evangelical students are interested in being a part of the PC(USA). As far as I could tell, after this meeting and this article, nothing changed at my seminary, except that it embraced religious pluralism and Religious Liberalism more and more.

As my final observations for this appendix, I include the following excerpt from my journal, dated Thursday, 7/22/99:

> Yesterday at the end of Bible Study I got a call from Dr. John Leith. That was truly a surprise. I'm sure he does not remember what I look like, he barely knew I existed at all when I was at Union, but he sure knew that I had gone up to sit with Dr. Kingsbury at that meeting from which I was turned away. I mentioned the meeting, and he said, "And _____ _____ wouldn't let you in."

The main reason for his calling was to thank me for sending him a copy of the manuscript of the meeting with the Trustees. "_____ _____ is a liar!" he proclaimed to me. "His wife is the one who fought to bring Rosemary Reuther to _____ Church!" In fact, according to Leith, _____ was not the only one lying that day. "They just lie." He said _____ is like Bill Clinton. He said a lot of things, many of which I can't even remember now.

He invited me to come see him at his home, but it's a very rare thing for me to go to South Carolina. I never got those kinds of invitations when a seminarian. He asked who I graduated with, and the one I knew he would know was _____ _____, whose father and grandfather were big names in the old southern church. I remember him talking to _____ a lot! But honestly, the biggest sense I got from Dr. Leith was one of sadness, of someone who feels betrayed by many people he trusted and supported in the past. He particularly seems to mourn for his relationship with _____ _____, for whom he went to bat so _____ could get into graduate school, and who will not speak to him now, and was instrumental in driving him from teaching a decade or so ago.

Maybe "mourn" is too tender a word. He's angry. But he's also nearly 80, and there's not a lot he can do with his anger; maybe sadness is what I feel for the lion in winter. _____ thinks Leith is particularly disappointed with his own people, "Leith's Army", a phrase I have heard tossed around through the years. They talk a lot, but they don't seem to do very much, at least not like what Westminster has done or what Doug Brandt did, or what the Forum is doing. I don't know. Maybe we young pastors are too dumb to know when to quit. How audacious we are, to take on such an entrenched foe! Storming the gates of hell. Father, help me to do my duty, and never, never to take myself too seriously.

The Forum is going to publish my "one church can make a difference" article on-line now. I faxed them a copy this week after talking with Parker Williamson to see if it was OK to pull it from the Layman's backlog, which it was. Parker seemed pleased that I called to check first, and said they really liked the article, but the sooner it got out, the better, so let the Forum take it first. The Layman may run it later. As I said in an e-mail to Parker, I do think that the story will get stale if it waits more than a year after the meeting before being published.

BIBLIOGRAPHY

Book of Church Order of the Presbyterian Church in the United States, The. Atlanta, Georgia: The Office of the Stated Clerk, 1981-1982, 1982-1983.

Book of Church Order of the Presbyterian Church in the United States, The. Richmond, Virginia: The Board of Christian Education, 1964.

Book of Church Order of the Presbyterian Church in the United States, The. Richmond, Virginia: John Knox Press, 1950.

Constitution of the Presbyterian Church (U.S.A.), The. Part I, The Book Of Confessions. Louisville, KY: The Office Of The General Assembly, 1996.

Constitution of the Presbyterian Church (U.S.A.), The. Part II, The Book Of Order. Atlanta, Georgia and New York: The Office Of The General Assembly, 1987-88.

Constitution of the Presbyterian Church (U.S.A.), The. Part II, The Book Of Order. Louisville, KY: The Office Of The General Assembly, 2009/2011, 2011/2013.

Covenant Network's www address, covnetpres.org/. Nave, Douglas, "Guidelines for Examination of Church Officers", 2011.

Fellowship Of Presbyterians, The, www address, fellowship-pres.org/. "Narrative on the Health of Mission and Ministry (for congregations)", 2011.

Hodge, Charles. Systematic Theology. New York: Scribner, Armstrong, And Co., 1872.

Presbyterian Layman's www address, layman.org/. Adams, John H, "Two cases established precedents for today's battles in PCUSA", 2004.

Presbyterian Layman's www address, layman.org/. Reagan, Jason P. "California Church Files Complaint Against Santa Barbara's Union-Presbytery Plan", June 26, 2012.

Smith, Egbert Watson. <u>The Creed Of Presbyterians</u>. New York: The Baker And Taylor Company, 1901.

Trinity Foundation, The, www address, trinityfoundation.org/journal. "The Horror File, Theology", May/June 1982.

Wright, Robert. "Infidelity—It may be in our genes. Our Cheating Hearts." Time 1995